Happy Days Are Here Again!

A Short Interpretative History of the New Deal

Happy Days Are Here Again!

A Short Interpretive History of the New Deal

GEORGE WOLFSKILL

HOLT, RINEHART AND WINSTON

New York Chicago San Francisco Atlanta Dallas
Montreal Toronto London Sydney

Copyright © 1974 by The Dryden Press
A division of Holt, Rinehart and Winston, Inc.
All Rights Reserved
Library of Congress Catalog Card Number: 73-2098
ISBN: 0-03-086681-4
Printed in the United States of America

234 008   9 8 7

Happy Days Are Here Again!

A Short Interpretive History of the New Deal

For my parents

"Train up a child in the way he should go;
and when he is old, he will not depart from it."

—Proverbs 22:6

Preface

Warm Springs, Georgia. April 12, 1945. Roosevelt appeared weary and exhausted. He had lost weight, his face was gaunt and ashen, his sinuses were still acting up. The burden of the presidency during the worst of wars, the pressure of decision making at the Yalta Conference, sorrow at the death of "Pa" Watson on the trip home— all this, and more, had drained him. He would bound back, of course; Warm Springs would work its miracle. It always had. But after nearly two weeks (the presidential party had arrived on Good Friday, March 30) he had improved little.

Roosevelt sat at his desk in the Little White House. With his secretary, Bill Hassett, he was catching up on neglected work. As Roosevelt signed letters and papers Hassett laid them on chairs, the floor, the couch—waiting for the scrawled signatures to dry—a ritual known as "waiting for the laundry to dry," according to the President.

Miss Margaret Suckley, a cousin to Roosevelt, sat on the couch to the President's left, quietly crocheting. Miss Laura Delano, another cousin, was arranging flowers in vases about the room. Mrs. Roosevelt's former secretary, Mrs. Winthrop Rutherfurd, whose enduring relationship with the President had very nearly caused the dissolution of the Roosevelt marriage some years before, sat to his right. To one side was Madame Elizabeth Soumatoff, an artist of some reputation, at work on a portrait of the President. It was 1:15 p.m.

Roosevelt looked up from his papers, reached for his holder, inserted a cigarette, lit it, and pressed his left hand to his temple. The hand moved to his forehead, then dropped. Miss Suckley stepped to his side. "Did you drop something?" she asked. "I have a terrific headache," Roosevelt answered in a whisper. With that, the magnificent torso sagged in the chair.

The sudden death of Roosevelt shocked a nation still at war. Roosevelt was a cripple; he had been since 1921. Somehow, in the back of his mind, everyone knew he was a cripple. And everyone—when he thought about it—knew Presidents were vulnerable as other men. Even so, as the years slid by Roosevelt seemed to acquire an immunity from the vagaries of life. He had a kind of indestructibility, an air of immortality, especially for the young and impressionable who seldom thought of death, who really could remember no other President.

I was one of that young and impressionable generation. Nineteen-thirty-three had been a year of new beginnings for both of us; Roosevelt had become the thirty-second President of the United States while I had become a freshman in high school. My generation would know depression and war and a lot more, firsthand, with Roosevelt the proprietor of the nation's business the whole time.

I had never met Roosevelt, and had seen him in the flesh but once in my life, yet his passing moved me like a death in the family. Becoming reconciled to the finality of it meant, in part, remembering the many ways his life had affected mine. One memory always stood out from the rest. It involved my closest boyhood friend, whose mother, in desperation, wrote a letter to President Roosevelt asking him what to do to save the family home from foreclosure. The father had been without steady work for years during the worst of the depression; lights and gas had been cut off at one point for nonpayment of bills. With stub pencil and dime-store tablet paper she wrote a letter to the President of the United States. The letter received a prompt reply, a word of encouragement, and an explanation of how to get in touch with the local Home Owners Loan Corporation office to refinance the mortgage and forestall foreclosure. A widow now, she still lives in that house.

I remembered that the day Roosevelt died. It was experiences like this that led me, like so many of my generation, to remember Roosevelt with much fondness, to measure all Presidents by Roosevelt, all administrations by the New Deal. I was finally attracted to the period as a field of special study by a desire to revisit my youth, to test memories and impressions of those years against what I had learned and was learning. Roosevelt and the New Deal, I found, were not always as I had remembered them, confirming Lincoln Steffens' conclusion that the process of maturing consists in unlearning.

This book is a short interpretation of Roosevelt and the New Deal as I have now come to understand them. It is meant primarily for undergraduate college students and casual readers as an introduction, not a finale, to an era—the Roosevelt years. It is not a history of "the Crash" or the Great Depression, although the Crash and the Great Depression are the backdrop. It is not a biography of Franklin Roosevelt, although there is a lot about Roosevelt in it. It is not a history of the New Deal, although it is about the New Deal. It is not a history of the Roosevelt foreign policy and World War II, although both figure in the conclusions.

The book touches on many things because the New Deal touched many things. But whatever the New Deal was, and whatever may have been the pervasiveness of its influence, it was first and foremost an economic and political fact of life. Accordingly, this is where I have put the emphasis—on the economic and political implications of the New Deal.

The book has purposely been written without the usual trappings of scholarship; there is not a footnote in sight. It consists of a prologue, three interpretive sections, an epilogue, and a bibliographical essay. The prologue attempts to set the mood for the coming of the New Deal. Part 1 contains a fast sketch of the New Deal years through 1945. Part 2 takes a look at the New Deal through the eyes of its contemporaries and tries to answer the question: What did Roosevelt, New Dealers, and curbstone observers—both friends and foes of the New Deal—think it was? Part 3 deals primarily with the economic, social, and political consequences of the New Deal. In the epilogue I have tried to summarize some of my own thoughts on the New Deal as an economic and political event.

As might be expected, the bibliographical essay is at best a partial assessment of Roosevelt and the New Deal by those who claim some expertise. However, it has the added virtue of attempting to analyze and synthesize the views of major interpreters of the New Deal.

In the preparation of this book I have incurred personal debts along the way: to Miss Gwen Robertson, Mrs. Marjorie Burden, Mrs. Sally Stoffregen, and Miss Shelia Renfro for checking elusive facts and for typing the first draft of the manuscript; to Mrs. Glyndean LaPlante, who typed the final draft. I am also indebted to my colleague, John A. Hudson, head librarian at the University of Texas at Arlington, with whom I collaborated on a study of New Deal critics, *All but the People*, published in 1969. He read the entire manuscript and criticized it with his customary lack of reverence. He is my favorite critic. As always, I am indebted to Alberta, my wife, who has been unobtrusively present at the birth of our six children and our three books.

It is also customary for authors to mumble something under their breath about assuming full responsibility for errors in their book—all the while hoping to hell no one finds any. I am unwilling to go that far. I assume only a partial responsibility for this book, a responsibility that I share with Robert E. Burke, general editor of the Berkshire Studies in American History, who knows more about the New Deal than most people, and Seibert G. Adams, Jr., director of Dryden Press, who is no amateur either.

Epigraph

On Thursday, the nominations. Roosevelt's old friend, John E. Mack of Dutchess County, placed his name before the convention in an uninspired address. As he concluded, the first of the demonstrations began: the organ blared "Anchors Aweigh," the banners rose, the delegates marched and cheered, the chairman vainly pounded his gavel. Louis Howe, doubled up with asthma on his bed at the *Congress*, suddenly felt he could stand the naval song no more. "For God's sake, tell 'em to play something else," he said, between hacking coughs, to Ed Flynn. "Tell 'em; oh, tell 'em to play 'Happy Days Are Here Again.'" The order was quickly transmitted to Arthur Mullen, and Franklin D. Roosevelt was given a new anthem.

Arthur M. Schlesinger, Jr. *The Crisis of the Old Order*

Contents

Prologue

A Time To Weep: The Coming of the New Deal

> *To every thing there is a season,*
> *and a time to every purpose under the heaven: . . . A*
> *time to weep, and a time to laugh; and a time to mourn,*
> *and a time to dance.*
> *—Ecclesiastes 3:1, 4*

> *Everything nailed down is coming loose.*
> *—Marc Connelly,* The Green Pastures *(1930)*

> *We have done all we can do; there is nothing*
> *more to be done.*
> *—Herbert Hoover March 4, 1933*

March 4, 1933. Inauguration Day dawned bleak, matching the mood of the country. It had rained off and

on; now it was misting. Sleet clung to the trees; sullen clouds hung low, threatening more rain. The raw wind blew across Capitol Plaza, where shortly Franklin D. Roosevelt would take the oath of office. It was bitter cold—the penetrating cold of despair. Cold for the throngs already beginning to gather; cold for the troops manning the machine guns strategically located—just in case. Everywhere there was a sense of foreboding, heavy and oppressive, as New York *Times* reporter Arthur Krock wrote later, "comparable to that which might be found in a beleaguered capital in war time."

Shortly before noon Hoover and Roosevelt set out from the White House in an open car for the drive to the Capitol. President Hoover sat motionless, eyes lowered, the anguish and frustration of the past four years clearly etched in his expression. He made no gesture, no nodding of the head, no waving of the hand, to acknowledge the scattered, indifferent applause and cheers from the crowds lining the streets. The efforts of Roosevelt to engage the President in conversation produced only inaudible murmurs or no reply at all. On they rode in painful silence, each perhaps lost in his own thoughts of the events that had brought him to this fateful moment in history, a moment of cruel rejection for the one and unlimited opportunity for the other.

When he accepted the Republican presidential nomination in 1928, Hoover had said: "We in America are nearer to the final triumph over poverty than ever before in the history of any land." In the election that followed he gave Alfred E. Smith, the highly successful and popular four-time governor of New York, an awesome drubbing, winning by more than six million popular votes and carrying forty states, including five from the usually solid Democratic South.

In a losing cause, Smith had polled more votes than any previous Democratic candidate, winner or loser. And with overwhelming support by voters with foreign backgrounds, Smith broke the Republican hold on most of the big cities. But Smith was a Roman Catholic and his parents were Irish immigrants. His big-city background, his religion, and his open opposition to Prohibition made him suspect in the eyes of rural, Protestant Americans. These liabilities, coupled with a booming economy (which Republicans, during the campaign, translated into "a chicken in every pot and two cars in every garage"), meant that Smith was beaten from the start. Hoover won big in 1928, according to one historian, because of "Rum, Romanism, and Prosperity."

By 1932, all the news was bad—if you were a Republican. In a hopeless, lackluster, always-on-the-defensive bid for reelection, Hoover was overwhelmed by Roosevelt, who had made the country a promise: "I pledge you—I pledge myself to a new deal for the American people." Roosevelt won by more than seven million votes, carrying all but six states. The result of the presidential election of 1932, perhaps not so much an endorsement of Franklin Roosevelt as a repudiation of Herbert Hoover, was convincing evidence of how quickly political fortune could change in a democracy. "Democracy," Hoover would write later, "is not a polite employer."

The explanation was simple. Between Hoover's "triumph over poverty" and Roosevelt's "new deal for the American people," disaster had struck. Not famine. There was food everywhere except in people's bellies. Not pestilence. The dread of epidemic disease had vanished with the spinning wheel and muzzle loader. Not foreign foe. The outsider with mischief in his heart had not set foot on our shores for more than one hundred years. There was drought. Soon there would be winds that would carry away the rich earth in great dark clouds, depositing some of it on decks of ships miles at sea and leaving behind the Dust Bowl. But the real disaster was not a cruel and indifferent nature on the rampage. The disaster was economic: total collapse—unexpected, unprecedented, beyond the comprehension of good honest folk, who did not know what had hit them.

For the confident Hoover, the Crash of 1929 and the Great Depression that followed what Gilbert Seldes so aptly described as the "years of the locust"—had been like a kick in the groin. And, like any good athlete, he reacted by trying to let on that he was not hurt, that nothing was wrong. For a while, at least, he convinced himself that nothing was wrong. The country listened to cheerful chatter from the White House and Wall Street about how this was just a period of readjustment; the economy would rebound stronger than ever; this was only a temporary setback, like 1907 and 1921. And, of course, there was eventually the famous put-on about "prosperity just around the corner."

Eventually, Hoover took action. As will be seen later, he went beyond any previous President in combating economic depression, with what amounted to a limited "new deal" of his own. But in the early stages of the disaster, Hoover laid on the line his confidence in businessmen and bankers, his faith in spontaneous cooperation and voluntary action to halt the economic collapse. In the fall of 1929, in a series of White House conferences, he wrung pledges to maintain production and wages from leaders of railroads, industry, construction, finance, and trade. Labor leaders promised no strikes, no new wage demands.

Similar meetings with state and local government officials produced commitments to cooperate with the federal government in expanded programs of public works and with the recently organized Committee for Unemployment Relief. Almost daily, it seemed, the country's newspapers featured pictures of self-assured political leaders or self-conscious, camera-shy businessmen and labor leaders, posing on the White House steps after conferences with President Hoover.

These efforts produced meager results. The ordeal continued, got worse. The Great Depression, it appeared, was a contradiction of everything Hoover stood for. It mocked him; it branded him—with no small amount of help from Democrats—a fool, helpless and inept. Hoover was destined for the history books as the fall guy of the Great Depression.

His inability to cope with the economic crisis was a bitter disappointment to Hoover; failure was a new experience. His road to the White House had begun with an engineering career that had taken him all over the world, had made him rich, and had earned him a reputation for coolness under pressure and level-headed efficiency. His first experience in government came during World War I, and the reward for his expert handling of Belgian relief was gratitude in Europe and applause at home. No one asked to see his political credentials when President Wilson offered him the job of Food Administrator after the United States entered the war. And having declared himself a Theodore Roosevelt Progressive in 1912 (he was out of the country at the time), Hoover was compromising no principles in accepting. He became Secretary of Commerce in the Harding administration in 1921, and his success in the office had prompted President Coolidge to refer to him, in private, as the "wonder boy."

Even after eight years in Republican cabinets, Hoover was offered to the country not as a partisan or as a Republican who had earned the right to run for President. He was presented to the nation in the election of 1928 as an uncomplicated patriot, a humanitarian, "the Great Engineer," an efficient administrator above the din of politics. He had held no elective office, had not been active in politics, had hardly thought through the matter of party affiliation, and just might have had the nomination of either party in 1920. His principal qualification for the presidency was his capacity for getting important work done in orderly fashion amid chaotic situations.

This is not to imply that Hoover had moved through the history of his times without a point of view. He had a philosophy, a philosophy that was so vital a part of his character that—when the crisis of the Great Depression was upon him—he was shackled by it. The ethical idealism of his rural, Quaker background was certainly a part of that philosophy. But the greater part was derived from an innocent, simplistic view of the world, a view in which five or six basic philosophies were in conflict: Communism, Socialism, Syndicalism, Capitalism, Autocracy, and Individualism—each spelled with a capital letter. Having carefully analyzed each, he said, he emerged "an individualist—an unashamed individualist." Not just an ordinary individualist: "I am an American individualist. For America has been steadily developing the ideals that constitute progressive individualism."

Thus Hoover's philosophy had a label: progressive individualism; and the essence of progressive individualism was equality of opportunity, which Hoover, in 1922, defined in less than deathless prose:

Our individualism differs from all others because it embraces these great ideals; that while we build our society upon the attainment of the individual, we shall safeguard to every individual an equality of opportunity to take that position in the community to which his intelligence, character, ability, and ambition entitle him; that we keep the social situation free from frozen strata of classes; that we shall stimulate effort of each individual to achievement; that through an enlarging sense of responsibility and understanding we shall assist him to this attainment; while he in turn must stand up to the emery wheel of competition.

Men, according to Hoover, were obviously not equal in talent, character, brains, or guts; to argue that they were, he held, was "part of the claptrap of the French Revolution." Such being the case, the only thing government could assure an individual was "liberty, justice, intellectual welfare [meaning education], equality of opportunity, and stimulation to service."

Hoover admitted that circumstances, particularly the realities of the Industrial Revolution, required government to take an active role in the daily lives of people. But that role had to be carefully drawn, so as to curb forces in business that would endanger equality of opportunity, and to nurture the initiative and creative faculties of the people. "To preserve the former," wrote Hoover, "we must regulate that type of activity that would dominate. To preserve the latter, the Government must keep out of production and distribution of commodities and services. This is the deadline between our system and socialism." In Hoover's solution to the problem of the relationship of government to the national economy the litmus test was two questions: Does this act of government safeguard equality of opportunity? Does this act maintain the initiative of the people?

By the time Hoover published *American Individualism* in 1922, these views had become dogma. And they suited the growing public mood of the 1920s. Much of the country, weary and disillusioned after two decades of reform and war, tired of "God in the White House" (as Mark Sullivan put it), wanted no more government-sponsored heroics and sacrifice. Allowing for the usual amount of rhetorical fall-out, Hoover was saying that the Progressive spirit should not be revived in the 1920s. He would have none of the New Nationalism, with its notion of government-regulated monopoly, or the New Freedom, with its trust-busting implications and regulated competition. Herbert Croly's views about conscious national purpose and planned progress, he believed, were dead wrong.

But Hoover's philosophy of progressive individualism was no disguise behind which lurked an old-fashioned conservative, an obsolete Social Darwinist with a heart like a pawnbroker. Hoover's philosophy was finally put to a practical test during the years he served as Secretary of Commerce. In practice, progressive individualism meant that Hoover would put his faith and sweat into getting business, with gentle persuasion from government, to police itself. He dedicated his considerable energies and talents to promoting trade associations and codes of fair trade practices, to reducing the waste of competition, to improving the efficiency of business. The success of these efforts was dependent upon the voluntary cooperation of business, and the backslapping camaraderie that developed between government and business in the 1920s was a marked change from the antitrust campaigns of the Progressive years.

Bricks—strange to say—were frequently offered as proof that Hoover's voluntary cooperation approach was working. Brickyards had once turned out endless sizes of building bricks (amid mighty blasphemous and obscene oaths by contractors), but Hoover had arranged an agreement on standard sizes—a feat hardly less remarkable than Mussolini's getting Italian trains to run on time.

It was fitting that Hoover should be nominated at a time when, according to the boast of some, America was entering a "New Era," in which business efficiency would be applied to the affairs of government, in which private profit, individual effort and initiative, social conscience, voluntary self-restraint, and benign government would reinforce each other and poverty would soon be left behind. Hoover was shocked and surprised when the system stumbled and faltered in 1929. But his faith was not shaken. Resorting to voluntary cooperation in the early stages of the depression crisis was not spur-of-the-moment on Hoover's part; it was a conditioned reflex.

Franklin Roosevelt's road to the presidency had been quite different from the one Hoover had trod. Roosevelt had acquired a considerable amount of practical training for the presidency, much more than Hoover. In 1910 he won election to a seat in the New York senate from a Hudson Valley district that had elected but one Democrat since the Civil War. In the senate, Roosevelt fought Tammany Hall to a standoff over the selection of a United States senator. Later, he helped organize anti-Tammany Democrats behind Wilson's nomination in 1912. His support of Wilson earned him a spot in the Navy Department as Assistant Secretary—the same post filled by Theodore Roosevelt on his way to the White House.

Roosevelt was an able and popular administrator in the Navy Department. He made peace with the new Tammany leadership; supported Alfred E. Smith in his bid for governor of New York in 1918; and was nominated for Vice President in 1920—a dubious reward for being the best available Wilsonian Democrat in New York acceptable to Tammany Hall. Experience in wartime Washington was invaluable, alerting Roosevelt to the possibilities of federal government, to what it could and could not do in time of crisis. Experience in the 1920 campaign, although a losing proposition from the start, was excellent training in the tricky business of national politics. Roosevelt had met lots of people, made many friends, and was privy to the inner circles of Democratic party leadership.

In August 1921, personal calamity struck. Roosevelt contracted polio. Courageously he fought to regain the use of his withered legs, a fight he continued to wage throughout the remainder of his life. (He walked again, with crutches, canes, and the aid of heavy braces.) The infirmity, visually minimized by careful staging of his public appearances, did not handicap his performance of his duties. As Al Smith would say later, when Roosevelt became a candidate for governor, the governor of New York did not have to be an acrobat.

While convalescing, Roosevelt kept in touch with party leaders, gently urging reform and reorganization of the Democratic party. The party was in awful shape. Since the election of 1920 it had become so atomized that it all but ceased to exist as a national party. At the heart of the trouble were the rural-urban tensions that had been building at least since the turn of the century. The rural-urban split pitted the majority element, southern Protestants (mostly Methodists and Baptists), against Democrats of the northern cities, who were, in overwhelming numbers, foreign born and Roman Catholic.

This rural-urban, Protestant-Catholic confrontation within the party was particularly evident in attitudes toward critical issues of the 1920s. Rural Protestants demanded strict enforcement of Prohibition; Catholic constituencies in the northern cities wanted repeal. Rural Democrats, particularly those of the South, either feared or sympathized with the Ku Klux Klan; urban Democrats opposed everything the Klan stood for. And the feelings went deeper, to issues such as the League of Nations, social reform, and relief for farmers and workers. How deep were the splits within the party was revealed in 1924, when a disgusted Democratic convention finally nominated John W. Davis on the 103d ballot.

Franklin Roosevelt was the only one to come out ahead in 1924. On crutches, he had electrified the convention with his now famous "Happy Warrior" speech nominating Al Smith. By the time he nominated Smith again, at Houston in 1928, Roosevelt had discarded his crutches. Smith won the nomination this time. And when Smith needed a vote getter to help him carry New York, Roosevelt was reluctant but ready. Smith lost New York in the presidential election, but Roosevelt won the governor's race by a narrow 25,000 votes. Two years later he won reelection by a whopping 725,000 votes, enough to capture the attention of every Democratic party leader in the land. It was his vote-getting capabilities, his reputation as a winner, that made Roosevelt the leading Democratic presidential contender in 1932.

In later years his enemies would sneer and say that Roosevelt had spent his time as governor running for the presidency, but that was not true. Roosevelt performed exceedingly well in Albany. During his two terms he attacked depression problems with experiments that were strongly laced with Progressive flavoring, particularly in matters of relief, labor, farm aid, hydroelectric power, conservation, and banking—all signs of things to come during the New Deal.

After reelection in 1930, Roosevelt, of course, planned in earnest to capture the Democratic nomination for President. Louis Howe, who had stuck with Roosevelt since the early days in the New York legislature, and James A. Farley, an untainted organization man, began the laborious task of lining up delegate votes. Farley toured the West, organizing support. Roosevelt could not crack the city organizations of the Northeast; they remained unshakably loyal to Al Smith. But Farley —traveling everywhere, writing countless letters in the green ink that would become his trademark, piling up astronomical telephone bills— rounded up more than enough strength in the farm states to overtake Smith.

Roosevelt was likewise the choice of most of the Southerners who mattered. Southern Drys, who had fought Al Smith every step of the way in 1924 to prevent his nomination and who had deserted him in the election of 1928, now rallied to Roosevelt. In 1932, men like Cordell Hull of Tennessee, Alben Barkley of Kentucky, North Carolina's Josephus Daniels, Mississippians John Rankin and Pat Harrison, and Louisiana's colorful Huey Long worked untiringly for Roosevelt. By convention time they had succeeded in putting all of the southern delegations in his column (except Maryland, Virginia, and Texas), a total of 210 convention votes of a possible 296.

The Republican National Convention, meeting in Chicago in June 1932, had all the gaiety of a wake. Renominating Hoover implied approval—meant pointing to the record as the overriding argument for reelecting him. Not to renominate him would be open admission of failure. Little wonder, then, that the convention renominated Hoover and Curtis without enthusiasm on the first ballot and went home without offering any new ideas for curing the depression.

A few days later the Democrats streamed into the same city, cheerful, confident, full of razzmatazz. The Democratic platform, not unexpectedly, blamed the depression on the Republicans. It also had some ideas for easing economic distress: proposals for federal unemployment relief, control of farm surpluses, regulation of holding companies and stock and commodity exchanges, separation of investment from commercial banking, and state unemployment and old-age insurance.

With the country falling apart, perhaps on the brink of armed revolution, the part of the platform that brought down the house was the plank on Prohibition, urging repeal of the Eighteenth Amendment. The lawless trafficking in bootleg alcohol and the hopeless task of enforcing laws on a public unwilling to accept the notion that a cocktail before dinner was a felony had combined to cripple the "noble experiment" of Prohibition begun in 1920. In some broader sense, the attempt to legislate morals, to intrude into an area of human behavior beyond the normal range of government, symbolized the rural-urban split in the Democratic party and the resurgence of religious fundamentalism in the 1920s. As the decade wore on, the conflict had grown more intense, the Wets urging outright repeal, the Drys demanding stricter enforcement and tougher legislation. The Democratic convention in 1932 was taking a forthright stand on one of the hottest issues of the day. Little wonder the rafters shook.

Roosevelt had formidable opposition for the nomination. There was Al Smith, who thought he deserved another chance at vindication after the defeat in 1928. Smith had strong backing from the eastern cities, especially the Tammany Hall organization in New York City, and a sizable faction of wealthy eastern conservatives led by Democratic National Chairman John Raskob. Speaker of the House John Nance Garner, the candidate of publisher William Randolph Hearst, and California Senator William Gibbs McAdoo controlled the big delegations from Texas and California. Woodrow Wilson's Secretary of War, Newton D. Baker, though short on delegates, seemed the likeliest compromise candidate should the convention become deadlocked.

Roosevelt received 661 votes on the first ballot—one hundred less

than the two-thirds required for nomination. Two more ballots changed
the total only slightly in Roosevelt's favor. Farley managed an early
morning adjournment, and a bargain was struck (the versions of how
this was accomplished are numerous and conflicting) that guaranteed
the California and Texas votes. On the fourth ballot, William Gibbs
McAdoo (who, in 1924, had dueled Smith for the nomination through
103 ballots before both lost to a compromise candidate, John W. Davis)
told the convention that California had come to nominate a President,
not to deadlock the convention, as in 1924. Remembering the bitterness of 1924, according to one wit, "McAdoo buried the hatchet—in Al
Smith's neck." All of the candidates gracefully yielded (except Al
Smith); Roosevelt was nominated; and John Nance Garner of Texas
settled for the vice presidency.

Roosevelt broke with tradition by flying to Chicago (through a thun-
derstorm) to accept the nomination in person. This, he told the howling
convention, should be a symbol of the Democratic party's future, the
breaking of foolish traditions. And then the promise that would mark
the beginning of a new era, the Roosevelt era, in American history: the
promise of "a new deal."

No novelist could dream up a plausible way for Roosevelt to have
lost the election of 1932; the result was foregone. Clearly, the country
was voting for change. But not revolutionary change. It was one of the
ironies of the Great Depression that, in the midst of the worst economic crisis in the history of the country, those who advocated radical
solutions—the Socialists and the Communists—would become as scarce
as whooping cranes. The Socialist candidate, Norman Thomas, and the
Communist candidate, William Z. Foster, received only 885,000 and
103,000 votes respectively—about 2.5 percent of the total.

The failure of Thomas and Foster to make capital of the depression
dramatized a significant aspect of the American tradition: ideologues
get nowhere in the United States, not even during depressions. Ideologues may sometimes influence the major parties but they do not
defeat them in elections. One reason for this is obvious. Third parties
operate only at the top, with no local base and no way to satisfy local
needs—and have always lost in the winner-take-all structure of the political system in the United States. But more important was the country's
devotion to middle-class values, which, as one historian has said, "set
the tone of American society, democratic politics, and capitalist eco-

nomics." In the American political tradition, "there was, historically, no political left or right on which to build, no important base from which to operate when the Depression thrust opportunity upon revolutionists of both extreme persuasions."*

The car in which Hoover and Roosevelt were riding pulled up at the Capitol and the President-elect was wheeled quickly past the shoving throng to the Military Affairs committee room. Roosevelt, surrounded by confusion, sat serenely, quietly glancing at the text of his speech. In the Senate chamber, John Nance Garner, the new Vice President, was taking the oath of office. A few moments later, as if from a long way off, Roosevelt could hear the Marine Band as it struck up "Hail to the Chief" for President Hoover, who emerged from the rotunda and walked gravely to the inaugural stand, built above the steep steps on the east side of the Capitol. Hoover settled back in his leather chair, which had been placed a little left of center on the podium.

Dignitaries came from the ceremony in the Senate chamber and out onto the inaugural stand. Vice President Garner arrived without a topcoat, defying the cold. In contrast, the retiring Vice President, Charles Curtis, seemed almost lost in his great fur coat. Senators, congressmen, cabinet officers, congressional clerks, Capitol employees—the great and the not-so-great—crowded the white-column inaugural stand, stood huddled along the ramp, and jammed the east doors through which Roosevelt would come. Eleanor Roosevelt, wife of the new President, appeared, flanked by her sons and daughter (all but James). The plan was to wheel Roosevelt to the east door, from which he would walk the more than thirty yards along the ramp to the lectern, slowly, painfully, leaning on the arm of James, his eldest son. Chief Justice Hughes was already in his place, looking like an Old Testament prophet with his black skull cap, white whiskers, and black robe. The crowd fell silent in anticipation. A solitary bugle sounded; then the drum roll. As Roosevelt moved haltingly toward the white balustrade at the front of the inaugural stand the Marine Band once more played "Hail to the Chief," this time for the new leader. A roar went up from the huge crowd, spontaneously—the day's first genuine demonstration of emotion,

*George Wolfskill and John A. Hudson, *All but the People* (New York: Macmillan, 1969, p. 314.

according to one observer. Now Roosevelt's hand was on the family Bible, and he was breaking another tradition: he was repeating the entire oath after Justice Hughes instead of the customary "I do."

"This is a day of national consecration," he began. "This great nation," said the unsmiling new President, "will endure as it has endured, will revive and will prosper." And then, with head flung back in a gesture the whole world would soon come to recognize, he spoke his most memorable line: "So first of all let me assert my firm belief that the only thing we have to fear is fear itself—nameless, unreasoning, unjustified terror." "This nation," he asserted, "asks for action, and action now."

Was Roosevelt implying there had not been action before? Hoover thought he had given the country action—as much as his conscience and a hostile Congress would allow.

After 1930, Hoover faced the certain knowledge that the depression was not temporary, and that his voluntary cooperation techniques were not producing the desired results. After the elections of 1930 he also faced a rebellious Congress. Even then he approached the problem of depression with a strategy designed to save capitalism but not to alleviate social misery—with measures loaded in favor of the economic aristocracy, measures that made it clear he did not intend to overhaul the economic machinery.

For farmers, Hoover had two answers to their prayers. Throughout the 1920s, while the rest of the country rode the crest of prosperity, farmers had been experiencing hard times. During the campaign of 1928, Hoover had promised farm relief and upward revision of the tariff rates on agricultural products. Soon after his inauguration, Hoover called the Congress into special session to honor those campaign promises to the farmers. Despite strong opposition from those who favored some form of price fixing and who had lost faith in tariff revision, Hoover had his way. Congress passed the Agricultural Marketing Act on June 15, 1929. The next year he got revision through the Hawley-Smoot tariff.

The Agricultural Marketing Act created a Federal Farm Board with a revolving fund of $500 million for loans to cooperatives to improve marketing, to build warehouses, to hold products during price declines. The Federal Farm Board could establish corporations that, in turn, could stabilize prices by large purchases of surpluses. The Hoover farm program collapsed during 1931, when domestic markets dried up, and Argentina, Russia, and Australia dumped enormous crops on the international market. By 1932 the Federal Farm Board had squandered $354 million on a program which had failed to control the American farmers' habits of daylight-to-dark production. The new Hawley-Smoot tariff confirmed the ancient American conviction that the way to aid agriculture was to build our own version of the Great Wall of China.

Hoover also was willing to cushion the depression through public works. In the spring of 1930 Congress approved $145 million for rivers and harbors, $75 million for highway construction, and a whopping $530 million for public buildings. And the brakes were set on immigration, although it was not really necessary. In 1929 some 280,000 had entered the country, but by 1932 immigration had slowed to a trickle, when only 36,000 entered. More significantly, 103,000 left the country that year.

For the time being, this was as far as Hoover was willing to go. If the country was losing confidence in him, the elections in the fall of 1930 did not improve the situation. The "smear Hoover" campaign mounted by the Democrats was in full cry. The consequence was a hostile, impatient Congress and a country pressuring the administration for more action.

The first two years had been bad enough, but the situation worsened in early 1931. Part of the trouble was foreign in origin. The United States had about $1.5 billion in foreign gold, mostly British and French, which American banks were holding. In early 1931, faced with troubles of their own, England and France called for their gold. American banks were also holding another billion dollars in short-term German paper, which Germany could not, or would not, pay. The foreign securities market, with Europeans dumping United States securities after the Crash of 1929, had all but vanished.

If bankers and stockbrokers were having their troubles, so were little folks. People who would not have known the difference between a bond and a balance of trade (or cared, for that matter) knew only that they were out of a job, or were working only part time, that they had exhausted their credit and good will, had cashed their insurance policies, sold their furniture and family heirlooms, pawned their jewelry—done everything desperate men can think of to keep their heads above water. Across the land breadlines were forming, young people were hitting the road to ease the burden of feeding extra mouths at home, and forlorn, pathetic, nondescript shacktowns were springing up—Hoovervilles, they were called—wherever there was vacant land on riverfronts, along railroad embankments, and by city dumps.

Hoover responded to the worsening situation in 1931 with a program of action that was too little and too late: additional lending to federal farm banks, creation of home-loan banks to reduce foreclosures, more federal works, drastic cuts in government spending, new taxes, and the Reconstruction Finance Corporation, with capital of $500 million and authority to borrow $1.5 billion. The RFC opened offices in thirty cities, started money flowing to banks, railroads, savings and loan associations, and related businesses. Through 1932 the RFC loaned $1.5 billion to more than 5,000 businesses.

This helped. But Hoover was adamant about tariff changes, vetoed the Garner-Wagner relief and public works bill because it would have put the federal government in the relief business, and threatened to veto the Patman Bonus Bill, a proposal for immediate benefit payments on the national insurance policies of World War I veterans. He slashed government spending by $700 million. Congress wanted to expand the currency, wanted a program of government work relief. Hoover would not hear of it.

Congress and the President also clashed over new taxes. Hoover wanted a manufacturers' sales tax, which, of course, would merely have been passed along to consumers. Southern Democrats were willing to support the manufacturers' sales tax idea because it would not burden the people of their states nearly so much as some other forms of taxation. But the majority in the Congress opposed the tax. There was some sentiment, especially among Democrats, for a national sales tax. But Hoover was less than lukewarm toward the idea. A handful, eager to use taxation to chastise the wealthy, agitated for increased income and inheritance taxes. They got nowhere. In the end, Congress and the President compromised on a revenue bill that raised the income tax and introduced a series of regressive nuisance taxes.

Hoover's defenders argued that Congress was dragging its feet, hamstringing the presidential program. The implication was that Democrats, biding their time until 1932, were causing the mischief. But Democrats were only partially responsible. As a result of the 1930 elections there were forty-eight Republicans, forty-seven Democrats, and one Farmer-Laborite in the Senate. In the House, Democrats had a majority of four. Hoover was getting rough treatment from a Congress in which Democrats and Republicans alike were straining for the chance to go beyond him, well beyond him, in attacking the depression.

But Hoover had already gone further than his conscience dictated. Not the "bonus marchers," or the Farm Holiday Association, or any of the other threatening groups of those depression years could shake his ideological commitments. In his Lincoln Day speech in 1931, Hoover stuck to his principles when he told the nation: "Victory over this depression . . . will be won by the resolution of our people to fight their own battles in their own communities, by stimulating their ingenuity to solve their own problems. . . . This is not the easy way, but it is the American way."

If it took nerve to say words like those in 1931, it took suicidal courage to repeat them in 1932. Yet repeat them he did. At Detroit, during the presidential campaign, he said: "In dealing with the present emergency I have insisted that we shall as a nation rely upon the initiative and responsibilities of our citizens, of our institutions and of our fabric of local government." It did little good for the defenders of Hoover to point out that Roosevelt seemed to be saying essentially the same thing, embellishing his position with pledges to balance the budget, cut federal spending, and prune the bureaucracy. By this time no one was listening to Hoover.

Roosevelt's inaugural address was not much, really; in cold print it was pretty thin stuff. But it was not what he said that mattered; it was how he said it. This was a new, a different Roosevelt. This was not the smiling, shadow-boxing candidate talking; this was the President of the United States, and there was steel in his voice. He spoke with authority. Hoover had been telling the country it had nothing to fear, repeating it until he was blue in the face, and no one believed him. Roosevelt said the same thing, in just one line, and the whole country believed. But a direct warning had evoked the most spirited applause of the day. If Congress faltered, Roosevelt said pointedly, he would ask for "broad Executive power to wage a war against the emergency, as great as the power that would be given to me if we were in fact invaded by a foreign foe."

Much of what Roosevelt said in the speech was so vague as to be open to any interpretation. For example, his reference to bankers and financiers, those whose business was money: "The money changers have fled from their high seats in the temple of our civilization. We may now restore that temple to the ancient truths." But in this instance the country did not have long to wait for a translation. On his first night in office, Roosevelt directed the Secretary of the Treasury, William Woodin, to draft an emergency banking bill. Roosevelt gave him less than five days—until the following Thursday, when Congress would meet in emergency session. Sunday afternoon, March 5, he signed an edict, resting on the rather doubtful legal authority of the Trading with the Enemy Act of 1917, that halted transactions in gold and proclaimed a national bank holiday.

On March 9 the special session of Congress convened in an atmosphere suggesting wartime crisis. Shortly before 1:00 p.m., Chairman Henry B. Steagall of the Banking and Currency Committee began reading aloud the proposed banking legislation from the only available copy, while some of the new members of the Congress were still trying to find their seats. Debate was limited to forty minutes. But, with a unanimous shout, the House passed the bill—sight unseen—after thirty-eight minutes. The Senate, over the objections of a small band of Progressives—men like Bronson Cutting of New Mexico, Edward Costigan of Colorado, and Wisconsin's Robert LaFollette, Jr.—approved the House version unamended, 73 to 7, at 7:00 p.m. At 8:36 that same night it received the President's signature. The whole affair, from introduction to final signature, had taken less than eight hours.

On Sunday night, March 12, an estimated sixty million people sat around their Philcos and Atwater-Kents to hear the first of Roosevelt's "fireside chats." The President, in the warmly comforting tones the country would soon learn to lean on, assured everyone it was now safe to return their savings to the banks. In simple language he summarized the banking problem and explained the steps being taken to correct it. Roosevelt took a complex subject like banking, quipped Will Rogers, America's favorite humorist, and made everybody understand it, even the bankers. "The whole country is with him," drawled Rogers, "just so he does something. If he burned down the capitol we would cheer and say, 'Well, we at least got a fire started anyhow.' "

The next morning banks opened their doors, their cash drawers filled with Federal Reserve notes issued against the banks' assets. The Roosevelt magic worked. Deprived of cash for days, people had been expected to withdraw their funds to meet immediate needs. Yet in every city deposits exceeded withdrawals.

No one, not even the most optimistic, had expected Roosevelt to move with such speed and self-assurance. "In one week," wrote Walter Lippmann, "the nation, which had lost confidence in everything and everybody, has regained confidence in the government and in itself." But the banking act was only the start, only a sample of what would follow during the next 104 days of the emergency session—the famous "100 Days" of the New Deal. Arthur Krock, reporting on that hectic session, wrote: "There is danger in the pace, and we know we may not land precisely where we intend to. But we are getting somewhere. . . . Never was there such a change in the transfer of a government."

The "100 Days" were in sharp contrast to the final four months of the Hoover administration, between Roosevelt's election and his inauguration, when the stricken country staggered and reeled. To escape the paralyzing delay before the start of the Roosevelt administration it was even suggested that Hoover appoint Roosevelt Secretary of State and then resign (along with Vice President Curtis), which would make Roosevelt President immediately. The idea was plausible, possible, constitutional—and unprecedented. Which meant it was also unthinkable.

So the country had waited. Waited while the index of production dipped lower and lower. Waited while banks failed. Waited while mounted police tried to keep order during runs on other banks. Action to save sound banks from ruin had begun when Governor Balzar of Nevada decreed a "bank holiday" of twelve days commencing October 31, 1932. But runs on banks spread, multiplied, picked up momentum in the Middle West and spread eastward to stronger institutions, whose very names had always inspired awe. On February 4, 1933, Governor Allen declared a bank holiday in Louisiana. Ten days later Governor Comstock closed all the banks in Michigan. Other governors followed these examples, until, on the morning of Inauguration Day, Governor Lehman declared a two-day bank holiday in New York.

Hoover blamed Roosevelt for the banking crisis. He based this singular conclusion on public fear that Roosevelt would take the country off the gold standard, unbalance the budget, and engage in assorted fiscal hanky-panky. By "public fear," Hoover meant bankers, and maybe those who depended on bankers. The nearly twenty-three million who had voted for Roosevelt in November were not fearful of what he might do. They could hardly wait for Hoover's term to end so that Roosevelt could start doing whatever he was going to do in the name of his New Deal.

But money orthodoxy was deeply ingrained. The efficacy of the gold standard and balanced budgets fell somewhere between that of a rabbit's foot and infant baptism. How deeply this was ingrained is reflected in the story of Lewis Douglas, Roosevelt's Director of the Budget, who had his differences with Roosevelt and eventually resigned. Early in the New Deal, when informed of Roosevelt's decision to cut the gold content of the dollar, Douglas warned William C. Bullitt: "Bill, this means the end of western civilization."

In November, shortly after the election, Hoover invited Roosevelt to the White House to confer. Roosevelt, deciding that Hoover was trying to tie his hands by trying to commit the next administration to Hoover's monetary policies, was noncommittal. In December 1932 and again in January 1933 Hoover urged Roosevelt to make public statements reassuring the country that he would pursue sound, conservative monetary policies. Again, Roosevelt hedged. He said he supported the Democratic party's platform pledge to preserve "a sound currency." But he would go no further, even though this meant that Carter Glass of Virginia, "father" of the Federal Reserve System, refused to become his Secretary of the Treasury, because Roosevelt would not assure him that "a sound currency" meant preservation of the gold standard. The currency issue gave Glass an excellent excuse, for it is doubtful that the aging senator would have accepted in any case.

Roosevelt, of course, refused to accept responsibility or blame for the banking crisis. The crisis, he believed, was the cumulative result of unsound banking practices of the past. At the time, a steady stream of bankers was making daily headlines with their confessions of stupidities and malfeasance to Ferdinand Pecora and the Senate Committee on Banking and Currency. Roosevelt also refused to rule out emergency monetary measures, which, if they were intended to stimulate the economy, would have to be inflationary. His announcement of William H. Woodin, president of the American Car and Foundry Company, as his Secretary of the Treasury was another clue that Roosevelt would be more flexible than Hoover. Woodin's open-mindedness on the money issue was common knowledge.

Hoover's insistence that Roosevelt promise to balance the budget was one of those "do as I say, not as I do" propositions. Throughout the 1920s, budgets were not only balanced but significant headway was made toward reducing the national debt. Under Hoover, annual deficits had grown to almost $3 billion by 1932. Hoover also sought vindication by trying to get commitments that Roosevelt would not repudiate the foreign policy of the waning administration. Roosevelt publicly promised to maintain the Stimson Doctrine, the nonrecognition of conquests by aggressor nations, which was first applied to the Japanese puppet government in Manchuria. And he promised to follow through on plans for United States participation in the economic conference to be held in London in June 1933. But he refused to commit himself to Hoover's thesis that the depression was essentially European in origin, or the corollary that the war debts due the United States should be traded off for international currency stabilization and disarmament agreements.

On February 17, three days after the Michigan bank holiday, Hoover wrote a long letter that was delivered the next day by Secret Service courier to Roosevelt in New York. (The President, in his haste and agitation, even misspelled Roosevelt's name on the envelope.) The letter chewed the same fat: the national crisis was one of confidence, not of policy, values, or economic machinery. The banking crisis was psychological, not economic. "The major difficulty," wrote Hoover, "is in the state of the public mind."

And how did he propose to restore national morale? "I am convinced," he told Roosevelt, "that a very early statement by you upon two or three policies of your Administration would serve greatly to restore confidence and cause a resumption of the march of recovery." For instance? "It would steady the country greatly," Hoover lectured the President-elect, "if there could be prompt assurance that there will be no tampering or inflation of the currency; that the budget will be unquestionably balanced, even if further taxation is necessary; that the Government credit will be maintained by refusal to exhaust it in the issue of securities."

In short, in the name of "cooperation" Roosevelt was supposed to go to bed with Hoover and call it a New Deal. In a letter to Senator

Simeon Fess of Ohio, Hoover listed the evil practices Roosevelt must forsake to consummate the marriage: "such proposals as the bills to assume Federal responsibility for billions of mortgages, loans to municipalities for public works, the Tennessee improvements and Muscle Shoals, are of the order." He must also, wrote Hoover, disavow opposition to a sales tax and to an increase in the tariff. And in a letter to Senator David A. Reed of Pennsylvania, Hoover wrote with uncommon candor: "I realize that if these declarations be made by the President elect, he will have ratified the whole major program of the Republican Administration; that is, it means the abandonment of 90% of the so-called new deal."

To suppose Roosevelt would scrap the New Deal before he took the oath of office was the scrambled logic of a desperate man. According to Roosevelt, Hoover's letter to him was a "cheeky" document. In his reply he ducked again, saying that "[the banking crisis] is so very deep-seated that the fire is bound to spread in spite of anything that is done by way of mere statements." It really did not matter. For some unexplained reason, Roosevelt's reply was delayed ten days and did not arrive at the White House until March 1.

On Friday afternoon, March 3, the four-month stalemate between the two men made the White House tea (Hoover's substitute for the traditional dinner) a trying and embarrassing experience. The conversation was desultory. Hoover continued to urge some kind of public assurances. Roosevelt continued to reject responsibility without power.

Hoover, a tragic figure, was never able to cope with the depression or rise above its shock. The calm detachment that had always characterized the man—that had, in fact, been the basis of his appeal—now made him appear cold and indifferent to human suffering. But what people took to be coldness was inflexible dedication to principle; Hoover was deeply moved by the nation's suffering. Despite his torment and anguish, he clung tenaciously to principle, to logic as he saw it. Indeed, his logic required that he pursue policies that seemed to be responsible for the depression: balanced budgets, high tariffs, governmental economy, and—above all—the proposition that people, not the government, must overcome the depression. It was heroic, he thought, to stand resolutely for those values when they were under attack.

It was not that Roosevelt was philosophically all that much different from Hoover, but he was adept at assimilating and synthesizing, and could attract the support and loyalty of people with ideas. Gregarious, he liked all sorts of people and made everyone, great and humble alike, feel at ease. His polio attack seemed to mark the development of more serious qualities in Roosevelt, to match his extraordinary personal charm and magnificent speaking voice.

Even so, Roosevelt was not a convincing liberal, and certainly not a radical. Nor was he an ideologue; he was not wedded to a philosophy. At one point, early in his first term, after Roosevelt was accused of being a Communist and a newspaperman asked him point-blank, Roosevelt replied: "I am a Christian and a Democrat." The answer reveals a good deal about the man, a disarming flexibility, almost an intellectual flippancy, which Hoover would have found insufferable. Unlike Hoover, Roosevelt could bend, and did. It was this quality, the ability to adapt quickly, without missing a beat, that was the significant difference between the two men.

One writer reported that, in the gathering darkness after Roosevelt's inauguration, "Mr. Hoover was weeping as his train drew out of the station toward obscurity." "We have done all we can do," said the bone-weary ex-President; "there is nothing more to be done." Others might do more, much more. But Hoover was right; he had done all he could do, all that his philosophy of government would let him do; and he had failed. Little wonder that he wept. But the people were not weeping with him. The new leader said there was nothing to fear, and they believed him. The time for weeping had passed.

Part One.

"This Great Nation Will Endure"

The country needs and, unless I mistake its temper,
the country demands bold, persistent experimentation.
It is common sense to take a method and try it:
if it fails, admit it frankly and try another.
But, above all, try something.
—Franklin D. Roosevelt
Oglethorpe (Georgia) Speech, 1932

This nation asks for action, and action now. . . .
This great Nation will endure as it has endured,
will revive and will prosper.
—Franklin D. Roosevelt
Inaugural Speech, 1933

CHAPTER ONE

Nothing to Fear: A New Deal Panorama, 1933-1945

> We did not dare to breathe a prayer,
> Or to give our anguish scope;
> Something was dead in each of us,
> And what was dead was Hope.
> —Oscar Wilde
> The Ballad of Reading Gaol

> The intellectual and spiritual climate was Roosevelt's
> general attitude that the people mattered.
> —Frances Perkins
> Secretary of Labor

Hoover's legacy to Franklin Roosevelt in March 1933 was a beleaguered land and a people without hope, a people beaten and dispirited. In contrast, it was a prosperous land and a people reclaimed—a people brimming with vigor and purpose—that the bewildered Harry Truman suddenly inherited from Roosevelt in April 1945. How could that be? After all, the intervening twelve years were years of depression and war for the United States— and years of suffering, privation, violence and destruction, tyranny, and death for the world.

The answer, in a word, was Roosevelt. "That nation or state," he had once said, "which is unwilling by government action to tackle new problems . . . is headed for a decline and ultimate death from inaction." The country was asking for action, quick action, he had said in his inaugural speech. And it was implicit that the action would not be just to alleviate—or hopefully solve—the larger problems besetting the country and the world. It was to solve the problems of individuals as well. In a sorry world, the world of the 1930s and the 1940s, the United States would seem the last place where a national leader was acting to revive the hopes of people. "Those suffering hardship from no fault of their own have a right to call upon the government for aid," said Roosevelt, "and a government worthy of its name must make fitting response." The American public understood Roosevelt to mean that the meek might yet inherit the earth.

With each problem met, with each crisis faced, with each evidence of concern, with each sign of improvement, hope grew. It grew until, from the worst of wars to have afflicted mankind, there blossomed in the United States the hope of a "brave new world." Roosevelt's greatest gift of leadership may well have been his talent to turn adversity to advantage, to inspire hope from each new travail. Shall we continue in sin, Saint Paul had asked, that grace may abound? It sometimes seemed as if Roosevelt needed the counterpoint of trouble so that hope could abound.

At any rate, one description of the New Deal is that it consisted of trial, action, and hope.

"Proclamation No. 2038. March 5, 1933. Whereas public interests require that the Congress of the United States should be convened in extra session . . ."

When Congress convened for the special session, Roosevelt, as already noted, had an Emergency Banking bill ready. During the next three and a half months—the first "100 Days" of the New Deal—he would have many other bills ready ("must" legislation, it would eventually be called) for aid to agriculture, labor, business, the unemployed, homeowners, beer drinkers, and more.

By the time Congress adjourned in mid-June, Roosevelt had everything he asked for: the Beer and Wine Act, Farm Credit Administration, Civilian Conservation Corps, Federal Emergency Relief Act, Securities Act, Tennessee Valley Authority, Home Owners' Loan Corporation, Agricultural Adjustment Act, National Industrial Recovery Act, Federal Deposit Insurance Corporation, and the repeal of the gold payment clause for government obligations. It was quite a haul. The effect on the country was like a stiff belt of bourbon on an empty stomach. Drooping spirits began to revive, a new spirit of optimism began to build, and there was a flurry of business activity even before the emergency recovery measures could possibly have been felt.

Execution of the New Deal recovery program was carried on with flair by a team the likes of which Washington had never seen. This did not mean the cabinet, however. The Roosevelt cabinet—the usual assortment of politicians, the well intentioned, and the well heeled—was not much; it was distinguishable from previous cabinets only by its inclusion of a couple of hard-working reformers. Governor George Dern and Senator Claude Swanson made little contribution as Secretaries of War and Navy, if only because their departments were in a stage of eclipse. Henry Wallace, son of a former Secretary of Agriculture, steadily grew in stature, despite his strangely detached and mystical personality. Postmaster General James Farley was the dispenser of patronage for the new administration; Daniel Roper, the Commerce Secretary, who spoke for the party faithful, and Henry Morgenthau, who succeeded William Woodin at the Treasury Department in 1934, were defenders of the conservative economic viewpoint. Homer Cummings of Connecticut, a last-minute replacement for Senator Walsh, who died en route to the inauguration, stayed on as Attorney General until 1939.

There was one hell raiser, Harold Ickes in Interior, an old Bull Moose Progressive who was once president of the *NAACP* in Chicago. He shared the reform label with Frances Perkins, who, as Secretary of Labor, was the first woman cabinet member in history. The new Secretary of State, Cordell Hull, a Tennessean with a long career in Congress, had strong support from the southern wing of the Democratic party. Hull came close to resigning in 1933 when Roosevelt jerked the rug from under him at the London Economic Conference, but Hull stayed on until 1944, steadfastly promoting his low-tariff, freer trade policies. After 1939, Roosevelt became his own Secretary of State, and Hull had little to do with major decisions. Ickes, Morgenthau, and Perkins stayed with the team until the end, although with some regularity Roosevelt had to talk Morgenthau and Ickes out of resigning—"holding their hands," Roosevelt called it. Wallace served as Secretary of Agriculture until he resigned to run for Vice President in 1940. After a term as Vice President to Roosevelt, he returned to the cabinet as Secretary of Commerce.

Excitement was stirred in the early days of the New Deal by the Brain Trust, a term coined by John Kieran of the New York *Times* during the 1932 campaign to describe the group of specialists from whom Roosevelt sought advice. The Brain Trust group, most of whose members held only minor posts in the government for purposes of getting on the federal payroll, was always unofficial, informal, and changing. Its members were expendable after Roosevelt had "picked their brains," a device he had used while governor of New York. The method functioned well during and after the Democratic National Convention of 1932, and Roosevelt continued it when he got to Washington. Throughout his years in office Roosevelt continued to draw on advice from uncommon sources; but the Brain Trust, as a group, ceased to function after 1933.

The chief recruiter for the Brain Trust was Columbia University professor Raymond Moley ("Moley, Moley, Moley, Lord God Almighty," according to a parody of the traditional hymn). Another was Felix Frankfurter of the Harvard Law School, whom Roosevelt would appoint to the Supreme Court in 1939. (It was inevitable that his protégés would be referred to as Frankfurter's "Little Hot Dogs.") The Brain Trusters and the lesser New Deal lights who began populating the departments and agencies baffled and worried a lot of people. George Peek, a veteran campaigner for farm relief programs in the 1920s and administrator of the Agricultural Adjustment Act, expressed the reaction of some: "A plague of young lawyers settled on Washington. They all claimed to be friends of somebody or other and mostly Felix Frankfurter and Jerome Frank. They floated airily into offices, took desks, asked for papers and found no end of things to be busy about. I never found out where they came from, what they did or why they left."

Among the best known of the Brain Trust were the controversial Columbia professors, Rexford Guy Tugwell and Adolf Berle, Jr., both of whom were suspect because of their strong stand in favor of national planning. Others included James M. Landis of Harvard and Judge Sam Rosenman, an old New York friend of Roosevelt. A special Roosevelt favorite was Thomas "Tommy the Cork" Corcoran, who, in addition to his other talents, could sing Irish ballads and play the accordion. Corcoran presided over "the little red house in Georgetown" (the residence of Corcoran, Landis, and Benjamin Cohen), where other New Dealers and Brain Trust types congregated to drink beer and talk of plans for making over the world. Hanford MacNider, a former American Legion commander, speaking in Jackson, Michigan, on the eightieth anniversary of the Republican party, described the Brain Trust as "brilliant young men of no admitted party allegiance, dizzy with sudden and unrestricted power . . . experimenting with every phase of national life. The industrial and business body of America is securely strapped to the classroom table." MacNider may have had a point. Benjamin Cohen, the most impressive of the Little Hot Dogs, was responsible for drawing no less than seven major bills during the first session of the Congress in 1935, which led one critic to suggest changing the spelling of Congress to C-o-h-e-n-g-r-e-s-s.

Besides the Brain Trust there was Louis Howe, who had been with Roosevelt since 1912. Sacrificing his newspaper career and neglecting his family, Howe had devoted his full time to one goal: promoting Franklin Roosevelt to the presidency. This accomplished, Howe moved into the White House with the Roosevelt family, and died there in April 1936. Small, sickly, addicted to the ponies, and a chain smoker of vile-smelling cigarettes, Howe may have been the only man in the world who could call Roosevelt "dumb Dutchman" to his face and say no to the President with impunity. Totally loyal to Roosevelt, he demanded the same degree of loyalty from everyone else.

Howe had unerring instincts, and could spot phonies and promoters from afar. He could not have cared less about issues or policies or the clash of ideologies; the well-being of Franklin Roosevelt was all that mattered. Although his influence on Roosevelt began to wane after 1934, one can speculate whether Roosevelt would have made fewer blunders if Howe had lived.

In any case, after his death advisers came and went and rose and subsided, none filling the void, until Harry Hopkins. Hopkins, a veteran social worker, who had also been with Roosevelt in New York, came to Washington in charge of New Deal relief programs. He was a frail, cadaverous, ulcer-ridden cynic who, like Howe, was fiercely loyal to Roosevelt. Hopkins, too, eventually moved into the White House, and became part of the family in 1940. Hopkins had more depth than Howe, and after the United States entered World War II he exercised more power than Howe had ever exercised, but he did not try to influence Roosevelt as Howe had done. To Hopkins, Roosevelt was always "the boss."

"Well, suh, I don't know nothin' about the New Deal, but if it's that what's gettin' us bigger tips then I'm for it."

The redcap at Washington's Union Station described the effect of the 100 Days much better than Walter Lippmann, who pontificated: "At the end of February we were a congeries of disorderly panic-stricken mobs and factions. In the hundred days from March to June we became again an organized nation confident of our power to provide for our own security and to control our own destiny."

While the redcaps and the Lippmanns across the land were savoring those exciting days, the emergency recovery program took off like a roman candle. Roosevelt was counting on the National Industrial Recovery Act to rescue business, and fireworks were guaranteed when Roosevelt, acting on Moley's advice, appointed Hugh Johnson director of the National Recovery Administration. Johnson ("Old Iron Pants," he was called), with a general's star and an amazing vocabulary and capacity for alcohol to show for his years in the cavalry, was a protégé of Bernard Baruch and a proven administrator with the Moline Plow Company. Johnson promoted the *NRA* with missionary zeal; "I regard *NRA* as a holy thing," he said.

The land suddenly sprouted "Blue Eagle" emblems, and it was proclaimed on flags, signs, placards, banners, and labels that "We Do Our Part." Governors, local officials, chambers of commerce, service clubs, boy scouts, school children, housewives, labor leaders, editors, and preachers were exhorting each other to do his part. The ballyhoo that went with launching the *NRA* was climaxed in mid-September with one of the biggest parades New York had ever seen, complete with a Navy blimp trailing an enormous "We Do Our Part" banner.

The *NRA* enjoyed its greatest popularity before it started; once its cumbersome machinery swung into action, its most consistent product was trouble. Small-scale businessmen, who had little to do with drawing the codes under which each business would operate, got much the worst of it. Despite heroic efforts by people like New York Senator Wagner, Lloyd Garrison, dean of the Wisconsin Law School, and Francis Biddle, the Philadelphia attorney, to make the program work, labor eventually became disenchanted because of the ineffectiveness of the collective bargaining guaranteed under section 7(a) of the NIRA. Price fixing, allowed under the codes, got no standing ovation from consumers. Statistically, there was little net increase in employment or in economic activity. And by the time the Supreme Court declared the *NRA* unconstitutional in the spring of 1935, its effectiveness, largely psychological in the first place, had about vanished.

For sustained public support and achievement of goals, the Agricultural Adjustment Act was more successful than the NIRA. The AAA was the New Deal answer to farm problems that had been a long time in the making. The demands on the American farmer during World War I had led to expanded productivity accompanied by higher farm prices and higher income. Farm prices and income dropped precipitously after 1920, however, and leveled off at precariously low rates throughout the rest of the decade.

Agricultural depression in the 1920s had led to serious consideration of a plan to alleviate the distress of farmers: the McNary-Haugen plan. The plan had evolved from a proposal by Hugh Johnson and George Peek, both of whom had been in the farm implement business in Moline, Illinois—a business usually hard hit by depression. Their proposal, explained in the pamphlet *Equality for Agriculture*, published in 1922, called for a "fair exchange value" for farm products. Under the McNary-Haugen plan, the federal government would purchase an entire annual crop and pay the farmers the world price plus the tariff on that crop. Any surplus beyond what was needed for the domestic market would be sold by the government at the world price. Whatever loss was incurred by the government would be offset by an "equalization fee" prorated among the farmers. Widely supported by farmers, the McNary-Haugen plan was twice vetoed by President Coolidge on constitutional grounds.

When the AAA went into effect in May 1933, it seemed fitting that George Peek should become the first director of the Agricultural Adjustment Administration. At the outset, there was trouble in the Department of Agriculture over policy. Some longtime McNary-Haugen advocates favored farm subsidies but not curbs on production; they wanted to sell or dump surpluses abroad. Others wanted production curbs and reduced acreage; they feared dumping would only drive agricultural prices down still further. While the argument simmered, Secretary of Agriculture Wallace planned the large-scale destruction of the cotton and hogs that would have glutted the market in 1933. Thus Wallace would forever be remembered as the "honorable Lord destroyer," the "assassin of little pigs." Among Wallace's casualties—along with the little pigs—was the federal treasury. It cost more than $100 million to plow under the 1933 cotton crop, an event that was immortalized in verse:

> For Wallace has spoken
> In his words of loud blunder,
> "Don't save for tomorrow,
> Just plow your stuff under."

The government's acreage allotment plan, the long-range method for cutting production and raising farm prices, was voluntary. The goal was to increase farm income by raising prices to 1909-14 levels—what the administration called parity. It did not take wits long to rephrase Saint Paul: "Faith, hope, and parity, and the greatest of these is parity."

Unprecedented opportunity to receive benefit payments for doing less work produced a high level of cooperation, and by 1934 there were significant declines in cotton, wheat, corn, and hog production, as well as spectacular (although erratic and unpredictable) increases in farm prices. Critics were quick to argue that it was the drought of 1934 rather than the AAA that was producing results. But it was hard to argue with a 25 percent increase in farm income. Under the AAA, large farmers did better than small farmers; farmers producing basic commodities did better than those who were more diversified; tenants and sharecroppers came away empty handed.

While the administration grappled with problems of farmers and businessmen, New Deal relief programs were getting under way. Farm and home mortgages were refinanced and Reconstruction Finance Corporation operations were expanded to help small businessmen and to make loans to the states. The Federal Emergency Relief Administration provided direct relief—a dole, actually—which did little more than provide bare subsistence. The Civil Works Administration, created in November 1933, provided work relief—everything from raking leaves to building airports. Hastily conceived, the CWA was abolished in 1934 and resurrected in a new form the next year, as the Works Progress Administration. And the Civilian Conservation Corps, one of the more widely approved New Deal measures, was getting young men into the woods and the fresh air for a salary of thirty dollars a month. While most people probably approved New Deal relief efforts on humanitarian grounds, the kindest verdict would seem to be that relief measures eased hunger and misery but were too meager to stimulate the economy very much.

Following the 100 Days, the pace of the New Deal slackened but took on a more rhythmic beat. When Congress convened for its regular session in January 1934, Roosevelt seemed content to stand pat on his program for recovery. He had a right to feel satisfied. On the anniversary of his first year in office the New York *Times*, with mock seriousness, noted only one major failure. Everything had improved except the weather; the winter of 1933-34 was the worst since 1888. The session was almost leisurely and the results reflected the easing of the crisis. Legislation created a Securities Exchange Commission and a Federal Housing Administration. With passage of the Reciprocal Trade Agreements Act, which permitted Roosevelt to pare existing tariff rates as much as 50 percent if other governments would make comparable cuts, the country seemed to be steering a new direction in tariff policy.

Congress adjourned in mid-June. On July 1 the President would board the U.S.S. *Houston* for a five-week trip to Hawaii by way of the Panama Canal. Before departing he set the tone of the off-year elections in another fireside chat. "The simplest way for each of you to judge recovery," he told his radio audience, "lies in the plain facts of your individual situation. Are you better off than you were last year?" That was the simple test, and Roosevelt was certain the people would respond. "I am inclined to believe," he told Vice President Garner, "that the voters as a whole are pretty well satisfied that we are going some place and that they still want action."

Even Roosevelt was not prepared for the results. To their 59 votes in the Senate the Democrats added 10; in the House the number of Democrats swelled from 313 to 332. It was virtually unheard of for the majority party to gain strength in an off-year election. It had last happened during the administration of Theodore Roosevelt, and was so uncommon as to justify Arthur Krock's verdict that it was "the most overwhelming victory in the history of American politics." "He [Roosevelt] has been all but crowned by the people," was William Allen White's bemused observation.

He [Huey Long] was high in our political thoughts."

Despite the obvious endorsement of the administration in the 1934 elections, the New Deal was not without its enemies. The Louisiana senator, Huey Long, with his Share Our Wealth organization, was only one of several who were "high" in the thoughts of Jim Farley and the New Dealers. There was also Father Charles Coughlin and his National Union of Social Justice, and Dr. Francis E. Townsend with his Old Age Revolving Pension plan. And there was Jouett Shouse and the American Liberty League, formed in the late summer of 1934 by leading businessmen.

Each had his own good reasons for disliking Franklin Roosevelt, reasons which will be discussed at length in a later chapter. And each could vent that dislike through organizations with broad appeal. Long, Coughlin, and Townsend spoke for those hardest hit by the depression, for those largely overlooked in New Deal plans for recovery, for a brand of social unrest that had been simmering far too long. They were tribunes for segments of society which would have agreed overwhelmingly that the New Deal had not gone nearly far enough. Shouse and the Liberty League reflected the views of those who were frightened at the direction the New Deal had taken, who were convinced Roosevelt had gone much too far.

Added to these mounting voices of discontent was the inescapable fact that, although conditions were better, the depression was not over. With the victory at the polls in 1934, what more should Roosevelt do; where was he to go from here? His State of the Union message in January 1935 seemed to provide the answer. It was a rousing affirmation of the social objectives of the New Deal in which he declared that security for the individual in an industrial society was an obligation of government: pensions for the aged, insurance for the unemployed, jobs instead of charity. "The federal government must and shall quit this business of relief," Roosevelt insisted.

The federal government did not quit the relief business, of course, but the President had to say something to head off the bad name relief was acquiring. A feud between Hopkins and Ickes over the relative merits of public works versus relief work, of carefully selected big public works projects versus small, hastily conceived relief projects, only made matters worse. Ickes was tighter than new shoes with public works funds while Hopkins was freer with relief funds than a sailor on shore leave. Hopkins (that "lawless individual," according to Ickes) finally won out over Ickes ("He is stubborn and righteous, which is a bad combination," Hopkins said sarcastically) as Roosevelt chose to go with massive work relief.

The feuding had endangered the President's relief bill for 1935, a "blank check" proposal totaling $4.8 billion. The bill finally passed in April, but the rest of the program languished in committee. Since the State of the Union message Roosevelt had grown strangely silent, becalmed, and the country seemed to be drifting. Certainly Congress was. Since January, Congress had plodded a leisurely course and was nearing its only apparent goal, adjournment.

Suddenly Roosevelt came alive again. For months he had been feeling the mounting pressure from all directions, from reformers, radicals, progressives, from demagogues like Long, from business and other conservative elements. What seemed to bring affairs to a head was the Supreme Court. In January the court had struck down the oil production controls of the NRA. In May the court torpedoed the Railway Pension Act and the Frazier-Lemke Farm Mortgage Act, and finished off the month with the "Black Monday" decision, which killed the NRA.

At a White House meeting in early June, congressional leaders were handed a list of "must" legislation by the aroused President. "Everyone could see," *Time* magazine reported, "that the winter of his discontent had ended." Hopkins was elated. "Boys—this is our hour," he is supposed to have urged. "We've got everything we want—a works program, social security, wages and hours, everything—now or never. Get your minds to work on developing a complete ticket to provide security for all the folks of this country up and down across the board."

Hopkins had every right to feel elated. Besides the relief bill, which had already passed, Roosevelt now wanted passage of a social security plan, the Wagner labor relations proposal, a banking bill, and a public utility holding company measure. To these four the President soon added a fifth, a new tax plan that critics very promptly labeled a "soak the rich" scheme. When Congress finally adjourned in late August, Roosevelt had—in some form, at least—everything he had demanded. It was, he said, a session of "memorable achievement."

But it had not been easy. The whole package, particularly the tax bill, had run the usual gauntlet of emotional adjectives—"shameful," "gigantic hoax," "unadulterated socialism," "un-American." The tax proposal was really insignificant so far as raising revenue was concerned—about $250 million more per year, or enough to run the government for maybe ten days. When Congress finished with the corporation and inheritance tax features the bill was no longer a significant device for redistributing wealth. What mattered was that the President's message to Congress recognized taxation as a means of social control even if the law, in its final form, did not.

The program that finally emerged from the long session set the tone of a new chapter in the history of the Roosevelt administration. The session was more than a "Second 100 Days." With social reform and social justice apparently taking priority over relief and recovery, some were willing to call it a Second New Deal.

"On the 4th of March, 1937, at the noon hour, on the front steps of the Capitol Building at Washington, Franklin D. Roosevelt will be inaugurated for his second term as President of the United States. That's as certain as sunrise tomorrow morning."

The editor of the Jackson (Mississippi) *Daily News* was wrong about one thing: neither Roosevelt nor anyone else would be inaugurated on March 4, 1937. Ratification of the Twentieth Amendment had changed Inauguration Day to January 20. And for a time, at least, there was some uncertainty whether Roosevelt would be reinaugurated at all.

Republicans, recovering from the shock of defeat in 1932 and 1934, were feeling optimistic. Their strategy for 1936 would be simple. Dominated by Hoover and the conservative wing of the party, Republicans would bear down hard on the New Deal threat to the virtue of the Constitution. Roosevelt, they would insist, was raping that precious document.

They would point to evasive actions and delaying tactics by the administration to avoid a showdown in the courts. They would remind voters what the courts had done to the New Deal program once given the chance. And they would quote from Roosevelt's letter of July 6, 1935, to Samuel B. Hill of the Ways and Means Committee, urging passage of the Guffey Coal bill: "I hope your Committee will not permit doubt as to its constitutionality, however reasonable, to block the suggested legislation." The anti-Constitution course of the New Deal, according to former Illinois Governor Frank Lowden, made "saving of the Constitution from the menace of those who would destroy it . . . the supreme issue of the hour." In his deliberate flouting of the Constitution, said House minority leader Bert Snell, "Mr. Roosevelt has come perilously close to what some people call impeachable grounds."

Roosevelt's assault on the Constitution, according to Republicans, was but a preliminary to changing the system of government. The air became thick with Republican charges of collectivism, socialism, dictatorship, and even communism—at least by implication. In November 1935 Hoover took his most vicious swipe at Roosevelt: "There are only four letters of the alphabet not now in use by the administration. When we establish the Quick Loans Corporation of Xylophones, Yachts, and Zithers the alphabet of our fathers will be exhausted. But, of course, the new Russian alphabet has thirty-four letters."

Perhaps Republicans were caught up in the enthusiasm of their own rhetoric. They may have been too much encouraged by the victory in a special election in mid-August 1935 of a relentless anti-Roosevelt Republican in a traditionally Democratic district of Rhode Island. The Boston *Evening Transcript* described the special election as "a change of popular sentiment of genuinely revolutionary proportions." They were impressed—perhaps overly impressed—with the "hate Roosevelt" campaign of the American Liberty League and the prospects of huge sums of money that the League and its business allies would use to oppose Roosevelt in 1936. Republicans may also have overestimated the importance of the discontent stirred by Long and others, the constant badgering of Roosevelt by extremists of the left and right, and the rumors of third parties and anti-Roosevelt coalitions. Whatever the reasons, Republicans believed the tide was running against Roosevelt—that they really had a chance in 1936. In December 1935 a poll by the *Literary Digest* indicated that 57.69 percent of the people were dissatisfied with the New Deal.

During the session of Congress in 1936 Roosevelt looked bad. It was a short and listless session, in which Roosevelt asked for little and got less. The veterans' bonus bill received a perfunctory veto by Roosevelt, which was promptly overridden. Three days after the session began the Supreme Court, in *U.S.* v *Butler*, ruled the Agricultural Adjustment Act unconstitutional. The administration responded with a new plan that met the court's objection to payments for curtailing production. In the new plan the farmer would receive subsidies for replacing soil-depleting crops with soil-conserving crops. In March the plan was enacted (the Soil Conservation Act)—to the accompaniment of the usual objections: slavery for the farmer, buying votes with "a gentle rain of checks," dictatorship, and worse. "It is communistic," said Congressman John Taber.

In June, Congress recessed temporarily for the Republican National Convention in Cleveland. The thought of bringing down Roosevelt quickened the pulse of every Republican has-been, might-be, and never-was. The list included Herbert Hoover, publisher Frank Knox, the aging Senator Borah, and Senator Lester Dickinson of Iowa. But the leading candidate was Alf Landon, governor of Kansas, the only Republican governor to have been reelected in 1934.

Publisher William Randolph Hearst, the strong man of San Simeon, claimed credit for "discovering" Landon. As early as October 1935 Hearst had sent trusted emissary John Lambert to Topeka to size up Landon. "Any ringbones on your pony that would show up in dry weather?" asked Landon—referring to himself—as Lambert, his scouting mission completed, stood on the platform waiting for his train. "You could have been more definitely against the League of Nations," Lambert replied. So began the presidential boom for the man James Farley described as "an inexperienced governor of a typical prairie state."

During the preconvention political jockeying Landon had been labeled "the Kansas Coolidge," but whoever was responsible for this comparison evidently did not know either man. Landon, born in Pennsylvania and reared in Ohio, had moved to Kansas in his teens. A lawyer who never practiced law, Landon had turned to oil and made millions. He was a veteran of the Bull Moose bolt in 1912, admired Wilson, supported the League of Nations, and had voted for the Progressives, La Follette and Wheeler, in 1924. A chain-smoking, card-playing fisherman, hunter, and horseman, Landon was anything but a Kansas Coolidge. He had even expressed some kind words for the New Deal. He was, as the Cincinnati *Enquirer* put it, "not so much a 'Kansas Coolidge' as a 'Republican Roosevelt.' '." When the time came, it was Landon on the first ballot.

Meanwhile there were what looked like serious Democratic defections. A prestigious group of anti-Roosevelt Democrats formed what they called the National Jeffersonian Democrats, made common cause with Governor Eugene Talmadge of Georgia and his "Grass Roots" anti-Roosevelt movement, and, from their headquarters in St. Louis, claimed they could divert at least three million votes from Roosevelt. The defection of Al Smith likewise seemed ominous. And there was the coalition of Coughlin, Townsend, and what was left of the Share Our Wealth movement under the banner of William Lemke and the new Union Party. But Roosevelt had eliminated one threat. After the assassination of Long, he had made peace with the Long political organization ("the Second Louisiana Purchase," according to the wags).

Roosevelt was probably not in as much danger of defeat as it seemed at the time. With what there was to choose from, Roosevelt and the New Deal looked better every day. Whatever mistakes he had made the people seemed willing to forgive. As Roosevelt said in his acceptance speech: "The Almighty weighs the sins of the warm-blooded and those of the cold-blooded in different scales." At any rate, Roosevelt campaigned as if his reelection was in doubt. In August and September he arranged what he called "nonpolitical" trips to various parts of the country just to "make news" talking about drought conditions, flood control, and the like. The New Deal also made news. Roosevelt kept before the public the achievements of the administration. ("Henry," he told Secretary Wallace, "through July, August, September, October and up to the fifth of November, I want cotton to sell at 12 cents. I do not care how you do it.")

In the campaign, Roosevelt went to the country, not just as a partisan Democrat but rather as a leader above the din of partisan politics. Appealing to a coalition of urban workers, farmers, young adults, blacks and other ethnic groups, and the unemployed, Roosevelt largely ignored the Democratic party, seldom mentioned it by name, accepted support from all sorts of groups and organizations not usually identified with the party, and campaigned "not as a Democrat, but as a New Deal liberal fighting not for party success but for a cause." The cause was the fulfillment of New Deal goals of social and economic democracy, the pledge to continue the struggle against "business and financial monopoly, speculation, reckless banking, class antagonism, sectionalism, war profiteering." What he was after, and what he got, was what one historian has called a "Grand Ratification" of the New Deal. The campaign of 1936 was an awesome performance, with Roosevelt at his very best.

By election day nearly everyone conceded that Roosevelt would be reelected; the only question was by how much, which would depend in large part on two significant developments during the campaign. One was the outspoken shift of black leaders from the Republican party to the New Deal camp. The other was the vigorous growth of political awareness by organized labor. Union leaders such as Sidney Hillman and John L. Lewis organized labor's Non-Partisan League, raised $1 million, and went all out to deliver the labor vote to Roosevelt. Democratic National Chairman Jim Farley predicted how much right on the button: Roosevelt 523 electoral votes, Landon 8. Only Maine and Vermont stood between Roosevelt and a clean sweep. Farley's explanation —"the over-powering personality of one individual"—was probably close to the truth. At least John D. M. Hamilton, Farley's Republican counterpart, agreed. In his appraisal of the election he said the same thing, only with greater poignancy: "The Lord couldn't have beaten Roosevelt in 1936."

"Very confidentially, I may give you an awful shock in about two weeks. Even if you do not agree, suspend final judgment and I will tell you the story."

The feeling appeared to be widespread that, in the wake of Roosevelt's overwhelming victory, there would be a period of conciliation, of consolidation, a period of good will and the healing of national wounds, an "era of good feeling." As usual, the prophets were wrong. Closer to the truth was the aging cynic, H. L. Mencken. "Give your mind seriously to the question of the Second Coming," he told a friend; "the signs and portents are upon us."

The year 1937, which began with such promise, would become the year in which the New Deal developed a case of the dry heaves. Roosevelt himself provided the issue with a top-billing item around which every malcontent on Capitol Hill with a score to settle with the White House could swarm like ants at a picnic. The "court packing" plan in

February—the "awful shock" to which Roosevelt's letter had alerted Felix Frankfurter—rallied New Deal opposition. His plan, the Judiciary Reorganization bill, would authorize the President to appoint an additional judge for each federal judge who did not retire upon reaching the age of seventy. The total number of such appointments could not exceed fifty; the maximum membership of the Supreme Court would be limited to fifteen. Even so, since the Supreme Court then had six justices over seventy years of age, Roosevelt could add six new justices immediately if the legislation were approved. The plan did not pass; but before his second term ended Roosevelt would appoint four judges, making the "Roosevelt Court" a reality despite Congress. But for the moment the enemy tasted blood. There would be other shocks, however, and considerable blood, before 1937 was over.

The first indication of Roosevelt's intentions had come in his inaugural address in January 1937. Had the nation during his first term, he asked, reached "the goal of our vision"? Roosevelt answered his own question:

I see millions of families trying to live on incomes so meager . . . .
I see millions whose daily lives in the city and on the farm continue under conditions labeled indecent. . . .
I see millions denied education, recreation, and the opportunity to better their lot. . . .
I see millions lacking the means to buy the products of farm and factory. . . .
I see one third of a nation ill-housed, ill-clad, ill-nourished.

In quest of "the goal of our vision," Roosevelt would attempt much in 1937, and would come away almost empty handed. "Why so lean a harvest," asked Democratic Senator Theodore Green of Rhode Island, "from soil that promised such abundant fertility?" Looking back on the first session of the 1937 Congress, the New York *Times* observed with cool detachment: "Rarely has an Administration met so many failures."

The casualty list read like an honor roll of reform legislation: a child labor bill, a stronger food and drug bill, a ship safety bill, crop insurance and other farm bills, proposals that would have made the Civilian Conservation Corps permanent, and extension of the TVA concept to other parts of the country. But the most dramatic defeats were the wages and hours proposal, the plan for reorganization of the executive branch, and, of course, the court plan.

After such a sweeping victory in 1936, what had gone wrong? Part of it was the general feeling, beginning to develop among both Republicans and Democrats, that the 1936 victory was Roosevelt's last. Republicans would not have to face such a campaigner again and Democrats had better find a successor. Part of it was resentment, and a deterioration in relations with the Congress, largely because of Roosevelt's great popularity with which he could pressure Capitol Hill. Congressman Herron Pearson of Tennessee went to the heart of the matter when he pointed out that only eighteen of the seventy-seven major bills passed during Roosevelt's first term had originated in Congress, "where all ought to have originated." The other fifty-nine bills, said Pearson, the resentment boiling over, "had an illegitimate birth, conceived in sin and shapened in iniquity somewhere downtown, and were brought up here and the bastards laid on our doorstep with the command of the Executive that we acknowledge parentage."

Part of it was disenchantment. Roosevelt was embarrassed and deeply disturbed by a sudden outbreak of labor disorders that began in the fall of 1936 and continued through the summer of 1937. Most of the labor troubles involved the new Congress of Industrial Organizations. The CIO had been born in November 1935, and John L. Lewis, president of the United Mine Workers, was the midwife. The two dozen or so industrial unions in the American Federation of Labor had become increasingly restive and disillusioned with what they believed were selfish and shortsighted policies of the craft unions that dominated the AFL. What finally brought matters to a head was the flat rejection at the AFL convention in 1935 of Lewis's proposals for moving more quickly on the unionizing of workers in mass production industries. When Lewis and other dissident industrial union leaders began making plans for a new and competing organization, the AFL made irrevocable the breach in the labor movement by expelling the industrial unions.

It was the organizing activities of the CIO that touched off trouble in late 1936, and it began with the effort of the United Rubber Workers to unionize the rubber industry in Akron, Ohio—an effort that introduced the country to a novel device for preventing strikebreaking and lockouts: the sit-down strike. The sit-down tactic was soon appropriated by the United Automobile Workers in their drive to unionize the industry. The climax came during January and February 1937, when strikers occupied a General Motors plant in Flint, Michigan, for six weeks.

Meanwhile efforts to organize the steel industry were moving along apparently without a hitch. In March, United States Steel, the industry leader, had quietly recognized the union, and it was assumed that the others would quickly fall in line. But the other companies ("Little Steel," they were called) refused. The resulting strikes in Massillon, Ohio, and Chicago, which left a dozen strikers dead and scores injured, caused the whole country to stir apprehensively. This was bad enough, but Roosevelt was in for further embarrassment.

For four years economic conditions had improved, until in the spring of 1937 levels of production exceeded those of 1929 before the great Crash. The moment Roosevelt attempted to cut back on spending and relief and to balance the budget in 1937, the economy began going sour again, wiping out most of the gains that had been made since 1933. The usual statistics—business and industrial indexes, car loadings, steel production, stock sales, inventories, exports, unemployment, and all the rest—bore evidence that the "Roosevelt Panic" (as Representative Ham Fish first labeled it) was on.

In November Roosevelt called a special session of Congress. His program to halt the distressing skid included new agricultural legislation, a wages and hours proposal, housing legislation, antitrust law revision, and a request for reorganization of the executive branch. "If private enterprise does not respond," Roosevelt warned Congress and the country, "government must take up the slack." But Congress adjourned a month later without acting on any of the proposals.

The outbreak of labor troubles, particularly the sit-down strikes with their implied threat to private property, and the sharp dip in the economy created serious doubts about the Roosevelt leadership. As if to compound his troubles, Roosevelt was faced with revolt in the ranks of southern Democrats in Congress, men of his own party who were never comfortable in the New Deal, who were alarmed at the trend of the New Deal, its lavish spending, its mounting debt, its expanding bureaucracy, its casual disregard for traditional policies and procedures.

What was more, they saw the New Deal as a threat to traditional race relations, to states' rights, and to the long-familiar power structure of the South. Southern Democrats, in addition to all else, resented the inferior position to which they had been relegated in the New Deal scheme of things. "Let me say in all candor to my fellow Senators, and to anyone else who happens to hear it," said Senator Josiah Bailey of North Carolina, "that this group is not going to run the Democratic Party." The result was a close working agreement in 1937 between southern Democrats and Republicans, a coalition that was capable of fighting Roosevelt to a standoff.

The Roosevelt leadership had received another staggering blow in 1937. In mid-August, when Roosevelt had the opportunity to make his first Supreme Court appointment since becoming President, his choice to fill the vacancy caused by the retirement of Justice Van Devanter was Alabama's Senator Hugo Black. Black, a consistent supporter of the New Deal, was certain to be confirmed by his Senate colleagues, although some agreed privately with former President Hoover's wry observation that his appointment would mean the court was "one-ninth packed."

The senator and his wife were in Europe when a reporter broke the story that Black had once been a member of the Ku Klux Klan. Cutting short his trip, Black returned and made a clean breast of it before a nationwide radio audience. Yes, he had belonged to the Klan. When he first entered local politics in Alabama, he explained, election was impossible without Klan approval. But he had never been active, had never attended Klan meetings after joining. The Senate accepted Black's explanation and confirmed the appointment, but Roosevelt's critics had a joyous time of it. "When Franklin Roosevelt is dead and buried and all his bones are rotted," wrote one, "the one thing for which he will be remembered is the fact that he played around with Black and appointed to the highest honorable office in American life a man who was a member of the Ku Klux Klan."

All these setbacks in 1937 had seemingly ended Roosevelt's hold over Congress. The President, Harold Ickes wrote in his diary in late summer, "is punch drunk from the punishment that he has suffered recently." The irresistible leader of 1936 had become the repudiated leader of 1937.

When the President turned up empty handed after the special session it was a sure sign that it was safe for members of the conservative coalition to move. In December 1937 they circulated their own recovery plan, which was largely a product of the bipartisan efforts of Democratic Senator Bailey of North Carolina and Republican Senator Vandenburg of Michigan. The plan was as old as the Ark of the Covenant: states' rights, balanced budgets, encouragement for business, tax cuts, and the other Ten Commandments of conservatism.

Now it was 1938, a year of brutal intramural strife among Democrats, fought out against a backdrop of continuing depression and impending elections. No motivating force in this world is more compelling, more likely to produce congressional action, than elections. Prospects of deepening depression during an election year had their sobering effect, bringing a halt to the stalemate, to the war of attrition between Congress and the President, long enough to avert near catastrophe among farmers.

In February 1938 Roosevelt signed into law a new Agricultural Adjustment Act that controlled production through soil conservation payments and acreage allotments. In addition, growers of the five leading staples—wheat, corn, cotton, rice, and tobacco—were to receive parity payments. That is, with 1909-14 as a base period (1919-29 for tobacco), farmers were guaranteed an income up to 75 percent of what those commodities had brought during the base period. The law likewise provided for crop insurance against natural disasters, export subsidies to stimulate foreign sales, and distribution of surpluses to those on relief.

In May, Congress finally approved Roosevelt's wages and hours proposal; but it took a last-minute public appeal by the President to get it. The Fair Labor Standards Act, as it was called, provided for a twenty-five cents an hour minimum wage, to be increased to forty cents in gradual stages. The work week, set at forty-four hours, would be reduced to forty hours over a three-year period, and workers were to receive time and a half for overtime work. The law also had the effect of abolishing child labor by forbidding the interstate shipment of goods produced by persons under sixteen years of age.

But the Congress defeated Roosevelt's reorganization bill, just as it had done in the special session of 1937. Presidents at least as far back as Theodore Roosevelt had recognized the need for reorganization of the administrative machinery, and just before leaving office Hoover had received from the Congress limited reorganization power, power that would be wholly inadequate for the sudden growth of administration during the New Deal. Every serious student of government knew that sooner or later there would have to be a major overhaul.

In 1936 Roosevelt had appointed a Committee on Administrative Management that included many outstanding authorities on public administration. It was an executive reorganization bill, embodying the Committee's recommendations, that was defeated in the special session of 1937 and again in 1938. It had been savagely attacked by the opposition press (Colonel McCormick's Chicago *Tribune* branded it a "dictator bill"), by Father Coughlin, who inspired an avalanche of letters and telegrams against it, and by congressional enemies who insisted on comparing it to the court-packing plan. In 1938, an election year, it had been subjected to the usual campaign aberrations.

(In 1939, after all the clamor had subsided, Congress, without undue opposition, passed an executive reorganization bill similar to the one that had been twice defeated. It provided for six executive assistants to aid the President, and it granted authority to streamline administration by abolishing some agencies outright, by placing unattached agencies in appropriate departments, by shifting others from one department to another, and by gathering others under new coordinating agencies. The reorganization steps under Roosevelt were crucial—so crucial, according to one expert in public administration, that they may have "saved the Presidency from paralysis and the Constitution from radical amendment." In any case, the reorganization converted the presidency into "an instrument of twentieth century government.")

The heavy black lines did not start climbing back up the economic charts until the summer of 1938, and then only with a massive transfusion of federal funds. "Pump priming" through the Works Progress Administration (WPA), the Farm Security Administration (FSA), the Civilian Conservation Corps (CCC), and other agencies reversed the downward spiral. But it took $3 billion to do it, and ended Roosevelt's brief fling at budget balancing.

The new economic emergency had been a contributing factor in the split between Roosevelt and the Congress. Working together under pressure to deal with the emergency had, if anything, widened the rift, especially between Roosevelt and the southern conservative bloc. And all efforts to close the gap had failed. "The Party is divided hopelessly," Senator Bailey wrote Wyoming's Joseph O'Mahoney; "the points of view and the respective interests, the objectives, cannot be reconciled."

The coalition of southern Democrats and northern Republicans became a permanent arrangement in 1938. Blocked in Congress by members of his own party, some of whom owed their elections directly to his popularity, Roosevelt slowly came to a decision: the time had come for a showdown with his own party. "An election cannot give a country a firm sense of direction," he told the country in a fireside chat in June 1938, "if it has two or more national parties which merely have different names but are as alike in their principles and aims as peas in the same pod." "As the head of the Democratic Party," he continued, "charged with the responsibility of the definitely liberal declaration of principles set forth in the 1936 Democratic platform, I feel that I have every right to speak . . . where there may be a clear issue between candidates for a Democratic nomination involving these principles."

The struggle over court packing may have planted the purge idea. Here was a fight, not with Republicans (they wisely stayed out of it) but between the President and his own party. Roosevelt stewed for weeks over the humiliation by a Congress that had gotten completely out of hand.

He could not forgive or forget a Vice President who had stood in the Senate lobby with one hand holding his nose and the thumb of his other hand turned down on the court plan. Garner had retreated to Texas during the worst of it. Nor could Roosevelt forget that Hatton Sumners of Texas, chairman of the important Judiciary Committee, had told his House colleagues "Boys, here's where I cash in." Nor that Tom Connally, Carter Glass, and other southern Democrats worked overtime with men like Burton K. Wheeler, Ed Burke, and Bennett Champ Clark in the common cause of undoing a Democratic President. For one who had been reelected in 1936 the way Roosevelt had, and with Democratic congressmen swarming about his coattails, the treachery was intolerable.

If the court fight suggested the purge, the announcement by Governor Phil La Follette in the spring of 1938 that he was launching a new party, the National Progressives of America, created a sense of urgency. Roosevelt genuinely believed the La Follette party was a threat, that it might attract those liberal and left of center groups on which Roosevelt had built a new coalition after the election of 1934. He felt compelled to remove any doubt that the Democratic party was the party of liberalism and reform.

Jim Farley and other party leaders were appalled by Roosevelt's purge plan. Twenty-three of the Democrats' thirty senators were up for reelection in 1938, plus, of course, the entire House membership. Roosevelt proposed to intervene, directly or indirectly, in a handful of these elections to help unseat men who had consistently opposed him. Other Presidents had tried their hand at intervening in local elections— to their sorrow. Roosevelt, egged on by Hopkins, Corcoran, Ickes, and some others close to the President (the "White House Janizaries," Hugh Johnson was calling them in his newspaper column), was inviting still another good licking.

There were ten—all Democrats, all with years of seniority and prestige—whom Roosevelt would have been delighted to see retired into the oblivion of private life: Senators Clark of Missouri, Adams of Colorado, McCarran of Nevada, Longeran of Connecticut, "Cotton Ed" Smith of South Carolina, Tydings of Maryland, Gillette of Iowa, Van Nuys of Indiana, and George of Georgia. John O'Connor of New York City, who as chairman of the House Rules Committee had done more than any one man in Congress to frustrate the President, was the lone congressman on Roosevelt's priority list. But as election time approached, Roosevelt may have had second thoughts. Despite his strong feelings toward them, Roosevelt refrained from any direct action against Clark, Adams, McCarran, Gillette, and Van Nuys. What at the start looked like a mass execution with blindfolds and a final cigarette had turned into a wrist-slapping exercise.

The most dramatic vignette in Roosevelt's attempted purge unfolded at an unlikely, out-of-the-way place: Barnesville, Georgia. Walter George, a fixture in the Senate since 1922, was being opposed in the primary by Governor Gene Talmadge, idol of the Georgia "crackers," and by the Roosevelt candidate, the colorless Lawrence Camp, an obscure United States district attorney from Atlanta. August 10 was a sweltering day in Barnesville, where a soggy, sweaty crowd gathered at a huge outdoor rally to see the fun.

Roosevelt and Harry Hopkins were there. A nervous Lawrence Camp and a poker-faced Walter George were there. Talmadge, who had vowed long ago never to be seen with Roosevelt, was somewhere else, campaigning against the "nigger loving" New Deal and "that cripple," Franklin Roosevelt. When he spoke to the crowd, Roosevelt minced no words:

Let me make it perfectly clear that he [Senator George] is, and I hope always will be, my friend. He is beyond any possible question a gentleman and a scholar ... but with whom I differ heartily and sincerely on the principles and policies of how the government of the United States ought to be run. I am impelled to make it clear that on most public questions he and I do not speak the same language.

As soon as the President finished his speech, Senator George approached him gravely and said: "Mr. President, I regret that you have taken this occasion to question my democracy and to attack my public record. I want you to know that I accept the challenge."

His duel with Congress—the "purge"—was a failure. All Roosevelt accomplished was the martyrdom of his enemies, who (except O'Connor) were reelected to a man. On the surface, the internecine strife between Roosevelt and congressional Democrats was along ideological lines, but what was actually at stake was control of an unbeatable party label. As one Michigan editor put it at the time, "We are witnessing in the Senate debate another turning point in the history of the country." "Out of this debate," he continued, "will emerge a New Deal Party and a Democratic Party ... it seems practically certain that the Democratic Party, as it has existed almost from the beginning of the country, will be doomed." "A party," he wrote, by way of clarifying the issue, "cannot exist half Roosevelt and half Democratic."

Despite all this, a *Fortune* poll early in 1939 indicated that more than 60 percent of the country, at least in some general way, approved of Roosevelt and his New Deal policies. "If the *Fortune* survey is even approximately correct," wrote journalist Ernest Lindley, "a great many Democrats in Congress have let themselves be stampeded into the anti-Roosevelt camp by trepidations based on incorrect readings of the public mind." Roosevelt's strength, as it had been from the beginning, was his love affair with the American people. So enduring was that bond, wrote Lindley, that it should serve as "a warning to the members of Congress, and especially to the Democrats, that they should think twice—or three or four times—before they flout him."

"I have said this before, but I shall say it again and again and again: Your boys are not going to be sent into any foreign wars."

Even had things been going well for Roosevelt at home—which they

were not—World War II would undoubtedly have required a severe cur-
tailment of his New Deal. The war would certainly make Roosevelt's
pledge to the parents of America concerning their boys an impossible
promise to keep.

Roosevelt, who came of age just when the United States was beginning to flex its muscles as a world power, was impressed with the
he-man style of diplomacy practiced by his famous cousin, Theodore
Roosevelt. Franklin, moreover, had a life long interest in ships, a great
love for the sea and the navy, and was admittedly influenced by the
ideas of Admiral Mahan. By 1933, Roosevelt had been to Europe more
than a dozen times.

Service in the Wilson administration gave him the opportunity to see
international policymaking and diplomacy close up. While Wilson had
been struggling to maintain neutrality, Roosevelt was working to build
the navy against the time when the United States would enter the war.
He was certain it would happen, believed it *should* happen, and was
committed to the use of United States power not for self-aggrandize-
ment but for international peace. Roosevelt shared Wilson's vision of a
League of Nations, and had made it a priority issue when he ran as the
Democratic vice presidential candidate in 1920.

Except for the positive accomplishments of the Washington Naval
Conference, Roosevelt deplored the drift of international affairs and
the sterility of United States policy during the 1920s. He ridiculed what
he considered the stupidities of Republican tariff policy and the preten-
sions of the Kellogg-Briand Peace Pact. But as the decade wore on, as
depression settled over the land, Roosevelt trimmed sail on the League
issue. As a candidate in 1932, he announced that he was opposed to
United States membership in the discredited League. Later, of course,
he would propose such an organization of his own, the United Nations.

He went through with a commitment made by Hoover to participate
in an international conference at London in June 1933. The aim of the
gold bloc countries at London, to stabilize foreign exchanges, was in-
compatible with Roosevelt's policy to raise commodity prices at home
by reducing the value of the dollar. He was roundly charged with
"wrecking" the London Economic Conference, and perhaps he did. But
in a choice between immediate benefits from domestic policy and long-
range benefits from international monetary cooperation, Roosevelt
chose to be nationalistic.

Except for poking his finger in the eye of the world at the London Economic Conference, Roosevelt was fairly consistently internationalist, but he had a healthy concern for isolationists in both parties. In retrospect, it may be that Roosevelt let isolationists deter him too much. At least there was a kind of timidity in his foreign policy, an unwillingness to jeopardize domestic programs by too vigorous a pursuit of international goals. The rationale was that, to whip the depression, Roosevelt had to have isolationist votes in Congress. The Reciprocal Trade Agreements Act of June 1934 was an example of Roosevelt's problem. The act permitted him, at his own discretion, to adjust tariff rates as much as 50 percent. It was a favorable start toward liberalizing United States policy, but it was also a warning. Only five Republicans voted for it, two in the House and three in the Senate.

Depression conditions were causing many Americans to see the Soviet Union in a new light. Businessmen, visualizing Russia as a potential market for surplus production, threw ideology to the winds and urged resumption of diplomatic relations. Besides, with the victorious Japanese armies in China whooping it up for the Emperor, being on good terms with Russia was not such a bad idea. Talks in October 1933 between Roosevelt and Maxim Litvinov, commissar for Soviet foreign affairs, paved the way. The resumption of normal relations was not a rousing success, but it marked an important break with past policy.

In his inaugural address Roosevelt had said he would "dedicate this Nation to the policy of the good neighbor." This was evidently one of those meaningless generalities that find their way into speeches. His first opportunity to be a "good neighbor" was in Latin America, and in time the Good Neighbor policy was understood to mean United States policy in the Western Hemisphere.

On the whole, his plan was a sincere effort to be what the label implied. In 1901, in the aftermath of the Spanish American War, Cuba had become at least a quasi protectorate of the United States. The most significant provision of the Platt Amendment, which defined the new relationship, granted the United States the right of intervention to preserve "Cuban independence and the maintenance of a government adequate for the protection of life, property and individual liberty." But United States claims to the right of intervention went much further. Since 1904, when Santo Domingo defaulted on its foreign debt, the United States had exercised in the Western Hemisphere what President

Theodore Roosevelt defined as "an international police power." This policy—the Roosevelt Corollary to the Monroe Doctrine—meant that while the Monroe Doctrine precluded intervention in the hemisphere by European powers, it was the responsibility of the United States to see that cause for intervention did not arise.

At the Montevideo Conference in December 1933 the United States surrendered the unilateral right of intervention under the Roosevelt Corollary, abrogated the Platt Amendment the next year, withdrew from Haiti, and, by recognizing the Martinez government in El Salvador, was apparently abandoning the traditional policy of withholding recognition of revolutionary governments in the hemisphere. New treaty arrangements with Panama in 1936 omitted the right of intervention and transferred to Panama responsibilities for operating and protecting the canal.

That the policy was working was reflected in the rousing welcome Roosevelt received when he arrived for the Buenos Aires Conference in December 1936. In 1938 the Good Neighbor policy was put to the supreme test by expropriations of American-owned petroleum lands by the leftist regime in Mexico. Roosevelt, who resisted pressures to intervene, gently urged the Mexican government to allow reasonable compensation. A commission of United States and Mexican representatives later arranged a quietly amicable settlement of the dispute. When World War II finally came, the Good Neighbor policy paid handsome dividends in the general response and cooperation of the hemisphere in the war effort.

Meanwhile the international structure, which had begun to collapse in 1931 with the Japanese attack on China, was about to receive another violent blow from Italy's tinhorn caesar. In October 1935, Mussolini's new Roman legions invaded Ethiopia. Roosevelt, doing what he had to do, declared United States neutrality and invoked an arms embargo.

The isolationist mood of the country had been made manifestly clear by public reaction to the Nye Committee investigation of the munitions industry in 1934 and 1935 and by the prompt and overwhelming rejection of Roosevelt's proposal in 1935 that the United States join the World Court. In the summer of 1935, when Mussolini's intentions toward Ethiopia became clear, that isolationist mood had also produced the Pittman Resolution in the Congress, intended to keep the United States from again being led up the garden path.

The Pittman Resolution, which contained a mandatory arms and credit embargo, prohibited American ships from carrying arms or munitions and withdrew the protection of the government from United States citizens traveling on belligerent ships. This meant, of course, that the policy would inadvertently penalize future victims of aggression. This was not the case, however, with Ethiopia, which did not have the shipping or financial resources to buy arms from the United States. Since the policy applied only to arms, Roosevelt did the next best thing: he appealed to the country to restrict, voluntarily, other exports —what he called a "moral embargo." Moral suasion had about as much effect upon American oil companies as the Ethiopians and their spears had against Mussolini's bombs and gas.

Roosevelt was not so opposed to the neutrality legislation as some, in retrospect, have let on. The mandatory arms embargo disappointed him; he had hoped it would be discretionary. But he approved the idea of a neutrality stand that would avoid the pitfalls that had been Wilson's undoing. If war came, Roosevelt did not want to have to defend American rights blindly—relying on history, on natural law, on the caprice of German submarine commanders, or whatever, as Wilson had been forced to do. Besides, the restriction was for only six months. Perhaps when it expired he could get more flexible legislation from Congress on the arms embargo.

Mussolini's Ethiopian adventure was the start of one international crisis after another. In March 1936, Hitler marched troops into the Rhineland, the German territory west of the Rhine River that had been demilitarized according to terms of the Treaty of Versailles after World War I. That summer civil war erupted in Spain, whose result, after more than two years of bloodletting, was the fascist regime of Francisco Franco. In 1937 the Japanese, not content with their earlier grab of Manchuria, resumed the war against Chiang Kai-shek. In 1938 Hitler swallowed Austria and, with the capitulation of Daladier and Chamberlain at Munich, the Sudetenland of Czechoslovakia.

The "peace in our time," which British Prime Minister Neville Chamberlain promised after Munich, lasted six months. In March 1939 Hitler seized the remainder of Czechoslovakia; in April, Mussolini invaded Albania; in May, the two nations joined forces in the Rome-Berlin Axis; in August, Hitler's nonaggression pact with Russia sealed the fate of Poland. On September 1, Germany invaded Poland and World War II was under way.

This course of events produced what one historian has called a "storm cellar" neutrality on the part of the United States. In the case of the Rhineland, if England and France were unwilling to risk war to stop Hitler—a war they were certain to win—there was not a whole lot the United States could do about it. On the other hand, United States involvement in the Spanish Civil War was unthinkable. Before it was over there would be intervention by others, by Germany, by Italy, by Russia, who would use that poor and ravaged land for a dress rehearsal of World War II. But with American public opinion badly divided, with Catholics supporting Franco and Communists supporting the Loyalists, Roosevelt (who privately sympathized with the Loyalist cause) kept hands off. The Congress responded to the Spanish Civil War by amending the neutrality legislation to include civil wars in the arms embargo.

In May 1937, with isolationist sentiment in the United States approaching high tide, Congress produced a new neutrality act. (The original act, in August 1935, was for only six months, but when the time came for it to expire, Congress, with Roosevelt's approval, had extended the term for another year, until May 1, 1937.) Its basic features —an arms and credit embargo and a ban on travel—were not questioned.

The question confronting Congress and the President in 1937 was how far the country was prepared to go in sacrificing its export trade (in goods other than arms) if a general war broke out in Europe. Was it possible to keep the United States out of war without endangering economic recovery? Could the country, through legislation, have the best of both worlds—peace with prosperity? The naive answer was yes. All Congress had to do was require that goods be sold on a "cash and carry" basis. The Neutrality Act of 1937, with its cash-and-carry formula, was, according to one historian, the only way the United States could "remain economically in the world and politically out of it."

The ink was hardly dry before the administration was faced with the question of invoking the new act when Japan resumed the rape of China. Roosevelt, on a technicality, had a choice—the technicality being the lack of a formal declaration of war by either Japan or China. Over loud protests from isolationists, Roosevelt refrained from applying the neutrality act to the Sino-Japanese conflict. Such a policy, while risky, and of little practical value to China, nevertheless satisfied the sympathetic feeling of most Americans toward China.

In October, at Chicago, Roosevelt launched what he later called a "trial balloon" when he proposed that the democracies "quarantine" the aggressors. But the country was never going to get a chance to find out what that might mean. Even before Roosevelt could get back to Washington there was talk among some isolationist congressmen of possible impeachment. And the *Wall Street Journal* ran a headline: STOP FOREIGN MEDDLING: AMERICA WANTS PEACE. "It is a terrible thing," said the President at his next news conference, "to look over your shoulder when you are trying to lead—and to find no one there."

The fact is, somebody *was* there. The isolationist press, as expected, uttered great cries of anguish over Roosevelt's quarantine speech, but the Washington *Post* and the New York *Times* endorsed the concept, as did the majority of editorial writers around the country. Because Roosevelt had expected his trial balloon to be shot down by isolationists, its widespread support had caught him by surprise. He obviously had not thought through the quarantine idea. When pressed to elaborate, he "retreated into ambiguity," according to one writer, rather than admit there was no "substance to his rhetoric."

Now it was 1938, and the United States continued its passive role, reacting to world events rather than trying to shape them. The Austrian *anschluss* and the Munich crisis inspired dread and foreboding, but little else. When England and France surrendered the Sudetenland of Czechoslovakia to Hitler at Munich, the feeling in the United States was one of immense relief. The Munich settlement marked the high tide of isolationism in the United States.

In some larger sense, isolationism had encouraged Hitler—had, in the words of a leading historian, made the United States "the handmaiden of European appeasement." On the other hand, the gutless policies of England and France in the 1930s were not likely to encourage material aid or moral support from the United States. A strong stand against aggression and dictatorship might have enabled Roosevelt to overcome isolationist opposition at home, but without some sign from England and France of fire in their souls it was asking too much to expect the United States to act unilaterally. European appeasement was no more commendable than United States neutrality.

The events of 1939—the fall of Czechoslovakia, the Albanian invasion, the Rome-Berlin Axis, and Hitler's assault upon Poland—prodded the United States into the first long step toward war. In November, Roosevelt signed the Neutrality Act of 1939. The loan and travel bans remained. But the United States could now sell the tools of war to all belligerents on a cash-and-carry basis. As a practical matter, repeal of the arms embargo meant United States aid for Hitler's foes; British control of the seas guaranteed that no swastika flags would fly on ships in United States ports.

The fall of the Low Countries and the imminent fall of France in the spring of 1940 precipitated the "Great Debate": Should the United States become an impregnable fortress or gamble on all-out aid to the Allies short of war? The issue was reflected in the noisy clash between the America First Committee and the Committee to Defend America by Aiding the Allies, organizations of concerned citizens who carried the debate from Madison Square Garden to the most obscure crossroads.

Support for the America First Committee came from an improbable mixture of isolationists—or "non-interventionists" as they preferred to call themselves. There were high-minded idealists who sincerely believed that the wisest policy for the United States was to avoid war at all costs. Included in their ranks were many clergymen and devout Christians, especially young people, who had embraced a pacifist philosophy of nonresistance. There were businessmen, particularly midwestern businessmen, who saw appeasement of the dictators as a way of stimulating trade, and other businessmen who joined in perhaps solely because of dislike for the New Deal. Some old Progressives, men like Gerald P. Nye and Burton K. Wheeler, thought they saw the hand of munition makers and Wall Street in the drift of events. Some of the foreign-born, German Americans and Italian Americans, opposed war with the Axis because it would strain their loyalties. The Socialists saw war—any war—as the fatal flaw of capitalism. The Communists held the same view of the war, until Hitler attacked the Soviet Union. The native fascist crowd likewise opposed intervention, because they favored an Axis victory and the resulting spread, they hoped, of fascist dictatorship to the United States.

The Committee to Defend America by Aiding the Allies, organized by William Allen White, the widely respected newspaper editor from Kansas, drew support from those who, for whatever reason, were Anglophiles, who were unwilling to see England and the British Empire go under. For obvious reasons, the White Committee had widespread sympathy from American Jewry. But most supporters of aid for the

Allies were simply patriotic Americans who disagreed with their counterparts in the America First Committee, and who believed that an indifferent foreign policy in the 1930s had left the country with only one meaningful choice short of war. There were even a few who wanted to go further and declare war on the Axis.

Roosevelt eventually chose "measures short of war"—which meant a scrape-the-bottom-of-the-barrel policy to provide arms to England after the Dunkirk disaster and a "destroyer deal" in which fifty United States destroyers were given to England in exchange for bases in Newfoundland, Bermuda, and the Caribbean.

Nineteen forty was a presidential election year, and the Great Debate was still raging when the Republicans assembled in Philadelphia—two days after the surrender of France. Leading contenders for the nomination were Senator Arthur Vandenburg of Michigan and Robert A. Taft of Ohio, both isolationists, and the vigorous young district attorney from New York, Thomas E. Dewey, who also had isolationist leanings.

But out of nowhere in the weeks just before the convention had come Wendell Willkie, Indiana-born president of Commonwealth and Southern, the huge public utilities holding company. Willkie, a Republican convert, had been a delegate to the Democratic convention in 1924, had supported Smith in 1928, and had voted for Roosevelt in 1932. Despite his tousled, puckish appearance, Willkie was a superb executive and hard-driving salesman, a "simple barefoot Wall Street lawyer" (according to Harold Ickes) whose monumental battles with the TVA had finally led him into the Republican camp.

Willkie went into Philadelphia with the backing of the *Saturday Evening Post*, of Henry Luce, publisher of *Time, Life*, and *Fortune* magazines, and with noisy support from the young, the liberals, and the internationalists in Republican ranks—and with very few delegates. On the first ballot he got only 105 votes. But with the galleries in bedlam, chanting "We Want Willkie!" he was nominated on the sixth ballot.

Roosevelt approached 1940 gingerly. He kept silent, and did not encourage any of the preconvention possibilities such as Farley or Garner. Chances are he intended all along to be the candidate; and once German panzers began to overrun France there was no doubt of it. But he had to proceed cautiously; the third term tradition, like all traditions with no particular rational basis, was a formidable obstacle. The stage was set for a draft. When one anonymous voice, yelling "We Want

Roosevelt!" set off a chain reaction in the hall, the convention was so relieved that it nominated Roosevelt by acclamation.

The Republicans did not repeat the error of 1936 by threatening to undo New Deal reforms. They could hardly have done so anyway, since their candidate had supported most of the New Deal. And on the war issue Willkie was closer to Roosevelt than to the die-hard Republican isolationists. Willkie hammered away at unemployment and the third term issue, but he was seriously handicapped by his "me too" background.

Early in the campaign he talked of a bipartisan foreign policy. He accepted the destroyer deal, although he deplored Roosevelt's method as "the most dictatorial and arbitrary act of any President in the history of the United States." As the campaign progressed, Willkie became increasingly reckless, calling Roosevelt a warmonger, promising no involvement in foreign war (which he later passed off as "campaign oratory"), and predicting that if Roosevelt were reelected he would have the country at war by 1941.

Roosevelt, stressing the achievements of the New Deal and the need for experience in building the defense needs of the country, nevertheless thought it prudent to counter Willkie's prophecy by reassuring the public: "Your boys are not going to be sent into any foreign wars." Roosevelt overwhelmed Willkie in electoral votes, 449 to 82, and by a margin of nearly five million in popular votes. The American people seemed to be endorsing his "measures short of war" approach, and this was reflected in the Gallup poll of 1940: 84 percent now favored an Allied victory, and 62 percent favored aid to the Allies short of war.

Through 1940 and into 1941, in fact right up to the eve of Pearl Harbor, Americans had clung to the belief that they could defend themselves by furnishing aid to England short of actual military involvement. The bottom-of-the-barrel policy and the destroyer agreement in 1940 had nevertheless marked the end of United States neutrality. When the war started, England had a dollar reserve of about six and a half billion. By the end of 1940 this had dwindled to roughly two billion. In a fireside chat late in December, Roosevelt called upon the American people to help the United States become what he called the "arsenal of democracy." He followed this, in his State of the Union message in January 1941, with a request for funds to build war materials for the Allies, 'the cost to be repaid by the Allies at the end of the war in goods and services. Roosevelt's proposal, quickly labeled Lend-Lease, was approved by Congress with an initial appropriation of $7 billion.

Public support of these policies meant the United States had departed from the Maginot Line mentality of the early neutrality acts, had moved from the passive role of neutral in the European conflict to one of friendly nonbelligerence. For years the United States had been wedded to a policy not of preventing war but of staying out of war if and when it came. By 1941 it was dedicated to the defeat of Hitler through all-out aid to England.

"I fling this challenge to America. If she, in her contentment, is going to stick blindly and stubbornly to the status quo in the Pacific, then we will fight America."

It was difficult to say for certain where or when relations began to go sour between the United States and Japan. As early as 1931 Japan had initiated a series of aggressive actions in the Far East by seizing Manchuria from China. This was followed by her repudiation of the Nine Power Pact, withdrawal from the League of Nations, and, in 1937, all-out war with China. In November 1938, shortly after Munich, the Japanese Premier, Prince Konoye, announced Japan's goals for a "New Order in East Asia" and a "co-prosperity sphere in Greater East Asia." What this might mean was not altogether clear, but it was certain to be on Japan's terms.

The turning point in relations with the United States may have arrived in July 1939, when recognition by the British government of Japanese conquests in China made it clear the United States could no longer count on help from England to protect its interests in the Far East. The United States now appeared to be faced with the choice of retreating in the Far East or of pursuing a more vigorous policy toward Japan on its own.

In 1940 the course of the war in Europe made Japan bolder. The fall of France offered Japan the opportunity to move into French Indo-China. The "Battle of Britain" enabled Japan to pressure England into closing the Burma Road. In September 1940 Japan joined the Axis, which carried the formal understanding that "Germany and Italy recognize and respect the leadership of Japan in the establishment of a new order in Greater East Asia." According to article 3 of the accord, the new partners "further undertake to assist one another with all political, economic and military means if one of the three . . . is attacked by a Power at present not involved in the European War or in the Chinese-Japanese conflict." Thus article 3 was a blunt and heavy-handed warning to the United States. A week later, Foreign Minister Matsuoka, certain that France, Holland, and England were passé in the Far East, and confident that Japan was now confronted only by the United States, uttered his fateful "we will fight America" challenge.

Negotiations between the United States and Japan were initiated in January 1941, but the pattern of these negotiations is too intricate for telling here. Suffice it to say that the two powers by this time had drifted dangerously close to war. To satisfy her legitimate needs, to assuage the appetite for glory of the extremists in the military, Japan had probably gone too far with her aggressions to stop or to return her gains. Over against Japanese ambitions was the United States with territorial possessions in the Far East considered vital to its own self-defense, a long-standing policy supporting the territorial integrity of China, and the immediate need to keep Southeast Asia, the world's principal source of rubber, tin, and quinine, as well as a rich supplier of oil, from falling into hostile hands. The dilemma, in simplistic terms, was that Japan could not turn back from her goal of a New Order and the United States could not permit her to proceed toward domination of Asia at the expense of China and the British Empire.

What Roosevelt needed in the Far East was time—a diplomatic stall, a holding action, a policy that would avoid the extremes of appeasement and provocation, a defensive policy that would not distract the attention of the country from the first order of business, the defeat of Hitler. The policy that seemed to fulfill these qualifications, which seemed to promise the best results, was gradual economic pressure.

While negotiations dragged on, strategic supplies and credits were extended to China, totaling more than $100 million from the beginning of 1940. Lend-Lease aid was extended to Malaya and the Dutch East Indies. And since passage of the Export Control Act in July 1940, which gave Roosevelt discretionary power to embargo anything necessary to the United States defense program, he had been gradually tightening the screws on the supply of aviation fuel, machine parts, scrap iron, steel, arms, ammunition, chemicals, and so on—with one major exception: an embargo on oil, the United States' ace in the hole. When, in July 1941, Japan forced Vichy France to surrender bases in south

Indo-China, the United States countered by freezing all Japanese assets, which meant a complete embargo and the severing of all trade relations. Negotiations and economic pressure proved fruitless. The United States, instead of agreeing to limited concessions, which might have strengthened the position of Japanese moderates and at least postponed war, adopted an adamant moral position on the issue of China that played into the hands of the Japanese extremists. United States inflexibility at the bargaining table and economic pressure, rather than deterring Japan, had the reverse effect of goading Japan into more reckless aggressions, including the fatal miscalculation of attacking American soil.

On November 25 the Japanese fleet began its secret voyage to Hawaii. For eleven more days the charade of negotiations went on. Indeed, bombs were falling at Pearl Harbor while the Japanese envoys, Nomura and Kurusu, were delivering their note rejecting Hull's most recent proposals. It was December 7, 1941, a date that Roosevelt, in asking for a declaration of war against Japan, prophesied "will live in infamy."

"When the nation is attacked every American must rally to its support. . . . All other considerations become insignificant."

The attack on Pearl Harbor meant the United States was in World War II all the way. Honoring their Axis commitments, Germany and Italy declared war on the United States on December 11 and the United States reciprocated the same day. Pearl Harbor, disaster that it was, ended the bitter debate between isolationists and internationalists and inspired a national unity that had been absent for years. "When the nation is attacked," said labor leader John L. Lewis, "every American must rally to its support."

In the early months after Pearl Harbor the war went badly, as the Japanese followed up their initial advantage with almost simultaneous attacks on a wide front, on the Philippines, Wake Island, Guam, Hong Kong, British Malaya, Singapore, Thailand, and Burma. Thailand fell almost immediately. Guam's surrender, less than a week after Pearl Harbor, was followed a few days later by Wake Island, and then Hong Kong on Christmas Day. In February 1942 England lost Malaya and the important naval base at Singapore. Most of Burma was under Japanese control by April 1942, closing off aid to China over the Burma Road. In the Philippines, combined United States and Philippine forces held out for several weeks on the Bataan Peninsula near Manila but were eventually forced to withdraw to the island of Corregidor, and finally surrendered in May 1942.

Before 1942 was over, however, the war took a more encouraging turn. The United States, by its victory in the battle of the Coral Sea, relieved the threat to Australia, broke the back of Japanese naval power in the battle of Midway, and began the long road back with the invasion of Guadalcanal and other smaller islands in the Solomons. Russia held at Stalingrad. The British held at Alexandria in North Africa.

Meanwhile, at home, the buildup was beginning, in manpower, ships, planes, and the tools of war that would produce military might unprecedented, undreamed of. War and preparation for it brought countless irritations and disruptions of normal living: endless hours of volunteer work by people serving on draft boards, by personnel of the OCD (Office of Civilian Defense), by performers and entertainers of the USO (United Service Organization); overcrowded transportation; housing shortages; overtime work; rationing. But far worse were the fear, the anxiety, the mounting casualties, and the steady stream of bad news from the war fronts, until the tide of battle turned late in 1942.

Converting from peacetime to wartime production, building new plants and facilities, and establishing priorities for the use of manpower and materials necessitated centralized control and planning unprecedented in the American democratic experience. Despite snarls and foulups, the system responded, it worked; the country reached the seemingly impossible goals set by the President. After several false starts, the ultimate device for getting things organized on the home front was the Office of War Mobilization, headed by James F. Byrnes, former senator from South Carolina, who resigned from the Supreme Court to take the most significant job in the domestic war effort. It was with good reason that Byrnes was referred to as "Assistant President." The OWM supervised and coordinated controls over civilian consumer purchasing, wages, salaries, prices, rents, profits, rationing, and "all related matters." The power granted the OWM and the auxiliary agencies that were created for implementing the mobilization was enormous.

Along with all this came problems of marshaling shipping, rail transportation, labor, and farm production and of dealing with the very sensitive matters of censorship, espionage, disloyalty, and civil liberties in time of war. Underwriting the whole war effort were astronomical expenditures. By the time Germany and Japan surrendered in 1945, the United States had spent more than $300 billion. A substantial portion of this enormous sum was derived from the purchase of war bonds by the American public—approximately $100 billion by the end of the war. Another source was the highest taxes ever imposed on the country, in the form of corporate income and excess profit taxes, excise taxes, estate and gift taxes, and personal income taxes and surtaxes collected on a pay-as-you-go basis through payroll deductions that commenced in 1943.

Before the end of 1943 the Axis had lost the initiative. Danger of invasion of England passed. On the eastern front the Russians began rolling back their German invaders. The surrender of the Germans in North Africa paved the way for the conquest of Sicily and Italy. In the Pacific, the United States neutralized Rabaul and overwhelmed the Japanese at Tarawa, the Gilberts, and Makin. And the Allies finally gained the upper hand in the struggle with German submarines for control of the Atlantic shipping lanes. It was a good year, one in which momentum shifted to the Allies and victory in the war was only a matter of time.

Meanwhile Roosevelt was facing trouble on the home front. Results of the off-year elections in 1942 reflected the ugly mood of the country, which was engendered by dissatisfaction with the war effort and the indignity of defeats sustained during the first months of the struggle. But fear and frustration, producing an anti-administration mood and a rising conservative tide, were not the only reasons for the 1942 results. There was a significant drop in the total vote, which hurt Democrats more than Republicans. The war effort was causing a mass migration of people into the armed services and into defense industries. Many people who might normally have supported Democratic candidates found voting inconvenient, were distracted from voting, or simply could not fulfill certain qualifications (such as residence requirements) in their new environment. In 1942 all of these causes combined to produce the slimmest majorities for the Democrats in both houses of the Congress since Roosevelt had become President.

In 1943, trouble between Roosevelt and the new Congress began almost immediately, but not over conduct of the war on the battlefield. Congress was one with the President in its desire for victory and for peace-keeping machinery after total victory. There was, however, con-

tinuous friction between Congress and the White House over the policies of the Office of Price Administration, the agency that had authority over prices, rents, and rationing. And congressional attacks on the
Office of War Information with resultant cuts in its appropriations, led
in late 1943 to the virtual liquidation of OWI facilities for coordinating
war news through the media at home. OWI activities in neutral and
enemy countries, however, continued unimpaired. The principal cause
for opposition to the OWI was suspicion that the agency would be used
by Democrats for unfair advantage during the campaign of 1944.

Roosevelt also had trouble with Congress over wartime tax proposals.
Indeed, in 1944 Congress rejected his tax recommendations. And with
considerable relish Congress used the war emergency as justification for
dismantling such venerable New Deal agencies as the Civilian Conservation Corps and the National Youth Administration.

The presidential election of 1944 was the first held in wartime in
eighty years. Willkie, who had run such a strong race four years earlier,
was beaten badly in the Wisconsin primary, leaving the Republican
nomination wide open for Thomas Dewey. Young, aggressive, famous
as a prosecutor who had sent a host of miscreants like vicelord "Lucky"
Luciano to prison, Dewey had been elected governor of New York in
1942—its first Republican governor in twenty years. At the national
convention in Chicago he was nominated on the first ballot.

Although there was serious anti-Roosevelt sentiment in Texas and
parts of the South, it was inevitable that Roosevelt would be nominated
for a fourth term if he wanted it. Although he was reluctant—"All that
is within me cries out to go back to my home on the Hudson River," he
said—when he at last indicated his willingness the only serious question
was his running mate. Henry Wallace, who had replaced John Nance
Garner on the ticket in 1940, was anathema to the party bosses, to
many Roosevelt backers in the West, and to conservative Democrats
everywhere, particularly the southern wing of the party.

Wallace, however, had the support of the extreme liberals in the party
and of important elements of the powerful CIO labor organization, and
particularly CIO vice president Sidney Hillman. In 1943 Hillman was
responsible for organizing the Political Action Committee (PAC), an
arm of the CIO, to rally workers, to combat anti-labor sentiment in the
country, and to gain more leverage for labor within the Democratic
party.

Roosevelt, concerned about party unity, and concerned that he would need southern votes to win, was willing to sacrifice Wallace for a compromise candidate. He suggested several, including James F. Byrnes and Senator Harry Truman of Missouri. Hillman warned Roosevelt that Byrnes, because of his southern background and because he had quit the Catholic church, was unacceptable to labor, to blacks, and to Roman Catholics. Truman became the choice after Roosevelt ascertained that he was acceptable to Hillman.

Democrats campaigned on the proposition that the country more than ever needed reliable, experienced leadership to see the war through to victory and to deal with postwar problems. The simple appeal was "Don't change horses in the middle of the stream." Dewey campaigned vigorously, leaning hard on the theme that the country needed "a house cleaning," new blood, an end to government in the hands of "tired old men."

Republicans chided Roosevelt with the taunt "Clear it with Sidney"— a not-so-subtle allusion to Roosevelt's having taken the reading of Hillman and the CIO leadership on the acceptability of Truman. But the most serious charge was the old "dictatorship" refrain. "Four years more of New Deal policy," read the Republican platform, "would centralize all power in the President and would daily subject every act of every citizen to regulation by his henchmen."

Roosevelt was elected again, of course, overwhelming Dewey in the electoral vote, 432 to 99. But the election was closer than it looked. In the popular vote, Roosevelt's winning margin was the narrowest since 1916. Wartime Washington was spared the usual inauguration hoopla. There was a simple ceremony on the White House grounds, and, soon after, Roosevelt was off to the Crimea and the Yalta Conference.

If 1944 had been a year of domestic trials and a troublesome presidential election, it was also a year of uninterrupted victories in the war. With one exception. In the Pacific, United States marines, with relentless naval and air support, swarmed over the Japanese at Kwajalein, Saipan, Tinian, and Guam. In October, American troops landed on Leyte in the Philippines. On the eastern front in Europe, the Russian armies had begun to chase the Germans across the continent, through Bulgaria, Rumania, Hungary, Yugoslavia, Czechoslovakia, and into Poland. In the west, the long-awaited Allied invasion of Europe across the English Channel, Operation Overlord, began on June 6.

The massive campaign in France went well, and by mid-September the Allies stood poised all along the western front for the final assault on the German homeland. At this point Hitler made one last desperate bid to postpone the inevitable: a counterattack using everything available against the Allied center in the Ardennes Forest—the six-week Battle of the Bulge, it would be called. The German gamble failed. By late January 1945 the Allies were on the move again.

Roosevelt returned from Yalta in early February. Finally yielding publicly to his infirmity, he delivered his report to the Congress sitting down. It was an explanation of as much of the Yalta agreements as seemed judicious at the time, and an appeal for public support of the forthcoming United Nations meeting in San Francisco.

There was still one fight to be waged with Congress before Roosevelt could retreat to Warm Springs for his spring vacation. He dismissed Secretary of Commerce Jesse Jones and replaced him with Henry Wallace. The fight for confirmation of Wallace by the Senate was a dilly. And it was Roosevelt's last victory.

"The story is over."

Early in 1945, in February, American forces stormed the Japanese-held island of Iwo Jima in what would be the bloodiest battle in the history of the Marine Corps. The struggle for Iwo was scarcely over when the assault on Okinawa began. With Iwo Jima and Okinawa in American hands, the Japanese home islands were within easy range of heavy bombers with fighter escorts. Meanwhile reconquest of the Philippines was moving smoothly, fulfilling General Douglas MacArthur's dramatic pledge: "I shall return." All was going well. In Europe and the Pacific the end was in sight. Then, without warning, came the AP flash: WASHINGTON—PRESIDENT ROOSEVELT DIED SUDDENLY THIS AFTERNOON AT WARM SPRINGS, GA. 4/12/45.

"The story," Eleanor Roosevelt sadly told a reporter, "is over." But shock and grief were betraying her. Tangible signs of the Roosevelt presence were everywhere. So, too, were the intangible signs. In the last days before his death Roosevelt had been preparing a speech for the United Nations meeting in San Francisco. In retrospect, its closing lines seemed almost a valedictory for just such a time: "The only limit to our realization of tomorrow," he wrote, "will be our doubts of today. Let us move forward with strong and active faith."

The Roosevelt years—depression years during which Roosevelt presided over the beginning of a modern welfare state, war years during which Roosevelt directed the most phenomenal economic growth in history—ended where they had begun twelve years before, on a note of high hope and expectation that would buoy the American spirit during the troubled times ahead. The Roosevelt style, the new goals he set for the land, and his techniques for achieving those goals would serve as models for many years.

The impact on the country of the Roosevelt presence and his enduring legacy are the substance of the chapters that follow. The evidence is compelling: the Roosevelt story is *not* over.

Part Two

I Look for a Circus

CHAPTER TWO

As They Saw It: The New Deal and Its Contemporaries

"Yes," the man replied, "they're [economic conditions] mighty bad. But ain't we got a great President?"
—*Quoted in Wilma Dykeman and James Stokely,* Seeds of Southern Change *(1962)*

"The dirty son-of-a-bitch!"
—*Quoted in Jerome Davis,* Character Assassination *(1950)*

By 1939 the domestic New Deal was over. With the Nazis and the Russians swarming all over Poland, World War II had begun. The international structure was collapsing everywhere and Roosevelt and the American people found themselves giving less and less attention to domestic affairs. All eyes were turned to the horizons, to Europe, to the Far East. The verdict was long since in on Roosevelt and the New Deal anyway. The man would have been hard to find who was so oblivious to what had gone on in the 1930s that he had not made up his mind one way or another.

With the majority, the overwhelming majority, the verdict was favorable. Many who admired Roosevelt, who approved the New Deal, could not have given any rational explanation for this if their lives had depended on it. Their response was uncalculated, intuitive; it had something to do with Roosevelt's ability to communicate concern, with his enthusiasm, his optimism, his self-confidence. It also had something to do with his supposed feeling for "the little fellow" (look at the enemies he had made—and was making—among all those millionaires).

Some liked the smile, the reassuring voice, the jauntiness, the triumph over personal misfortune. Or they liked his wife, Eleanor, and the passel of high-spirited Roosevelt children who always seemed to be in trouble —mostly in traffic court and divorce court. Or they liked the Brain Trusters and other new faces in the administration—a welcome change from the stereotypes who usually haunted the halls of government. Hopkins, Ickes, Johnson, Tugwell, Corcoran, and others were interesting, were "characters"; they added color, and were occasionally good for a belly laugh. Some liked the excitement, the sheer exuberance of the New Deal after the sullen passivity of the Hoover years. Some, of course, liked Roosevelt simply because he wore the Democratic label. It had been a long time since Democrats could enjoy Republican discomfiture, could find satisfaction in a calamity that had overtaken the Republicans.

Maybe Roosevelt was making some mistakes. Maybe some of the things done in the name of the New Deal were foolish or absurd. But he was trying—and apparently succeeding—in the face of terrible odds; this was the way many people saw it. They could not have cared less about ideologies. Whether or not the New Deal was some dreadful "ism" that would ruin the country, would embarrass and shame the founding fathers, did not cross their minds. They felt involved for the first time in the great destiny of the country. With Roosevelt in the White House, they felt for the first time that they mattered. Over the years there developed between Roosevelt and literally millions of Americans a love affair that was simple and uncomplicated—that bordered on worship, that approached idolatry.

Theirs was essentially an emotional, a visceral response to Roosevelt and the New Deal, which may have been best summarized in the words of the hitchhiker who was picked up near Decatur, Georgia, by Will Alexander, a longtime champion of better race relations in the South and administrator of the Farm Security Administration:

> Alexander drove him [the hitchhiker] to Decatur listening, wondering, and when he pulled up in front of the courthouse he offered him a word of sympathy.
>
> "Things are mighty bad. I'm sorry you're having it so tough."
>
> "Yes," the man replied, "they're mighty bad. But ain't we got a great President?"
>
> A tenant farm shack outside Winder, Georgia, seemed a long way removed from the White House, but somehow, as Alexander later said, "that strange man in Washington [Roosevelt] had reached across everything that divided them and had done something for that fellow."*

Others liked Roosevelt and approved of the New Deal on a more conscious level; their reaction was more clearly defined. It was Roosevelt, after all, who guaranteed the next meal for some of their neighbors, a job of sorts, change in their pockets, a chance for a movie, an occasional glass of beer. They could see improvement in conditions close to home: the price of cotton was up some, there was an extra day of work now and then, there seemed to be fewer apple peddlers on downtown street corners. They could see the New Deal was providing some help at least to people who usually got lost in the shuffle—old folks, blacks, dependent children, sharecroppers, farmers, unskilled laborers.

With still others, admiration and approval of Roosevelt was more intellectual; they thought they saw in the New Deal a revival of the reform ideal and a continuity that ran back at least to "Sockless" Jerry Simpson, Mary Elizabeth Lease, and William Jennings Bryan. Whether

*Wilma Dykeman and James Stokely, *Seeds of Southern Change* (Chicago: The University of Chicago Press, 1962), p. 192.

there was a continuity in the reform tradition, whether the New Deal was the logical successor to Populism and Progressivism, was beside the point. Some thought so, and that Franklin Roosevelt deserved to be named in the same breath with Theodore Roosevelt, Woodrow Wilson, Robert La Follette, George Norris. The New Deal, they thought, was a fulfillment of liberal impulses, a tackling of problems the country had been fending off for years, a start on reform long overdue, a shift away from the business-oriented government of the past.

Not all reformers from the old days were in Roosevelt's corner. A surprising number of Progressives who remembered fondly those golden years before World War I were anti-Roosevelt. They gagged on New Deal planning, bureaucracy, concentrated federal power, and the emphasis on economic security. These were men who had once dreaded the consequences of big business and big labor, who dreamed of reform and social uplift, through politics and preaching, in a white, Protestant, and rural and small-town America.

Perhaps an equal number of the old Progressives, however—particularly those who had translated dreams into action in the slums and ghettoes and the community houses, who had their hearts broken in the teeming cities—were pro-Roosevelt. Those who knew urban problems firsthand, the social worker types, saw the New Deal in a different light, and in a much more favorable light than their Progressive brothers.

Not only was there widespread approval of the apparent philosophical bent of Roosevelt and the New Deal, there was approval of specifics. The "three Rs" of the New Deal—immediate relief, long-range recovery measures, basic reforms—deserved applause. So did the deemphasis of states' rights. And so did the reliance upon close cooperation between states and the national government—"cooperative federalism" the political science professors would call it. Reliance upon national planning by the New Deal, something virtually unheard of in the past, made a great deal of sense to many. So did Roosevelt's apparent willingness to apply Keynesian economic principles to the recovery program. While "spending your way to prosperity" was often ridiculed as an absurdity, like "drinking yourself sober," there were those to whom "pump priming" and compensatory spending by government were the shortest route to recovery. The apparent goals of the New Deal—that is, major responsibility for the health of the national economy and for providing security for the individual—won approval in many quarters.

Special-interest groups—ethnic minorities, blacks, farmers, labor, and others—had their own, private reasons for approving Roosevelt and the New Deal. Among those special-interest groups there was considerable diversity. Perhaps it goes without saying that people in need of relief supported Roosevelt overwhelmingly, but his support went well beyond the grateful poor to include those who, for the first time, felt some sense of recognition, of having a place in a system that heretofore seemed to respond only to the needs of a white, Protestant, property-owning, Anglo-Saxon America.

Racial and ethnic minority groups strongly supported Roosevelt and New Deal reformism. Somehow they sensed that part of the New Deal fight to end the depression was also one to end inferiority and second-class status for hyphenated Americans. "If I could do anything I wanted for twenty-four hours," Roosevelt had once said, "the thing I would want most to do would be to complete the melting pot." In the 1930s they took him at his word; Jews, Italians, Poles, Czechs, and others (mostly Jewish or Catholic, mostly those who were politically ignored) swarmed to the Democratic party. Politically, the sons and daughters of the "New Immigration" came of age in the 1930s, and Roosevelt was their champion.

The wholesale transfer of black allegiance from the Republican party to the party of Roosevelt was part of the phenomenon. Three factors were primarily responsible for the blacks' switch. In the first place, during the decade of the 1920s blacks left the South in droves and headed north and west. Between 1920 and 1930 the number of blacks living outside the South increased by one-third and constituted 20 percent of the total black population. This black migration was more than just a matter of direction; it was a mass movement from a rural to an urban environment. With jobs in industry luring them, blacks settled in the cities, in what Samuel Lubell called the "Urban Frontier." The urbanized black in the North and West could vote. Because of the concentration of black voters, politicians were forced to pay attention for the first time.

In an urban setting the conversion of blacks to the party of Roosevelt was relatively simple. Although Roosevelt remained cautious where southern white feelings were at stake, he nonetheless accepted the black and took steps that would eventually lead to a remarkable improvement in their social and economic status. "Our Negro citizens," according to the Democratic platform of 1940, "have participated actively in the economic and social advances launched by this Administration." The claim was at least partially true, and black votes for Roosevelt were the symbol of their gratitude.

Farmers also shifted their allegiance from the Grand Old Party to Roosevelt. Of the major farm organizations, the oldest, the National Grange, was consistently lukewarm toward the New Deal. The Farm Bureau Federation, organized by the Department of Agriculture during World War I, became independent in 1920. It had the largest membership and had played a decisive role in framing the first Agricultural Adjustment Act. Thereafter the Federation usually offered at least a qualified approval of New Deal agricultural programs. The National Farmers' Union, headed by the fiery Milo Reno, was the newest and smallest of the major farm organizations. Initially, Reno was suspicious of Roosevelt, fearful that the farmers were in for more of the same. During the early stages of the New Deal the National Farmers' Union adopted a wary "wait and see" attitude. Eventually, it became the most enthusiastic supporter of New Deal farm measures among the "Big Three."

Individually, farmers in the 1930s were more ardently pro-Roosevelt than their spokesmen. They sometimes fumed because of New Deal regimentation of agriculture and the tendency toward overcentralization of government that went with it. And they were often outspoken in their criticism of specific New Deal policies, such as the tariff and farm credit. But when the time came to vote on election day, farmers joined the coalition and voted for Roosevelt.

Another of the well-established facts of the 1930s was the generous support given the New Deal by workers and their unions. It is probably true that labor showed a greater and more consistent sympathy toward the whole New Deal program than any other social or economic group.

By the 1930s the major goals of labor, which were unabashedly economic, had crystallized into "rights"—to work, to organize, to bargain collectively, to win security. Roosevelt and the New Deal were vindicating those rights in simple and obvious ways that a worker could understand. The worker knew that social security was good for him. He knew that a minimum wage and maximum hour law was a step in the right direction. He might not understand the nuances of section 7(a) of the NIRA, but he certainly understood signs that said "The President wants you to unionize." The worker might not comprehend all the implications of government planning and regulatory legislation, but he sensed that the New Deal was trying to promote industrial democracy, was trying to curb the rapacity of his employer. He knew what his fellow worker meant by the oft quoted remark: "Mr. Roosevelt is the only man we ever had in the White House who would understand that my boss is a son-of-a-bitch."

With the amount of criticism the New Deal generated over the years it was easy to forget that the vast majority approved Roosevelt and the New Deal, and both his domestic policies and his wartime leadership. That approval was expressed daily, and also at four-year intervals in a blizzard of votes—not once but an unprecedented four times.

But there was criticism. Lots of it. In the preface to his book *On Our Way*, published in 1934, Roosevelt admitted that some people were calling the New Deal fascism while others branded it communism. It was neither of these, he insisted, because the New Deal was being executed "without a change in fundamental republican method." "We have kept the faith with, and in, our traditional political institutions." Later, when the New Deal was under heavy attack, Roosevelt returned to the same proposition. People who were calling the New Deal fascism, communism, socialism, regimentation—whatever- were making complex what was really very simple. "I believe in practical explanations and in practical policies," he explained. "I believe that what we are doing today is a necessary fulfillment of what Americans have always been doing—a fulfillment of old and tested American ideals."

For Roosevelt, "practical policies" and "old and tested American ideals" meant that he was steering the New Deal on a course slightly left of center. But there were many people who did not think the New Deal was all that simple; they were going to test the New Deal with a different set of bench marks. Some were uneasy about Roosevelt; somehow he did not ring true. Some were skeptical about the people around the President—people performing in government for the first time, people unknown to the country's sidewalk superintendents. Some would judge the New Deal within an extremely limited field of vision: this piece of legislation, that policy, or—worse—an unguarded remark by one or another New Dealer. Some would judge the New Deal against preconceived notions, measure it against some ideology, weigh it in the fixed scales of political dogma. Others would judge the New Deal in terms of its goals, real or imaginary. Some others would set it alongside the American past and judge it in terms of what once was—or what they thought once was. Others would compare it to existing systems in Europe or to systems long since dead and all but forgotten.

In every such case Roosevelt and the New Deal came off second best. From whatever perspective, using whatever criteria, the verdict by these people developed a steady rhythm with three fairly consistent themes. In the first place, their verdict seemed to justify criticism of Roosevelt that was incredibly vicious and personal. In the second place, there was the paranoid proposition, stated or implied, that the New Deal was conspiratorial, bent on destroying the Constitution, subverting the federal system, betraying the country into the hands of those who would despitefully use her. Roosevelt, they insisted, was a fraud; worse, he was a fraud with treason in his soul. Finally, among the balanced critics, those who judged fairly, who shared none of the boorishness or aberrations of the others, the New Deal was a failure either because it went too far or because it did not go far enough.

With some who disliked Roosevelt the reasons were often quite irrational and unaccountable. There were people who simply disliked and distrusted the man; their opposition to Roosevelt was based on intensely personal grounds that usually had little to do with the merits of the New Deal. They did not like his smile (the "grinning Dr. Roosevelt," H. L. Mencken would call him). They did not like his cigarette holder (which he waved around "as though the thing were a conductor's baton," according to Malcolm Bingay of the Detroit *Free Press*). They did not like the way he tilted his head and appeared to be looking down his nose at people (a habit acquired after long years of maintaining the precarious balance of pince-nez glasses). In the Age of Aquarius, it now seems strange that anyone would object to the President's attire, yet there were those who did not like his wearing a cape in cold weather, although it should have been evident that, for a man with paralyzed legs, a cape is easier to manage than a coat.

They did not like it because Roosevelt had not sprung from grinding poverty, or resented him because he was from a prestigious family, a family of substance. The country was to hear a lot about pampered childhoods, spoiled brats and "silver spoons," about never having earned a living, or met a payroll, or lived within a budget. "You cannot take men," insisted Congressman Rich of Pennsylvania, "who have inherited things from their forefathers, who do not know the value of a dollar, and have them run a great country like the United States."

Others expressed their hostility through that ageless (and mindless) device of name calling. During his years in office Roosevelt was called about every name imaginable. One of the more spectacular name-calling episodes occurred at the annual banquet of the Military Order of the Loyal Legion in New York in 1937, a glittering affair at which Bainbridge Colby, once Secretary of State in the Wilson administration was the featured speaker. The proceedings began with an invocation during which a New York cleric prayed for providential blessing upon the President. At this point, according to Jerome Davis in *Character Assassination*, "a portly gentleman called out, in a voice that could be heard all over the dining room, 'The dirty son-of-a-bitch.' The minister was so dumbfounded by this occurrence that he paused for what seemed a full minute before he regained his composure and finished his prayer."

This was not the first, last, or only time that Roosevelt was called a son of a bitch. And he was called a good many other things. A short list of the milder epithets includes Communist, fascist, dictator, revolutionist, crackpot, weakling, opportunist, renegade Democrat, unprincipled charlatan, simpleton, swollen-headed nitwit, destroyer of capitalism, nigger lover, the Great Uncertainty, the Pied Piper of Hyde Park, the High Priest of Repudiation, "two-thirds mush and one-third Eleanor," and, perhaps meanest of all, "that cripple."

Personal animosity toward Roosevelt went well beyond name calling; no President in history was the victim of so many whisper campaigns, rumors, "poems," broad stories, and malicious lies. Part of the reason for this was that Roosevelt was an easy target. He was crippled by polio, a disease that was still mysterious at the time. The family name and fortune, which were equated with leisure, luxury, power and fame, inspired envy. But more important were the frustrations of the depression and the fears that the New Deal was some alien cure. Infantile as it may have been, vilification of the President was a satisfying form of release, of rationalization and self-justification, for the emotionally unstable.

The whisper campaigns and rumors usually revolved around Roosevelt's health. His paralysis made him fair game for all sorts of rumors that polio had affected his mind—including one wild story that Roosevelt had gone completely mad, had secretly been spirited away, and that an actor (appropriately made up for the part) was performing the executive duties.

Another common story had it that money collected from the President's Birthday Balls (annual events that developed into the March of Dimes) did not go into research and therapy for polio victims, it went into Roosevelt's pocket. Other stories had Roosevelt carrying on clandestine romances, the woman most often mentioned being Madame Perkins, Secretary of Labor. However, Roosevelt had no special immunity to women; in fact, his relationship with Mrs. Lucy Rutherfurd endured for years, and she was at Warm Springs when he died.

The numerous poems, jingles, doggerel, and stories were usually cynical and satirical, frequently vulgar, and sometimes quite obscene. A mild example that circulated widely at the time went:

> What man said to "that" woman?
> You kiss the negroes
> I'll kiss the Jews,
> We'll stay in the White House
> As long as we choose.

Another that turned up with regularity, usually on the back of business cards, was to the effect that "the President's wife is suing for divorce because she is not getting what he is giving the other people."

Mindless as all this might seem, it nonetheless represented the New Deal to many people; attacking and baiting the President was as far as some people got. It was with considerable justification that *The Nation* could say, in 1935: "Never in our history has an attack been so bitter. . . . No newspaper or journal would dare put into print even a hint of the charges about Mr. Roosevelt's mind and outlook." Or, as Marquis Childs wrote in 1936, "No slander is too vile, no canard too preposterous, to find voice among those who regard the President as their mortal enemy."

This kind of emotional, intensely personal response to the New Deal was not confined to the President. It reached out to his wife, prompting Gerald Johnson to write that "never before in American History had a respectable woman been subjected to such reckless and relentless attack"; to his children, who had "all the tricks of a carnival or circus outfit"; and to those close to him in the administration: "this horde of ravenous servants who batten on us, as maggots feed and grow fat on a dead dog."

Criticism of the New Deal, except in the first few months—the honeymoon to which every new administration is entitled—was steady, consistent, and ever increasing in tempo and temperature, until Pearl Harbor muted the strident voices of New Deal critics. The crisis of war was able to unite the country in common cause much more effectively than the crisis of economic collapse.

But between, say, 1934 and 1941 Roosevelt caught it from every direction. At some point during the course of the New Deal years Roosevelt would get an earful from Communists, Socialists, and (for lack of a better name) non-Marxists, who might be described as radicals, native fascists, the lunatic fringe of the extreme right, a substantial part of the American business community, the professions, the press, and— quite naturally—the Republican party. And there was serious criticism of Roosevelt and the New Deal from within his own Democratic party.

Criticism of the New Deal by all of these sources of opposition made some sense, had some inner logic, if one were willing to accept their premises. Take, for example, American Communists.

In 1933 and 1934 the Communists waged an incredible campaign of invective, a campaign that was part of a policy of international single-mindedness, of uncompromising militancy, laid down at the 1928 Moscow meeting of the Comintern. The party line required constant, unremitting opposition to local governments everywhere. And everyone who was not clearly identified with Marxism was, to hear them tell it, a "social fascist."

The American Communist party applied the party line to the New Deal relentlessly, with the fervor of religious fanatics. Reformed capitalism was impossible, according to Marx's "scientific" laws of history. A series of increasingly severe business crises, climaxed by devastating depression, would be the signal for "socialist" revolution. What was needed (and what would inevitably come), Marxists argued, was not another patch but a whole new garment. Evolutionary reform was futile. Revolutionary change was the only answer to the contradictions of capitalism.

Most of the time American Communists were grim and tight lipped about the New Deal. Roosevelt was the prince of social fascists, according to Earl Browder, general secretary of the party; he was "carrying out more thoroughly and brutally than even Hoover the capitalist attack against the masses." "The New Deal," he said, "is the rawest deal that the workers have ever received. . . . Industrial slavery stares us in the face from the hands of that great savior—the dictator."

Browder defined the program of the New Deal as "the same as that of finance capital the world over." It was, he insisted, essentially "the same as Hitler's program," a program of "hunger, fascization and imperialist war," differing only "in the forms of its unprecedented ballyhoo, of demagogic promises, for the creation of mass illusions of a savior who has found a way out." "Is not this trickery," asked the Communist *Daily Worker*, "the hallmark of this Wall Street tool, this President who always stabs in the back while he embraces? How unctuous is his empty solicitude for the ragged, hungry children . . . with the ruthlessness of a devoted Wall Street lackey spending billions for war and profits, and trampling on the faces of the poor."

The anti-Roosevelt, anti-New Deal line continued until late 1935, when Comrade Browder returned from the Seventh Moscow Comintern powwow bearing a new global plan (the "Popular Front," it was called) in which Leon Blum in France and Franklin Roosevelt in the United States—people who only yesterday had been social fascists—were now applauded by the Communists. And the new image that American Communists now attempted to reflect, and the new image they held of the New Deal, were both radical transformations. "[From] the bewhiskered, bomb-carrying, sinister figure in threadbare coat shouting revolutionary slogans and accusing liberals and moderates alike of fascism, the new Communist became the cleancut all-American boy, reasonable and self-effacing, calling for a United Front against a common foe."*

From 1936 to 1939, except when relief appropriations were slashed and when an arms embargo was imposed against Loyalist Spain, the Communists laid off Roosevelt. They became especially friendly after the "quarantine the aggressor" speech in Chicago in October 1937, occasionally implying in the *Daily Worker* that Roosevelt was almost as great as Earl Browder. In the election of 1936 the Communists had

*George Wolfskill and John A. Hudson, *All But the People* (New York: Macmillan, 1969), p. 126.

been urged to vote for Roosevelt in those states where Communists had been kept off the ballot. In 1939, when the Communists were urging Roosevelt to run for a third term, the *Daily Worker* sprang this dreadful verse on an unwary public:

> Mr. Roosevelt won't you please run again
> For we want you to do it
> You've got to go through it
> *Again.*

After 1941, by which time Hitler had violated the nonaggression pact and attacked the Soviet Union, and the United States had entered the war in an unnatural alliance with the Soviet Union, Roosevelt could do no wrong, to hear American Communists tell it—unless you raised the issue of when he intended to open the second front in Europe to take the heat off Russia.

But all of this was only a matter of Communist tactics. Roosevelt, they thought, was their best defense against home-grown fascism. He was certainly their best bet to provide relief for the beleaguered Soviet Union. So they supported him. But the Communists really despised Roosevelt, and in the early years of the New Deal, when their honest feelings were showing, they attacked him openly and relentlessly. They despised and hated him because they despised and hated the American system, despised and hated the capitalist future that Roosevelt was trying to ensure. They knew what was at stake. Roosevelt was insurance against Marxist revolution, and they knew it.

Although Norman Thomas polled nearly 900,000 votes in the 1932 presidential election, the Socialist party had a total membership of only 15,000. Even this small band was wracked by internal dissension. By 1935 factionalism and an infestation of ex-Communists resulted in mass exodus from the Socialist party—7,000 members, nearly a third of the total membership, by the end of the year. The problems that bedeviled the Socialists elicited from *Common Sense*, the organ of the League for Independent Political Action, a cry of despair: "The Left Wing leans to the side of revolution, the pacifists withdraw from the idea of violence, the Westerners get distrustful of the New York Jewish legal crowd, the trade unions resent the highbrows."

Even more serious, however, was the external threat to the survival of the Socialists—the threat from the New Deal. Roosevelt's efforts to save capitalism, to rejuvenate it, and to relieve the suffering brought about by its apparent failures eroded Socialist support. The decline of the Socialist party in membership and influence was directly related to the success and popularity of the New Deal. "What cut the ground out pretty completely from under us," said Norman Thomas later, "was Roosevelt in a word. You don't need anything more."

Although Roosevelt's critics often accused him of being a home-grown socialist, Norman Thomas (who should be considered an expert) disagreed. Thomas conceded that some of the public identified the New Deal with socialism; but Roosevelt, he said, "did not carry out the Socialist platform, unless he carried it out on a stretcher." Thomas was laying it on a little thick; the New Deal had, indeed, accomplished a significant number of the immediate demands of the Socialist platform of 1932. What Thomas meant was that the New Deal and socialism were worlds apart philosophically. Another reason for the case of mis-taken identity, Thomas explained, was because the public had been told the New Deal was socialism "in various accounts by Mr. David Law-rence, Mr. Alfred Emanuel Smith, and Mr. James P. Warburg."

This identification of socialism and the New Deal in the public mind may have been one reason why Socialists felt compelled to attack the New Deal so vigorously. The need to clearly establish a separate ident-ity was a matter of self-preservation. But Socialists were also honest. They criticized the New Deal for not being precisely what some others swore it was—socialism.

One might feel reasonably safe in assuming that the New Deal was not socialism if the Socialists said it was not. But whether it was equally safe to accept their definition of the New Deal is another matter. If the New Deal was not socialism, what did the Socialists think it was? Norman Thomas, in *The Choice before Us*, characterized the New Deal as "essentially State capitalism," which was only one step removed from fascism—and not a long step, either. In June 1933, in reply to the question "Is the New Deal socialism?" the New York *Times* quoted Thomas as saying that "Mr. Roosevelt's revolutionary achievement is emphatically in the direction of State capitalism and not socialism." And, he warned, "we shall not long have the economics of fascism without a considerable dose of its politics." As the decade wore on,

Thomas was still giving the same answer to the question: Roosevelt was no Socialist; his economic ideas "were too similar to those of Hitler and Mussolini."

If Communists privately hated Roosevelt, Socialists merely pitied him. To them, Roosevelt was simply a decent, well-meaning, half-hearted liberal. The New Deal was a mass of halfway, piecemeal reforms that were just effective enough to mute the voices of political and social protest. Socialists were frustrated by dreams of what the future could be. The golden opportunity, the opportunity to effect a Socialist revolution or at least a radical change, they lamented, was slipping through Roosevelt's fingers like sand. The consequences of this lost opportunity would, they feared, be some form of fascism.

Although some people insisted Roosevelt was a Communist or a Socialist, the Communists and Socialists never mistook Roosevelt for one of their own. Moreover, Roosevelt was so unconvincing a liberal that even liberals refused to claim him.

In the thirties the first concerted liberal movement (meaning non-Marxists who were left of center) was the League for Independent Political Action, organized in September 1929 with a slate of officers that read like a Who's Who of liberalism—John Dewey, Paul Douglas, Oswald Garrison Villard, Nathan Fine, Paul Blanshard, Harry Laidler, Reinhold Niebuhr, Stuart Chase, John Haynes Holmes, and W. E. B. DuBois.

What they stood for was vigorous, positive Progressivism: "the intellectual progressivism of the twenties," to quote one authority, "a progressivism anchored to a strong middle-class and national economic planning developed by such men as Dewey, Veblen, Lippmann, and Croly." For them, capitalism, he-man style, was doomed; but at the same time they insisted that a new society, built on the proletariat, Marxist style, was a cruel hoax. Toward the New Deal they adopted a wait-and-see attitude. Failure to enact the "right" legislation, they warned, would require them to reconsider their political posture—might in fact result in the formation of a third party, a new party dedicated to liberalism.

It did not take the LIPA long to reach a verdict. In September 1933, after only six months of waiting and seeing, it issued a call to farm and labor leaders for a meeting in Chicago. Thomas Amlie, Wisconsin Progressive and former congressman, told the conference that a $20 billion public works program was the only move Roosevelt might have made to save capitalism. But actually it did not matter. Capitalism, Amlie contended, was "not worth saving." Nor could capitalism be reformed; between capitalism and socialism in some form, argued *The New Republic*, "there is no longer a feasible middle course." The implication was that at some earlier time there was "a feasible middle course," but *The New Republic* did not indicate what it might have been. At any rate, that time was past; the New Deal was a failure; disintegration was just around the corner. "Unless we have an organization," Amlie pleaded, "it is clear that a movement . . . will come from the right, and this is what we have come to know as 'fascism.' "

Despite its fears and alarms, the Chicago conference adjourned in futility. Instead of uniting forces in a new national party, as planned, they settled for another organization, the Farmer-Labor Political Federation, which LIPA leaders hoped would have broader appeal among farmers, laborers, and intellectuals.

The LIPA and the FLPF blistered the New Deal, Roosevelt's backing and filling vacillation, and the inadequacies of his program. Both groups urged formation of a genuinely liberal party before it was too late. Alfred Bingham, co-editor with Selden Rodman of *Common Sense*, a new organ of liberalism (it was founded in December 1932) and the voice of the LIPA and FLPF, wrote often and with contempt of Roosevelt "liberalism"—with liberalism always in quotation marks. The New Deal was "whirligig reform" conjured by a politician "more renowned for his artistic juggling than for robust resolution." The consistent theme of *Common Sense* was that the New Deal, despite its well-meaning humanitarianism, was "a fraud and a sham." "When an egg is rotten," Bingham wrote, "painting it pretty colors won't improve it." Whatever else it may have been, the New Deal, according to *Common Sense*, was a hopeless attempt to make capitalism work. "And since it is impossible today to make capitalism work for long," wrote Bingham, "the New Deal is doomed to failure. With this in mind no intelligent or courageous radical can support Roosevelt."

Brave talk started the pulses pounding and juices flowing in the LIPA and FLPF faithful. The upshot was a call for a national third party convention. Delegates, meeting in Chicago in July 1935, formed a new party, the American Commonwealth Political Federation. Hopes ran high in 1936 that the ACPF might produce a groundswell of liberal support that would swamp Roosevelt. "We must have a new national third party," wrote Governor Floyd Olson of Minnesota, who had once told a reporter "You bet I'm radical. You might say I'm radical as hell." "1936 Is the Time!" was the exultant cry of *Common Sense* as late as April 1936.

The dream of a third party ended faster than it began when leaders of the ACPF finally faced up to their dilemma. Should they stand firm behind their radical principles, organize a third party (which would certainly siphon off votes from Roosevelt), and run the risk of delivering the country to conservatives and reactionaries? As Governor Olson put it for the less fastidious, should they risk electing a "Fascist Republican"?

A *Common Sense* poll of its people produced surprising results. It indicated that 50 percent were going to vote for Roosevelt anyway, 44 percent for Norman Thomas, and 4 percent for Lemke. The ACPF made its choice: it stayed with Roosevelt. Even Bingham, the conscience of the native radical movement and executive secretary of the ACPF, came to terms, announcing that he would give Roosevelt "a support limited only to the next few weeks, and withdrawn the day after Election Day." For all his bravado, Governor Olson confided to Harry Hopkins that he also planned to vote for Roosevelt. (But Olson never got the chance; he died in the summer of 1936.)

The day after the election found radicals even more disorganized than in 1932; but, on reflection, disorganization did not seem so serious in 1936. Roosevelt was better than farmer-labor groups and ACPF supporters had any right to expect. Besides, the New Deal coalition that Roosevelt had put together in 1936 looked very much like a third party that had been formed within the framework of the Democratic party.

Many rationalized their dilemma. Roosevelt, they told themselves, would push programs for a planned economy, and they would be more effective in bringing this to reality by working inside the Democratic party than in splinter movements. By 1938 *Common Sense* had come so far that it offered its support for a third term for Roosevelt.

In April 1938 Philip La Follette, governor of Wisconsin, tried his hand at the futile business of launching a liberal third party to unhorse Roosevelt. The National Progressives of America, despite Governor La Follette's disclaimer that "this is NOT a *third* party . . . [but] THE party of our time," got a lukewarm reception from radicals. *Common Sense* favored ignoring the new party and continuing support of the New Deal. National Progressives learned the truth early from embarrassing defeats in Iowa and California. To add insult to injury, La Follette was defeated in his bid for reelection as governor in November 1938. La Follette's defeat was more than the defeat of one man; it marked the end of the third party threats to Roosevelt and the New Deal.

Millions may have supported Roosevelt, millions may have endorsed the New Deal; but the real radicals of the country did not. Communists did not, although they pretended to after 1935 (expedience required it); Socialists did not, although Roosevelt cut deep into the ranks of those who were Socialists only on election day; radicals did not, although Roosevelt probably received over half their votes in 1936 and wrecked their third party plans.

For Communists, Socialists, and other left wingers, Roosevelt was barking up the wrong tree. "The essential logic of the New Deal," wrote Max Lerner in 1936, was "increasingly the naked fist of the capitalist state," which, as Tom Amlie had said, was not worth saving. Each group, for whatever motives, believed the system was faulty, that it had to be changed. Not just medication but major surgery, not just tinkering around but fundamental change—from top to bottom.

To proponents at the extreme ends of the political spectrum in the 1930s, left-wing radicals and right-wing reactionaries, the issue of national destiny was simple: the system would be some form of socialism or it would remain capitalistic. But capitalism was, by definition, fascism to the political left. "If we maintain the capitalist system," wrote John Strachey, the British Marxist, "there is no other possibility." The extreme right, agreeing that there were no alternatives, assumed it had already lost the first round: New Dealism was socialism and socialism meant communism. At least this was the way it looked in the world of signs and wonders of the native fascist crowd.

Activities of extremists in the 1930s prompted creation in 1937 of the Institute for Propaganda Analysis, a nonprofit organization to study propaganda techniques, to keep tabs on extremist organizations, and to conduct educational programs on propaganda and public opinion methods in schools and colleges. The Institute attracted to its support some of the country's outstanding scholars, including Charles A. Beard, Hadley Cantril of Princeton, Paul Douglas of the University of Chicago,

Malcolm MacLean of the University of Minnesota, and Columbia University's Robert S. Lynd of *Middletown* fame.

The Institute published the results of its research in monthly bulletins and special reports. According to *Propaganda Analysis* for January 1, 1939, there were some eight hundred organizations in the United States that could be called pro-fascist. Some of them had "Fascist" in the name of the organization. Most of them resorted to at least some of the flummery of fascism, using the swastika, or something approaching it, as part of their insignia. The members wore colored shirts with a paramilitary cut; the leaders mimicked the insufferable posturings of the European dictators. All of them posed a threat (some more than others), despite their claims to the role of savior: to save democracy, to save Christianity, to save individualism and free enterprise, to save the country from something or other. Their anxieties about the safety and preservation of the Bible, the faith of their fathers, the Constitution, and "the American way of life" meant, in translation, an anti-Semitic, anti-Communist, anti-Roosevelt campaign that, for sheer lunatic intensity, was without parallel in the American experience.

Where the New Deal was concerned, the 1930s spawned an alarming number of such people with a messianic mission, a divine call to arouse Americans to a new peril: a chief executive with treason on his mind, a black-hearted President who had seduced a desperate people for the purpose of delivering them to the enemy. Roosevelt, insisted the native fascists, was a Communist; the New Deal was a Marxist trick; "the crippled Judas would betray America with a kiss."

This is what the New Deal meant to the native fascist, to people like Gerald B. Winrod ("the Jayhawk Nazi"), William Dudley Pelley of the Silver Shirts, Howland Spencer ("the Squire of Krum Elbow"), George W. Christians of Chattanooga and leader of the White Shirts, Robert Edmondson (who boasted that the American Jewish Committee had voted him the most prolific anti-Semitic pamphleteer in the United States), Harry A. Jung, who headed what was called the American Vigilant Intelligence Federation, George Deatherage, fuehrer of the Knights of the White Camellia (which used the swastika for its insignia), James True, whose organization, America First, Incorporated, he said, was dedicated to frustrating "the Jew Communism which the New Deal is trying to force on America." The list could be extended almost indefinitely.

According to them, Roosevelt was not just intellectually a Marxist, he was a Communist. And more. Roosevelt was a Jew. His New Deal was dominated by Jews. The time would come when America would be delivered by that Jew, Rosenfeld (Roosevelt's "real" name), and his Jew-dominated New Deal to the Jew-dominated international Communist conspiracy.

How much of this arrant nonsense they (especially the leaders) believed is hard to say. But whether they believed it or not, one thing was certain. They hated Franklin Roosevelt. They hated him for essentially the same reason that Communists hated Roosevelt. Like the Communists, they were aiming for a new system. A new order. And Roosevelt stood astride their path.

There were others, men who attacked Roosevelt and the New Deal almost as viciously as the native fascists, men who were, in the long run, perhaps more dangerous because they were more calculating, less self-deceiving. Among them was Senator Huey Long, who ran Louisiana like a feudal baron.

Long, a supporter of Roosevelt in 1932, soon became one of his bitterest enemies when it became clear Roosevelt was not going to support his Share Our Wealth ideas or let him control the expenditure of federal relief and work relief funds in Louisiana. Before his assassination in September 1935, Long had organized the Share Our Wealth Society, believed by some to be only a thinly disguised attempt to capture the Democratic party. The organization eventually had more than 27,000 local chapters and claimed between six and seven million members. While allowing for the possibility that the membership figures were inflated, James A. Farley, Democratic national chairman, feared that Long, running on a third party ticket, might be able to draw between three and four million votes. In a close election, a vote of that size, Farley warned, "could easily mean the difference between victory or defeat."

Meanwhile Long's attacks upon Roosevelt became increasingly hostile, ever more extravagant. The New Deal was "the Empire of St. Vitus," "the united order of crooks, thieves, and rabble-rousers," the "blue buzzard government," a "brain-trust-bureaucratic-alphabetical conglomeration of everything except sense and justice." "Frank-lin De-la-no Roo-se-velt," Long would say, placing exaggerated emphasis on each syllable, "is a liar and a fake," a "no good" who "hasn't a sincere bone in his body." They should, he once suggested, "hold the

Democratic convention and the Communist convention together and save money."

After the death of Long, the Share Our Wealth Society was appropriated by one of his lieutenants, Gerald L. K. Smith. Smith was cut more from the native fascist cloth, a preacher-turned-patriot who saw Communists under every bed. Smith moved the headquarters of the organization to Detroit and eventually joined forces with two other phenomena of the decade, the Reverend Charles E. Coughlin and Dr. Francis Townsend.

Father Coughlin, a Roman Catholic priest who was destined to become the most famous cleric in the land in the 1930s, began weekly broadcasts over Detroit station WJR as early as 1926. By the time of the Great Crash he was already a radio celebrity with an enormous audience and a particular appeal to big-city ethnic groups. The popularity of his radio sermons—uncertain casseroles of politics, economics, and religion, with the main ingredient the salutary effect of inflation—led, finally, to his launching the National Union of Social Justice with some nine million members, according to Coughlin's loose-leaf bookkeeping.

Dr. Townsend, of Long Beach, California, was the founder of the Old Age Revolving Pension, better known as the Townsend Plan. By 1935 some five million people, organized into thousands of local Townsend Clubs, were waiting expectantly for the day when the federal government would adopt their plan to pay $200 monthly to all unemployed persons over sixty years of age. Both Coughlin and Townsend found compelling reasons for turning the full force of their personal popularity and their organizations against Roosevelt.

Coughlin, an inspired supporter of Roosevelt in the early stages, had praised him lavishly and extravagantly, had easy access to the White House, and was on "Dear Mac" terms with the President's secretary, Marvin McIntyre. In 1933 Coughlin had asserted that "the New Deal is God's deal"; it was "Roosevelt or Ruin," he warned the country.

But Coughlin's ardor cooled in late 1934 when he decided that Roosevelt "was making the same economic errors as had Hoover and Coolidge," that the "Old Deal" and the New Deal were more of the same: "One was the left wing and the other the right wing of the same bird of prey." By 1935 the New Deal was the "Pagan Deal" and the "raw deal." Coughlin came full circle, referring to Roosevelt as "that great betrayer and liar—Franklin Double-Crossing Roosevelt"; made a great spectacle of admitting how wrong he had been about Roosevelt; and in 1936 asserted that "if this is what we call a New Deal then this plutocratic, capitalistic system must be constitutionally voted out of existence."

Townsend's hostility toward Roosevelt apparently dated from a personal slight in late 1934, when he was denied an appointment with the President. The official Townsendite publication made much of the snub ("President Roosevelt even refused to meet Dr. Townsend. . . . We have aristocracy in the White House—not democracy"), and Townsend himself often referred to it. Roosevelt's public silence concerning the Townsend Plan and the passage of social security legislation was taken as conclusive evidence of the President's unfriendliness. The final insult was a congressional investigation into the Townsend movement in the spring of 1936, with strong implications that it was another California-based bunko game.

Townsend deeply resented the investigation, stalked out of the hearing, and was promptly cited for contempt of Congress. Townsend believed the whole business had been inspired by Roosevelt. As the election of 1936 approached, Townsend was after Roosevelt in full cry: "Roosevelt? He's just a soft, vacillating politician who is being used by Tugwell and the other Reds. I'd rather see Norman Thomas in the White House."

Eventually, Townsend and Smith agreed to pool their resources with Coughlin and they embarked upon a third party enterprise—the Union Party—with Coughlin bragging that they would enter the campaign of 1936 with more than twenty million votes committed against "the communistic philosophy of Frankfurter, Ickes, Hopkins and Wallace." "We here and now join hands," was the way Smith analyzed the unusual coalition, "in what shall result in a nationwide protest against the Communistic dictatorship in Washington."

The choice of a presidential candidate for the new Union Party was unfortunate. William Lemke, nominally a Republican from North Dakota, neither looked nor sounded the part. He was bald, had a glass eye, was badly marked from a bout with smallpox, wore ill-fitting clothes with a slept-in look, and had the general appearance of a man constantly harassed. But he had a good mind, was a graduate of Yale Law School, and, as a leader of the Nonpartisan League and attorney general of North Dakota, had won the support and admiration of the farmers.

As a congressman, Lemke had supported most of the New Deal. But his chief concern was farm legislation. With his friend, Senator Lynn Frazier of North Dakota, he had introduced a series of bills to stop farm foreclosures and to refinance farm mortgages with government help. Roosevelt's lack of enthusiasm for the Frazier-Lemke legislation turned Lemke against the New Deal. As the candidate of the Union Party, he was not long getting into the act. "I look upon Roosevelt," said Lemke in his high-pitched, flatland twang, "as the bewildered Kerensky of a provisional government."

Nothing came of the Union Party challenge. Coughlin's millions in July became 882,479 in November—less than 2 percent of the popular vote. The winds of social unrest which had blown so hard in 1935 were, by 1936, no more than a gentle breeze. The Republicans fared better, but not much better. Landon and the Republicans had only two states to show for their efforts; "As Maine goes, so goes Vermont" was the Democrats' taunt.

Roosevelt flattened the coalition of discontent in 1936 without the help of the press. Most of the daily press opposed Roosevelt throughout his first term, and in 1936 it opposed his reelection. That the press was anti-Roosevelt was not mere allegation, it could be demonstrated statistically. Of the one hundred and fifty major dailies (those having a circulation of 50,000 or more), eighty endorsed Landon, fifty-five endorsed Roosevelt, and fifteen endorsed neither. This gave Landon a numerical margin of about 3 to 2, an edge of 53 percent to 37 percent, with about 10 percent presumably neutral. The fact of the matter was that most of those in the "neutral" category supported Landon in every way possible, except by endorsement.

There appeared to be a direct correlation between circulation figures and editorial line: the larger the paper, the more likely it was to support Landon. Of the fifty dailies with a circulation of 135,000 or more, 75 percent were for Landon, 20 percent for Roosevelt. The fifty medium-size dailies, those within a range of 80,000 to 135,000, went for Landon 52 percent to Roosevelt's 36 percent. But the fifty smallest dailies, those in the 50,000 to 80,000 bracket, went 34 percent for Landon and 54 percent for Roosevelt. The eighty papers endorsing

Landon in 1936 represented 67 percent of the total circulation. Of the major dailies and the newspaper chains, the New York *Daily News* and the Stern papers (which included the New York *Post* and the Philadelphia *Record*) and most of the Scripps-Howard papers endorsed Roosevelt.

The conclusion seems inescapable that the press was strongly anti-Roosevelt and that such opposition did not recede perceptibly until the war years. Some newspapers, some very good newspapers, opposed Roosevelt on principle, opposed policies on their merits, fought honorably, and stuck to the issues. Others, ignoring issues, ignoring principles, resorted to vilification, personal abuse, and reckless charges of treachery and subversion. There were perhaps a number of reasons for this opposition, some more legitimate than others, but certainly one reason was Roosevelt's attitude toward the press.

Roosevelt, because of the NRA newspaper code, lost support among publishers fairly early in the game. The code imposed controls on newspapers similar to those on other enterprises: minimum wages, maximum hours, and restrictions on the employment of children. Enforcement of code restrictions, declared the publishers, speaking through the American Newspaper Publishers' Association, would strike a blow at freedom of the press. William Randolph Hearst instructed his editor of the New York *American*, Edmund D. Coblentz, to tell Roosevelt that his press code was "in direct violation of the Bill of Rights . . . an abridgement of the freedom of the press," and that he was prepared to fight it "with every means at my command . . . even if it costs me every nickel I possess." In reply to a similar statement by Colonel Robert McCormick, owner of the Chicago *Tribune*, Roosevelt said: "Tell Bertie McCormick that he's seeing things under the bed."

Roosevelt was not impressed by the opposition of the publishers to the code. The code reflected his attitude that newspapers were businesses, not sacred shrines, and because they were businesses they deserved no more consideration than any other money-making enterprise.

The President was right in at least one important particular: big newspapers were big business. The problems of the businessman were also the problems of the publisher. And not only was newspaper ownership big business, but publishers almost invariably had their hand in businesses other than publishing. Thus their economic interests were best served by defending the status quo. Roosevelt, with his questionable programs for recovery, his talk of a planned economy, seemed a threat to the status quo and therefore to business—the publishing business included.

Important allies of the large city dailies (major advertisers, business in general, and especially big business) took a jaundiced view of the New Deal; and Roosevelt gave most businessmen cause to be nervous. Their relationship at the outset, based on a mixture of hope and desperation, began on a note of good will. "Roosevelt is the greatest leader since Jesus Christ," a prominent businessman told John T. Flynn, economic writer for *The New Republic*; "I hope God will forgive me for voting for Hoover." James W. Gerard, an important industrialist who had served as ambassador to Germany during the Wilson administration, credited Roosevelt with saving the country: "If we continue to stand behind President Roosevelt, he will pull us through."

That was 1933. A year later, businessmen were "standing behind Roosevelt" with knives in their hands. According to *Time* magazine, "Private fulminations and public carpings against the New Deal have become almost a routine of the business day."

On the whole, business conditions were much improved by 1934. But as fear of the depression subsided, businessmen had time to take stock of the New Deal; what they saw frightened them, made them indignant. Senator Tom Connally of Texas was describing their reaction more than he was explaining it when he said on the floor of the Senate: "As soon as the businessman sees a slight improvement he keeps shouting 'the government must get out of business.' Businessmen do nothing but bellyache." The Roosevelt whom they had at first hailed as their deliverer was not attempting a recovery of things as they had been in 1929; he actually wanted to change the old order, they believed. The increasing militancy of organized labor, an ever expanding bureaucracy, the anti-business attitude of "visionaries and absent-minded professors" in government, and the rape of the Constitution were part of the visible proof.

In a simile once used by Governor La Follette of Wisconsin, the psychology of business reaction to Roosevelt was like that of a drunk, wallowing in his own vomit in the gutter, who resents the man who picks him up for having seen him in such sad shape. Roosevelt had seen businessmen in the economic gutter, and had picked them up. They resented having been saved. They burned with shame at having been exposed as mere mortals. And perhaps, as Eric Johnston, head of the United States Chamber of Commerce during World War II, observed later, they "had been convinced by the anti-business orations that they were really criminals at heart." Part of the early indignation of businessmen toward Roosevelt was therefore motivated by a desire to save face.

The apparent bad blood between the administration and business continued until the war years, when resentment toward Roosevelt began to cool, the feeling of imminent disaster because of New Deal policies receded, and business, by accommodation, found it could live with the New Deal after all. The measure of the new rapprochement could be seen in the voluntary role of businessmen in planning the war effort (the "dollar a year" men they were called) and in the cooperation between government and business, which resulted in the most astounding production job in all history.

Because of the war and the dependence on business for a victorious war effort, Roosevelt's attitude toward business "mellowed," according to Johnston. Business began recouping its lost prestige—"retrieving," as Johnston said, "a large measure of the public confidence that it had enjoyed before the depression."

Not all businessmen were anti-Roosevelt, of course; the President had friends as well as enemies. Roosevelt's friendship with Vincent Astor and his occasional cruises on Astor's yacht, the *Nourmahal*, raised hackles among some Roosevelt supporters. Edward A. Filene, the Boston department store owner, was a steady Roosevelt friend and contributor who did occasional unofficial chores for the President. There were men like Milo Perkins, the bag manufacturer from Houston, and Joseph P. Kennedy—whose son would one day be President—who wrote a laudatory book, *I'm for Roosevelt*, in 1936. In the summer of 1934, Rudolph Spreckels of the West Coast family of sugar producers called on Roosevelt to suggest the possibility of creating an organization of businessmen to support the New Deal. When A. P. Giannini, founder of the Bank of America, heard of Spreckels' idea he sent a telegram to Roosevelt saying that if such an organization was formed, "count me in."

And there were others. At least some businessmen realized that what Roosevelt was doing was preferable to more radical solutions to the depression emergency, solutions that might seriously endanger—perhaps even destroy—their business and industrial self-interests. For this reason Roosevelt often had support from leading businessmen on specific issues, such as the NRA, the Wagner Act, social security, and the Fair Employment Practices Act.

But in 1934 embarrassment and humiliation, coupled with genuine alarm concerning trends in the New Deal, produced in much of the business community a reaction that was truly formidable. Businessmen were concerned about the experimental nature of some New Deal recovery measures and the "rather heavy strain of Alice in Wonderland economics." "Business is the Administration's guinea pig," complained Colby M. Chester of General Foods. "American business is chloroformed with fear and then experimented upon by gleeful theorists who developed their economic and merchandising dreams behind ivy-covered college walls, but do not know if they'll work because no one had attempted to find out."

Businessmen warned that the reckless experimentation of the New Deal was destroying business confidence. "Where political uncertainty is the rule," declared Merle Thorpe, editor of *The Nation's Business*, businessmen cannot make long term contracts; they cannot plan ahead; they cannot expand." "Uncertainty of the Administration's next move," wrote John E. Dowsing, author of *The New Deal—Shadow or Substance* "what new experiments will be resorted to, what noxious nostrums some of the quack doctors will prescribe and cockeyed statutes force down the patients' throats, breed distrust."

Unorthodox economics was only one thing that was wrong with the New Deal. According to the economist Roger Babson, another serious danger was the development of bureaucratic "capitolism." Growing bureaucracy and the concentration of power in Washington, according to Virgil Jordan, president of the National Industrial Conference Board, meant that American business was faced with nothing less than a "centralized bureaucratic dictation of industrial management."

The President's distant cousin, Colonel Theodore Roosevelt, Jr., was getting close to what would become the most serious charge leveled at the administration by a large majority of the business elite: Roosevelt was a dictator. After several false starts and some early confusion as to what kind (some thought him a fascist), the threat became perfectly clear. Roosevelt was on his way to becoming a Socialist (maybe even a Communist) dictator.

Within a year after Roosevelt took office, spokesmen for business were reading socialism into everything. TVA, PWA, CCC, social security, and all the rest were giant strides toward a collectivist state. The so-called soak-the-rich tax bill of 1935 was described in the monthly letter of the New York National City Bank as "based upon the principles of Karl Marx and the *Communist Manifesto.*" The New Deal, asserted Merle Thorpe, "headed down the same road as Communism." America, he wrote, "was concerned about Communist agitators with whiskers and bombs but was in reality accepting their program under the brand of a new order guaranteed on the label to save democracy." "We have," Thorpe exaggerated, "given legislative status, either in whole or in part, to eight of the ten points of the *Communist Manifesto* of 1848."

Given their personal dislike for Roosevelt and their fear of certain trends in the New Deal, it was inevitable that business leaders would soon bring into play the powerful machinery at their disposal, with which they had customarily pressured government and administrations in the past. The signal that it was time to begin playing rough may have come from Edward F. Hutton, chairman of the board of General Foods. In 1935, in *The Public Utilities Fortnightly*, Hutton suggested that the only way to combat "the plans so carefully drafted by the radical Socialists" was to "gang up." By "gang up," he explained later, he meant only "get together."

In 1934 and afterwards, businessmen did a lot of "getting together" to discuss the New Deal menace, and this ultimately led to concerted action. In August 1934, when Jouett Shouse, former executive chairman of the Democratic National Committee, held a press conference to announce formation of the American Liberty League, a new organization "to defend and uphold the Constitution," businessmen were certain they had found what they were looking for. " 'That Man' is bleeding the country white," according to a prominent member of the Liberty League—which may have revealed a little more accurately the real concern of the organization.

The Liberty League quickly became the most important anti-Roosevelt organization in the country. Although it was never able to rally a significant grass-roots membership, its rolls included the cream of American business leadership. It had almost unlimited financial resources, most of which came from the du Pont family. From September

1934 to November 1936 the League spent over a million dollars in an attempt to destroy the New Deal. Money that was not spent on salaries and organizational work went into one of the most extensive propaganda campaigns of the twentieth century.

The publication program of the Liberty League, for example, rivaled that of the country's largest publishers. Between August 1934 and September 1936 the League issued 177 separate titles and distributed over five million copies. The potential audience far exceeded the number of copies distributed, for copies went to newspaper editors, press associations, radio stations, and libraries. In addition to its regular publishing program, the League provided canned editorials and news stories to approximately 1,600 newspapers in fourteen western, midwestern, and southern states.

Liberty League literature pictured the United States on the brink of chaos, threatened by bankruptcy, socialism, dictatorship, and tyranny. Few New Dealers or New Deal measures escaped the assault. By the time the Liberty League had finished telling its story, it had said, and said well, what businessmen had been unable to say for themselves. Roosevelt had to be defeated because (1) New Deal measures endangered the Constitution; (2) centralization of power tended toward tyranny and dictatorship; and (3) most New Deal measures were socialistic or fascistic, or both.

Certainly all of those who opposed Roosevelt and voted against him (that is, the more than sixteen million who voted for Landon in 1936) were not from the ranks of "economic royalists." Most were modest-income, middle-class Americans who clung fast to ancient virtues as they understood them: hard work, individual enterprise, thrift, responsibility for one's own welfare—who looked to the *Literary Digest, Time* magazine, the *Reader's Digest*, and the *Saturday Evening Post* for reassurance that they were on the side of righteousness.

The depression, and Roosevelt's approach to it, had caused them to doubt and fear. Some of those doubts and fears they shared only coincidentally with the rich, with the Liberty League types—the excessive spending and mounting national debt, the centralization of power in government, the shift from regulation to control, the bureaucracy, the apparent breakdown of separation of powers and checks and balances in government, the mushrooming practice of "legislating" through administrative law, the decline of individual rights. What was happening in

the name of labor—strikes, sit-downs, violence, the threat to property—
worried them. They simply could not accept the validity of New Deal
paternalism, the notion that it was the duty of government to provide
security against all the hazards and vicissitudes of life—unemployment,
illness, accident, old age, death. "Thoughtful men and women," according to a typical *Saturday Evening Post* editorial in 1935, "constantly
ask each other when Uncle Sam is to cease playing Santa Claus." A
good cross-section of middle-class Americans could nod in solemn
agreement to that nagging question.

Throughout the Roosevelt years the most effective opposition came
from the Congress, from Republicans and southern Democrats, and not
infrequently from a coalition of the two. "If you believe what you hear
around Washington," wrote Ernest K. Lindley in his Washington *Post*
column for March 3, 1939, "President Roosevelt and his policies have
lost the confidence of the country and the New Deal is all 'washed up.'
The Republicans and conservative Democrats [in Congress] have built
up such a bear market on Roosevelt that even some of the New Dealers
are selling him short."

The reason was easy to see. In the 1938 congressional elections Republican membership in the House had nearly doubled; the Democratic
majority shrank from 227 to 87, and some Democrats won reelection
by margins thinner than the ham in a drugstore sandwich. More important, Roosevelt did not have a working majority. The number of Republicans and alienated Democrats who forged an anti-New Deal majority was sufficient, according to one observer, "to defeat, or vitally
amend, important legislation, although it may have the aggressive, and
even the belligerent support of the White House."

At the other end of Capitol Hill there was, according to Drew Pearson
and Robert Allen's "Washington Merry-Go-Round" column of
August 4, 1938, more mischief in the making for Roosevelt: the formation "by die-hard anti-New Deal Senate Democrats of a secret parlia-
mentary organization of their own," an organization "with all the
trappings"—a floor leader, whips, and executive committee.

Roosevelt's trouble with Congress was not a phenomenon that developed overnight; the ingredients were present from the beginning. As
early as May 1933, Arthur Krock, New York *Times* correspondent,
wrote: "In 1934 there will be heard in the land Republican campaign

assertions that the President has put Congress . . . on the shelf . . . that the constitutional duties imposed upon Congress were generally surrendered to the Executive."

Most critics were not so euphemistic; Congress, they insisted, had become a rubber stamp. This was understandable. At the outset, Congress—like most of the country—was frightened, was willing to go along with Roosevelt, was willing to try almost anything that might cure the depression. And there were those in Congress who supported Roosevelt not because they were paralyzed by fear but because they agreed with him.

But serious deterioration of executive-legislative relationships began shortly after 1934, for several reasons. In the first place, Roosevelt finally ran afoul of institutionalized serenity. Calamity had forced Congress and the President to be nice to one another, to forget, at least temporarily, their traditional conflict. When the crisis eased, Congress grew restive, showed signs of wanting to get back to the old ways of doing things, of wanting to resume its badgering of the White House occupant, whoever he might be.

Congress had its quota of men who had come to Washington when the trolleys on Pennsylvania Avenue were horse drawn, who had seen Presidents come and go and who owed them nothing, who could win election upon election no matter who was President. There were some who were bungling the nation's business when Roosevelt was still a young law student at Columbia. Congressional customs and practices, particularly the seniority system, made serenity and obstinacy comparatively simple. This was uniquely the case when Democrats held the majority and southerners dominated the committees and controlled the machinery.

Roosevelt faced precisely this situation in 1933. As was noted in the preceding chapter, so long as Roosevelt remained on reasonably good terms with the southern wing of the party, the New Deal had a chance; if these men kicked over the traces, the New Deal was in trouble. Some did. The New Deal after 1935 was becoming increasingly radical, they thought. Those who had never really felt at ease in the New Deal were now genuinely alarmed.

They also resented their decline in power and prestige in the councils of the Democratic party, a decline that was symbolized by abolition of the two-thirds rule at the convention of 1936. The "radicalism" of the

New Deal meant, specifically, two things: a threat to states' rights and the traditional power structure and a threat to white supremacy. "I think there would be still greater differences," said Congressman Charles Gifford of Massachusetts, alluding to the split between Roosevelt and his own party in Congress, "if it were not for the plum tree. The tree is still shaken for your [southern] benefit."

The high tide of Roosevelt's influence in Congress came in 1935, when Roosevelt pushed through a program of social reform never before equaled. But the price of success came high; Roosevelt's first term, despite appearances, was not a public relations triumph with Congress. He had used the depression crisis until it was threadbare. To get action, he had piled up enemies and political debts along the way. The landslide victory of 1936 was deceptive; it was a badly disorganized and divided Democratic party, both in and out of Congress, that rolled over Landon.

In the Congress, the opposition had begun to form quickly in 1937, rallying around the court fight. From this point on, the coalition of Republicans and southern Democrats effectively stymied the domestic New Deal, effectively curbed New Deal "radicalism." Roosevelt's enemies in the Congress survived the attempted purge of 1938, survived the election of 1940, even though the country by electing Roosevelt to a third term was still supporting the New Deal in some broader sense. After the off-year elections of 1942, the Congress was more conservative than it had been since the 1920s. Now it was no longer a matter of stalemating the New Deal. There began a systematic dismantling of some old and familiar New Deal agencies and programs. Reform, as usual, was no match for the requirements of total war.

Not that it mattered much. New Deal reform inspired by the depression was over anyway, and Roosevelt knew it. His Jackson Day speech in January 1939 was a rousing reaffirmation of New Deal objectives, a fighting speech with all the right strokes about Democrats sticking together and keeping faith with the American people—the kind of speech expected at a $100 a plate affair.

A more accurate appraisal of the situation had come three days earlier in his State of the Union speech to the Congress. The meaning was not lost on reformers when the President spoke almost pleadingly of the need "to invigorate the processes of recovery in order to preserve our reforms." There would be no further reform; Congress would see to that. That New Deal reforms could even be preserved now seemed in doubt.

It is true that much would be done during the war which, at another time and another place, might have been applauded by reformers. This was not the case, however, where civil liberties were at stake. By 1942, the government had interned some 120,000 persons of Japanese ancestry. Of the more than 40,000 men officially classified as conscientious objectors, most accepted noncombatant duty in the armed services. Some, (approximately 12,000), were assigned to Civilian Public Service camps. The remaining 6,000, most of whom were Jehovah's Witnesses, went to prison. The treatment of conscientious objectors in federal prisons and in the Civilian Public Service camps was anything but gentle. The government also undertook, unsuccessfully, to prosecute for sedition some two dozen of the country's leading fascist sympathizers. In wartime, it was apparently easy to forget that citizens were entitled to their views, despicable as those views might be to others. All in all, the war years were not a happy time for people of Japanese background, pacifists, conscientious objectors, Jehovah's Witnesses, antiwar cultists like the Black Muslims, and those with profascist leanings. Geoffrey Perrett may have been overstating his case when he wrote, "As far as civil liberties were concerned, the war was a disaster."* In any case, the record—as in World War I—was none too good.

On the positive side, Congress enacted a veterans' rehabilitation law, popularly known as the G.I. Bill, which provided unemployment benefits for returning veterans, guaranteed loans for them to buy homes or start businesses, and underwrote their vocational training or college education. Farmers were assured a price of 110 percent of parity as a minimum for basic crops. Farm tenancy was significantly reduced. Organized labor, besides benefiting from wage increases and overtime pay, made important gains through sympathetic interpretation of the Wagner Act by the National War Labor Board. These important gains by labor were not offset by passage of the Smith-Connally War Disputes Act, passed over Roosevelt's veto, which authorized government seizure of war plants where strikes were in progress, provided penalties for

*Geoffrey Perrett, *Days of Sadness, Years of Triumph* (New York: Coward, McCann and Geoghegan Inc., 1973), p. 357.

trying to promote strikes in government-operated plants, required a thirty-day notice before taking a strike vote, and prohibited union contributions to political campaigns.

There were wartime changes in the tax structure that added millions of people to the tax rolls, contributed somewhat to a redistribution of wealth, and helped slow down inflation. But what many have forgotten is what happened when Roosevelt asked for sizable increases in revenue in 1943. The Congress balked. The modest increase voted by Congress so provoked Roosevelt that he took the unusual step of vetoing a revenue bill, only to have Congress override the veto by wide margins.

War mobilization stimulated government planning on a larger scale than ever before. Under pressure of war, the administration also produced public housing on an unprecedented scale. And in 1944, anticipating the end of the war, the President, in his State of the Union message, spoke of an economic bill of rights for the American people under which "a new basis of security and prosperity can be established for all—regardless of station, race, or creed."

Yet for reformers there was something a little sad about all this. As a "reform" movement, the New Deal was winning some of its most notable victories in the Congress as by-products of mobilization for war. But maybe these *could* be called reforms—provided it was understood that the definition was being stretched like a fat woman's girdle to include doing the right things for the wrong reasons.

In examining the reactions of contemporaries to the New Deal, one thing must always be kept in mind. Theirs was a decade in which the issues seemed uncommonly elemental. For many the issue was survival —a meal, a job, a roof over one's head. For others the issue was how to conserve and protect what one had against the ravages of depression—land, property, savings, profits, dividends. Self-interest and self-preservation had the highest priority. And everyone sensed in the 1930s that his self-interest was inevitably linked with a greater issue—the survival of the country, its form of government and its economic structure. More serious thought and overt effort would go into scrapping the political and economic system of America than at any other time in its history.

This was the setting in which the New Deal was to function: a time of deep personal travail and national crisis. It is little wonder, then, that

Franklin Roosevelt was a hero to some; to others he was a villain. To some the New Deal was cause for optimism; to others it was cause for alarm. Who was right? Who was wrong? As one historian said recently, "We can no longer vote for or against Roosevelt." Which is to say that Roosevelt and the New Deal can now be judged only in terms of results. It is time, then, to turn to the economic, political, and social consequences of the New Deal.

> *Fighting with a businessman is like fighting*
> *with a Polack. You can give no quarter.*
> *—Thomas G. Corcoran, quoted in Edgar Kemler,*
> The Deflation of American Ideals *(1941)*

the summer of 1934, in a speech at Green Bay, Wisconsin, Roose-
related how a prominent businessman had only recently asked him
abolish all government supervision over business. "My friends,"
osevelt told his Green Bay audience, "I told him and I tell you that
people of the United States will not restore that ancient order."
When Roosevelt spoke menacingly of not restoring that "ancient
order" he frightened the daylights out of businessmen, wounded their
pride, evoked anger. This was not the first and it certainly would not be
last important public statement by Roosevelt and other New
lers that sounded "anti-business," that had an ominous ring of im-
nt change in the economic order of things.

ere fear and anger justified on the part of businessmen and others?
Roosevelt endeavoring to make over the economic system? Was the
Deal, at least in the economic sense, a revolution?

ot to hear Roosevelt tell it in the campaign of 1932. Throughout
campaign he worked Hoover over for doing nothing about the
ssion that his policies had presumably precipitated. Typical was
peech at Columbus, Ohio:

So I sum up the history of the present Administration in four
entences:

First, it encouraged speculation and overproduction, through its
false economic policies.

Second, it attempted to minimize the crash and misled the people
as to its gravity.

Third, it erroneously charged the cause to other Nations of the
world.

And finally, it refused to recognize and correct the evils at home
which had brought it forth; it delayed relief; it forgot reform.

s was Roosevelt's oversimplified but nonetheless honest appraisal of
Great Depression, reiterated during the campaign.

Part Three

The New Jerusalem

*As a Nation we have rejected any radical
revolutionary program. For a permanent correction of
grave weaknesses in our economic system we have relied on
new applications of old democratic processes.*
—*Franklin D. Roosevelt (1938)*

*We shall be doing ourselves a disservice if we
reject out of hand the concept of the leader because
of the fascist taint that it now bears, or because
of our fear of the power that leadership carries
with it. Every decisive group effort needs leadership.*
—*Max Lerner,* It Is Later than You Think *(1938)*

*This election is not a mere shift from the ins
to the outs. It means deciding the direction our
nation will take over a century to come.*
—*Herbert Hoover (1932)*

CHAPTER THREE

Economic Royal...
Oth...
Economic Conseque...
of the New...

> As I see it, the task of Government in
> relation to business is to assist the developm...
> of an economic declaration of rights, an econo...
> constitutional order. This is the common task o...
> statesman and businessman. It is the minimum
> requirement of a more permanently safe order of th...ings
> —Franklin D. Roosevelt (1932...

> But the central idea of Mr. Roosevelt's economi...
> policies . . . is the gigantic shift of governmen...
> from the function of umpire to the function
> of directly dictating and competing in ou...
> economic li...
> —Herbert Hoover, America's Way Forward (19...

From this premise Roosevelt began unveiling what he proposed to do about it. Agricultural recovery, he said, would carry a high priority in the New Deal. Farmers were encouraged but also bemused by the vague remarks in his first speech on agricultural problems, delivered at Topeka, in which he compared the national economy to "a seamless web." The United States had the factories, the machines to satisfy every need; but "those factories will be closed part of the time and those machines lie idle part of the time if the buying power of fifty million people on the farms remains restricted or dead as it is today." So far so good. And how did Roosevelt propose to restore farmers' buying power? "We must have, I assert with all possible emphasis, national planning in agriculture."

National planning in agriculture, as Roosevelt developed the theme in later speeches, would be applied in three major areas: farm prices, farm taxes, and farm mortgages. Increased farm prices would be achieved through a plan "worked out in cooperation with the wisest leaders of agriculture"—which was his most obvious hint during the campaign of the Agricultural Adjustment Act. Farm taxes—he did not explain how—would be reduced. And he would see to it that federal land banks reduced interest rates and extended the life of mortgages to reduce principal payments. Where farm property had been repossessed for default of mortgage payments, the original owners would be given preference when the properties were resold.

In another area critical to farm recovery, the tariff, Roosevelt was ambivalent. He attacked the Hawley-Smoot tariff of 1930, claiming it was largely responsible for the surpluses, low prices, and declining farm income. "The principal cash crops of our farms," explained Roosevelt, "are produced much in excess of our domestic requirements. And we know that no tariff on a surplus crop, no matter how high the wall—1000 percent, if you like—has the slightest effect on raising the domestic price of that crop."

The tariff policy had, he argued, provoked retaliation by other nations and had virtually forced American firms to open plants in foreign countries. What was even more serious, it had hobbled foreign countries in their efforts to pay their American debts and purchase American goods, because they could not sell to the United States. "They just could not buy our goods," said Roosevelt. "These goods then were thrown back upon our markets and prices fell still more."

Roosevelt said nothing about the tariff that had not been said over and over by high school debaters. Yet even these comments set off a rash of letter writing that asked about specific tariffs and whether Roosevelt proposed to reduce them. Republicans, sensing an important political opportunity, began asserting that he would reduce tariffs on farm products. Hoover went right to the point, demanding to know just which tariffs Roosevelt thought were too high. Roosevelt, eager to reassure the farm bloc, sent a telegram to major farm organizations just before the election: "Let me make it clear that I have consistently stood for a policy of tariff protection that will adequately insure the domestic market for our American farmer."

His tariff statements also made many workers uneasy. If farm tariffs were not to be lowered, then it seemed to follow that tariffs on manufactured goods would be. Before the campaign was over, Roosevelt had to make his peace with the blue-collars and hard-hats. He favored a mutual lowering of tariffs by international negotiation, he explained, but "I have not advocated, and I will never advocate a tariff policy which will withdraw protection from American workers against those countries which employ cheap labor."

If Roosevelt felt it necessary to recant on the tariff issue to avoid losing votes, the tipoff to what tariff policy would be under the New Deal came after the election with the appointment as Secretary of State of Cordell Hull, long an advocate of tariff reduction by means of reciprocal trade agreements. In any case, Roosevelt's views on the tariff were matters of judgment, not ideology; traditional, not radical.

According to Roosevelt, if national planning was vital to agriculture, it was equally vital to railroads. The major problems besetting railroads —unfair competition from motor carriers, unprofitable services, unreasonable competition with each other, duplicated facilities, and holding companies that were bleeding them white—were the inevitable result of "the entire absence of any national planning for the continuance and operation of this absolutely vital national utility." During the campaign Roosevelt proposed a national transportation plan based on a survey of transportation needs, a plan to be developed and implemented by a rejuvenated Interstate Commerce Commission.

Roosevelt's proposals concerning public utilities were no more exceptional than those for agriculture, the tariff, and railroads. He was emphatic in his opposition to government ownership of utilities: "I state

Part Three

The New Jerusalem

As a Nation we have rejected any radical revolutionary program. For a permanent correction of grave weaknesses in our economic system we have relied on new applications of old democratic processes.
—Franklin D. Roosevelt (1938)

We shall be doing ourselves a disservice if we reject out of hand the concept of the leader because of the fascist taint that it now bears, or because of our fear of the power that leadership carries with it. Every decisive group effort needs leadership.
—Max Lerner, It Is Later than You Think *(1938)*

This election is not a mere shift from the ins to the outs. It means deciding the direction our nation will take over a century to come.
—Herbert Hoover (1932)

From this premise Roosevelt began unveiling what he proposed to do about it. Agricultural recovery, he said, would carry a high priority in the New Deal. Farmers were encouraged but also bemused by the vague remarks in his first speech on agricultural problems, delivered at Topeka, in which he compared the national economy to "a seamless web." The United States had the factories, the machines to satisfy every need; but "those factories will be closed part of the time and those machines lie idle part of the time if the buying power of fifty million people on the farms remains restricted or dead as it is today." So far so good. And how did Roosevelt propose to restore farmers' buying power? "We must have, I assert with all possible emphasis, national planning in agriculture."

National planning in agriculture, as Roosevelt developed the theme in later speeches, would be applied in three major areas: farm prices, farm taxes, and farm mortgages. Increased farm prices would be achieved through a plan "worked out in cooperation with the wisest leaders of agriculture"—which was his most obvious hint during the campaign of the Agricultural Adjustment Act. Farm taxes—he did not explain how would be reduced. And he would see to it that federal land banks reduced interest rates and extended the life of mortgages to reduce principal payments. Where farm property had been repossessed for default of mortgage payments, the original owners would be given preference when the properties were resold.

In another area critical to farm recovery, the tariff, Roosevelt was ambivalent. He attacked the Hawley-Smoot tariff of 1930, claiming it was largely responsible for the surpluses, low prices, and declining farm income. "The principal cash crops of our farms," explained Roosevelt, "are produced much in excess of our domestic requirements. And we know that no tariff on a surplus crop, no matter how high the wall—1000 percent, if you like—has the slightest effect on raising the domestic price of that crop."

The tariff policy had, he argued, provoked retaliation by other nations and had virtually forced American firms to open plants in foreign countries. What was even more serious, it had hobbled foreign countries in their efforts to pay their American debts and purchase American goods, because they could not sell to the United States. "They just could not buy our goods," said Roosevelt. "These goods then were thrown back upon our markets and prices fell still more."

Roosevelt said nothing about the tariff that had not been said over and over by high school debaters. Yet even these comments set off a rash of letter writing that asked about specific tariffs and whether Roosevelt proposed to reduce them. Republicans, sensing an important political opportunity, began asserting that he would reduce tariffs on farm products. Hoover went right to the point, demanding to know just which tariffs Roosevelt thought were too high. Roosevelt, eager to reassure the farm bloc, sent a telegram to major farm organizations just before the election: "Let me make it clear that I have consistently stood for a policy of tariff protection that will adequately insure the domestic market for our American farmer."

His tariff statements also made many workers uneasy. If farm tariffs were not to be lowered, then it seemed to follow that tariffs on manufactured goods would be. Before the campaign was over, Roosevelt had to make his peace with the blue-collars and hard-hats. He favored a mutual lowering of tariffs by international negotiation, he explained, but "I have not advocated, and I will never advocate a tariff policy which will withdraw protection from American workers against those countries which employ cheap labor."

If Roosevelt felt it necessary to recant on the tariff issue to avoid losing votes, the tipoff to what tariff policy would be under the New Deal came after the election with the appointment as Secretary of State of Cordell Hull, long an advocate of tariff reduction by means of reciprocal trade agreements. In any case, Roosevelt's views on the tariff were matters of judgment, not ideology; traditional, not radical.

According to Roosevelt, if national planning was vital to agriculture, it was equally vital to railroads. The major problems besetting railroads —unfair competition from motor carriers, unprofitable services, unreasonable competition with each other, duplicated facilities, and holding companies that were bleeding them white—were the inevitable result of "the entire absence of any national planning for the continuance and operation of this absolutely vital national utility." During the campaign Roosevelt proposed a national transportation plan based on a survey of transportation needs, a plan to be developed and implemented by a rejuvenated Interstate Commerce Commission.

Roosevelt's proposals concerning public utilities were no more exceptional than those for agriculture, the tariff, and railroads. He was emphatic in his opposition to government ownership of utilities: "I state to you categorically that as a broad general rule the development of utilities should remain, with certain exceptions, a function of private initiative and private capital." One exception was the right of communities to operate municipally owned utilities. Another, one that later would be the cause of endless controversy, involved state or federally owned power sites. Roosevelt saw no objection to these being developed by government, although "private capital should, I believe, be given first opportunity to transmit and distribute the power." He even suggested that the federal government undertake the development of the Colorado, Tennessee, St. Lawrence, and Columbia rivers as major power sources. "Each one of these," he explained, "in each of the four quarters of the United States, will be forever a national yardstick to prevent extortion against the public and to encourage the wider use of that servant of the people—electric power."

Pending the recovery of agriculture and business, Roosevelt realized that unemployment and poverty were the problems of greatest urgency. During the campaign he spoke of the need for new and improved legislation in areas such as public health, workmen's compensation, aid to crippled children, old age insurance, unemployment insurance, and unemployment exchanges. But in the matter of relief, Roosevelt thought the first responsibility should fall upon the local community. When local funds were inadequate, the state should take up the slack. The federal government should become involved in relief only as a last resort, "when it becomes apparent that states and communities are unable to take care of the necessary relief work."

Roosevelt was convinced that if an equitable distribution of income and wealth could be achieved, poverty would automatically be eliminated. The way to achieve this desirable goal—an obvious corollary to his underconsumption-overproduction "mature economy" theory of the origins of the depression—was simplicity itself. Government must systematically eliminate favoritism and special privileges "whether they come from tariff subsidies, credit favoritism, taxation or otherwise." "The way to distribute wealth and products more equitably," said Roosevelt, in words that he might have borrowed from Hoover, "is to adjust our economic legislation so that no group is unduly favored at the expense of any group or section."

These were understandably matters of importance and concern. The time was not far off when Roosevelt, as President, would have to do more than talk about them. But infinitely more important during the campaign was what he expected to do about the collapse of business. His speech to the Commonwealth Club of San Francisco on September 23, 1932, was his most candid statement on plans for business recovery.

The speech began with a historical prologue recounting the conquest of the frontier and the growth of industry. Inevitably, the closing of the frontier and the development of giant corporations raised monumental problems; there was, he explained, "no more free land and our industrial combinations had become great uncontrolled and irresponsible units of power within the state." It was not possible "to turn the clock back, to destroy the large combinations and to return to the time when every man owned his individual small business." Yet this "highly centralized economic system," said Roosevelt, was threatening to become "the despot of the twentieth century."

Now that "despot" was in deep trouble. And the first step toward getting out of the trouble was to admit that government had a new responsibility. The responsibility that government must inevitably accept, said Roosevelt, was one that would "assist the development of an economic declaration of rights, an economic constitutional order."

What Roosevelt went on to describe to his San Francisco audience seemed to be a mild version of the New Nationalism, a version for business recovery somewhat similar to the Swope Plan and proposals made by the United States Chamber of Commerce, which would permit business, under government supervision, to curtail competition for the sake of controlling production and distribution.

This approach to business recovery, which is as close as he came to describing the National Industrial Recovery Act, received several labels in the speech: "cooperation under government direction," "balance among the productive processes," "stabilization of the structure of business." But, said Roosevelt reassuringly, it "goes without saying" that maintaining the proper balance and stability should be "by cooperation within business itself."

With the advantage of hindsight, historians, political scientists, and economists—those who look to the past for fun or profit (and occasionally for enlightenment)—would argue that Roosevelt had foreshadowed much of the early New Deal in his campaign speeches. They could spot, they said, the Agricultural Adjustment Act, the Securities and Exchange Commission, the Farm Credit Administration, the Civilian Conservation Corps, the Tennessee Valley Authority, the Home Owners' Loan Corporation, the National Industrial Recovery Act, and a lot more.

Maybe some people could identify all of these in Roosevelt's remarks; possibly he was being more specific than appeared at first glance. At any rate, Roosevelt was playing it safe; no candidate with a grain of sense was going to jeopardize certain victory. So, to most people, Roosevelt's statements on future policy were optimistic, general, vague, ambivalent. There was little that was frightening. Which is to say that Roosevelt sounded quite orthodox, quite traditional, quite conservative. Yet it was not Roosevelt's *words* during the campaign that seemed to matter. To the words were added the magnificent voice, the contagious grin, the ingratiating amiability, the skills of the phrasemaker, the ability to exude confidence—a very special alchemy that made the words appear more significant than they were.

About the most that anyone could infer from Roosevelt's campaign statements was that the federal government was likely to assume a somewhat larger role in the direction and regulation of the country's economic activity; there was to be greater reliance, perhaps, on economic planning than the country had been accustomed to. Most political commentators and editorial writers in 1932—and most other people, for that matter—were not aware that Roosevelt's campaign speeches contained any real hint of what was coming, of what the New Deal was really going to be. Perhaps they did not analyze his campaign speeches carefully enough, or penetrate the generalities in which some of his more important proposals were cloaked. At any rate, Roosevelt waged a campaign marred by few mistakes, in which he reassured millions of people without tipping his hand, without raising hackles.

With one exception. Some people had been perturbed by the implications of a passage in Roosevelt's Commonwealth Club speech. Written by Adolf A. Berle, the speech was the nearest Roosevelt came during the campaign to a statement of a New Deal creed: "Every man has a right to life; and this means that he has also a right to make a comfortable living. . . . Our Government, formal and informal, political and economic, owes to everyone an avenue to possess himself of a portion of that plenty sufficient for his needs, through his own work."

That was not unduly frightening. Romantic, maybe—compared to the Hoover philosophy. But it was a little frightening when Roosevelt added:

But plainly, we are steering a steady course toward economic oligarchy, if we are not there already. . . . The day of the great promoter or the financial Titan, to whom we granted anything if only he would build, or develop, is over. Our task now is not discovery or exploitation of natural resources, or necessarily producing more goods. It is the soberer, less dramatic business of administering resources and plants already in hand, of seeking to re-establish foreign markets for our surplus production, of meeting the problem of underconsumption, of adjusting production to consumption, of distributing wealth and products more equitably, of adapting existing economic organizations to the service of the people. The day of enlightened administration has come.

"Enlightened administration"—there was the kicker. It sounded too much like Roosevelt the First and Woodrow Wilson. Since all sentences in speeches are not of equal value, it did little good that Roosevelt went on to say: "The Government should assume the function of economic regulation only as a last resort."

In retrospect, if a judgment could be based on past performance and what he had said during the campaign, the economic philosophy of the man upon whom the country waited in March 1933 was that of a reformer who accepted the general framework of contemporary economic institutions. The private enterprise-private profit economy should not be abolished but retained. Its operations, however, were not always benevolent, did not always promote the general welfare, and must be enhanced by state and federal efforts when the need arose. In short, Roosevelt accepted private enterprise but wanted to improve the performance of business.

In 1932 he still seemed willing to believe that businessmen could improve the performance of business through cooperation, that public service could be included as one of the goals of responsible business leaders. In this way business itself could set its own high standards, and reduce the influence of the speculator, the promoter, and the monopolist. What Roosevelt condemned about modern American business enterprise was the development of monopoly and the concentration of economic power; he was not anti-business, but was opposed to monopoly and financial promotions.

By far the most important aspect of Roosevelt's program in 1932 for achieving higher standards in business was his acceptance of the principle of planning. He had often spoken of planning in the years prior to his nomination. His record in New York included a widespread use of planning, particularly in land use. In the 1932 campaign he widened his horizons still further by applying the planning principle to many areas of the economy: to reforestation and power development, to agriculture, to industry, to transportation. Roosevelt did not advocate a system of comprehensive, central planning for the entire economy. But he did show a willingness to experiment with different kinds of planning to meet the needs of different areas of the economy.

The American people in 1932 were already well prepared for such an approach. For one thing, government intervention in economic affairs had been growing for decades. Beginning with intervention in a few areas of the economy on a piecemeal basis—public utility regulation, acts regulating working conditions in factories, and the beginning of conservation programs—the nation moved into the area of monetary controls with the Federal Reserve Act of 1913, a brief but unprecedented program of planning during World War I, and into the beginnings of farm relief in the twenties. Hoover went even further, especially in areas of finance and credit, trying to combat depression.

The depression was so severe, and recovery seemed so remote, that many lost faith in the idea that a natural recovery would come quickly. Maybe a freely operating market economy would, in the fullness of time, bring recovery; but it would take so long, and be so costly, that the nation could not wait it out. Roosevelt was thinking out loud along these lines in his speech at Oglethorpe University on May 22, 1932, when he advocated planning to avoid depressions. He recognized the mood of the nation, that it might be willing to experiment with new, maybe even drastic methods of economic planning.

In some broader—and necessarily vague sense (because he was no philosopher), Roosevelt seemed to be agreeing with the basic premises of evolutionary thought of the late nineteenth and early twentieth century, with the thinking of men such as Lester Ward, Thorstein Veblen, Oliver Wendell Holmes, John Dewey, and William James. They were committed to the proposition that society develops and evolves, that individuals have the capacity to guide the evolutionary process, and that institutions should be overhauled to meet society's needs. Men such as these believed that adjustment of institutions to environment required intelligent government planning, and had boldly advocated such views during the Progressive era. They thought the Industrial Revolution had outmoded the values of nineteenth-century individualism, requiring government to reconstruct institutions in the interest of democracy.

During the campaign Roosevelt talked of the restoration of democracy, but in a way that seemed to mean a transformation of democracy. Consciously or not, he seemed to identify himself with that earlier evolutionary-pragmatic tradition. His appraisal of existing institutions was frequently made in a critical vein, as if he assumed that historical developments had perhaps made them obsolete, that greater government activity was essential in the current state of industrial development.

To businessmen, the image of Roosevelt the campaigner was one thing; the image of Roosevelt the President was going to be quite another. Until the United States' entry into World War II, Roosevelt and the administration carried on what looked like a verbal vendetta with American business. Anti-business rhetoric had a high priority in the depression years of the 1930s.

A spot check would indicate that the battle of words began with Roosevelt's first inaugural speech, in which he accused "unscrupulous money-changers" and "rulers of the exchange of mankind's goods" of betraying the country into the Great Depression "through their own stubbornness and their own incompetence." In 1934 had come the "ancient order" speech. The State of the Union message in January 1936 was a slashing attack in which Roosevelt once again applied the term "unscrupulous money-changers" to those who offered to lead the United States "back around the same old corner into the same dreary street." "Give them their way" (this "resplendent economic autocracy," he called them), and they would "take the course of every autocracy of the past—power for themselves, enslavement for the public." The New Deal had broken off the romance between government and the private interests, and in accomplishing this had "invited battle," had "earned the hatred of entrenched greed."

Later in the year, in his acceptance speech before the Democratic National Convention at Philadelphia, Roosevelt returned to the attack. "The royalists of the economic order," he told the huge throng at Franklin Field, "have conceded that political freedom was the business of the government, but they have maintained that economic slavery was nobody's business." And then the challenge: "The economic royalists complain that we seek to overthrow the institutions of America. What they really complain of is that we seek to take away their power." "This generation of Americans," he prophesied, "has a rendezvous with destiny." The crowd left with the impression that a major part of that destiny was to cut business down to size.

During the presidential campaign that followed, Roosevelt gave businessmen cause for apoplexy. In Chicago, in mid-October, he attacked with withering sarcasm:

Some of these people forget how sick they were. But I know how sick they were. I have their fever charts. I know how the knees of all of our rugged individualists were trembling four years ago and how their hearts fluttered. They came to Washington in great numbers. Washington did not look like a dangerous bureaucracy to them then. Oh no! It looked like an emergency hospital. All of the distinguished patients wanted two things—a quick hypodermic to end the pain and a course of treatment to cure the disease. They wanted them in a hurry; we gave them both. And now most of the patients seem to be doing very nicely. Some of them are even well enough to throw their crutches at the doctor.

In his last speech of the campaign, at Madison Square Garden, Roosevelt fired off at American business the strongest words he had uttered since taking office. He ended with another challenge, an ultimate defiance:

Never before in all our history have these forces been so united against one candidate as they stand today. They are unanimous in their hate for me—and I welcome their hatred.

I should like to have it said of my first Administration that in it the forces of selfishness and lust for power met their match. I should like to have it said of my second Administration that in it these forces met their masters.

In 1938, in a message to Congress dealing with the problems of monopoly and concentration of economic power, a message which was the prelude to investigations by the Temporary National Economic Committee (the O'Mahoney Committee), Roosevelt spoke once more in menacing tones of "a concentration of private power without equal in history" which was "seriously impairing the economic effectiveness of private enterprise."

It was not just the anti-business cant of "that man" which caused businessmen to lie awake nights. It was the people around Roosevelt, members of the administration, who presumably reflected Roosevelt's thinking, or perhaps even spoke on cue. High on the list was Rexford Tugwell. The very mention of the Columbia University professor's name could cause tempers to flare in some quarters. His talk about a "Third Economy," about rolling up his sleeves and making the country over, whetted suspicions. Had Tugwell not talked as early as 1932 of "the abolition of business," adding "This is not an overstatement for the sake of emphasis; it is literally meant."

This, according to Senator Thomas Schall of Minnesota, could only mean Tugwell was a "Goddamn Communist"; after all, Tugwell had spent two years in Russia studying the Gosplan. Little wonder that Schall regularly referred to Tugwell as "Comrade Tugwell, Brain Truster No. 1." On one occasion, Senator Simeon D. Fess of Ohio quipped that Karl Marx "would, were he living, necessarily be compelled to apologize for his conservatism to Professor Tugwell." When, in 1934, Roosevelt submitted Tugwell's name to the Senate for appointment as Under Secretary of Agriculture, Senator Richard Russell of Georgia voted against him because "we have all but been completely Russianized."

Others in the administration, especially Brain Trusters—Benjamin Cohen, Thomas Corcoran, James M. Landis, Mordecai Ezekiel, Felix Frankfurter and his "hot dog" boys—were under a cloud because of unkind things they had said or written about businessmen, about business, about the American economic system. It was "Tommy the Cork" Corcoran, for example, who was supposed to have said "Fighting with a businessman is like fighting with a Polack. You can give no quarter."

When things began to go sour in 1937 (the "Roosevelt Recession," some were quick to call it), administration spokesmen attributed it to businessmen who had deliberately and artificially induced recession by "ganging up" on the administration. The day after Christmas, 1937,

Robert Jackson, head of the Anti-Trust Division of the Justice Department, delivered a radio speech in which he blamed "monopolists" for the renewed depression. A few days later, at the meeting of the American Political Science Association in Philadelphia, Jackson accused business of waging a "strike of capital" against the administration. The day following Jackson's speech to the political scientists, Secretary Harold Ickes let loose a broadside against "big business fascism" that was endangering the country. Ickes warned that a new depression had resulted from resumption of "the old struggle between the power of money and the power of the democratic instinct," waged by a relative handful of economic titans ("America's Sixty Families," Ickes called them) who were determined to topple Roosevelt.

And so it went. Until the demands of war caused the administration to start passing out patriotic bouquets to businessmen, there was a uniformly consistent disposition, from Roosevelt on down, to hurt their feelings and to scare them with anti-business rhetoric, rhetoric which often drew invidious comparisons between "Big Business" and "small [what Roosevelt frequently described as "legitimate"] business," rhetoric which seemed to threaten all sorts of dire things to the national economic order.

But words and deeds are not the same thing; if they were, we would all be under arrest. Despite what he and others in the administration may have said, despite the anti-business rhetoric, Roosevelt was not deliberately attempting to antagonize business, at least not in 1933 and 1934. On the contrary, he was anxious to retain the allegiance of business to the New Deal. Business support was important. And it should also be said that spokesmen for business, while growing increasingly restive and apprehensive, were quite circumspect in their public statements about Roosevelt and the New Deal in 1933 and 1934. In the early stages the verbal vendetta was largely one-sided.

Why, then, the verbal brickbats? Part of the reason was surely psychological. Beginning with his first inaugural address, Roosevelt sought to reassure the country that it was not in for more of the same, that the business of America was no longer just business, as Coolidge had asserted. During the 1920s business had basked in unrivaled supremacy in the American economy, waited on, hand and foot, by an obsequious federal government. When the needs of agriculture or labor were up for consideration during the decade of "Normalcy," government moved grudgingly, or not at all. When business spoke, government jumped to it. The policy of government, according to William Allen White, "was to do with alacrity whatever business wanted to have done." It was with considerable justification that the *Wall Street Journal* wrote: "Never before, here or anywhere else, has a government been completely fused with business."

"What we seek," said Roosevelt in 1934, "is balance in our economic system—balance between agriculture and industry, and balance between the wage earner, the employer and the consumer." If Roosevelt meant what he said—if the New Deal was indeed going to be a "partnership between Government and farming and industry and transportation," if there was going to be a balancing of interests, coalition government, government by consensus, "broker state" politics, due regard and concern for "the forgotten man"—then business would have to be demoted from its solitary splendor. It would have to put its head in the huddle, wait its turn in line. Anti-business rhetoric was a place to start the process, self-defeating as the technique may have been.

Businessmen never seemed to fathom the purpose which New Deal anti-business rhetoric served. And, as noted in an earlier chapter, they too had some very unpleasant things to say about Roosevelt and the New Deal, in an anti-Roosevelt, anti-New Deal rhetoric of their own, which was stronger than horse radish. It probably does not matter now who actually started the name calling. Nor is it possible even to guess how much of the rhetoric was nothing more than infantile response. Both sides had their pride.

What matters is that businessmen took Roosevelt seriously. So seriously, in fact, that businessmen would sigh and look back to 1933 as the fateful year when the United States traded its birthright of free enterprise and laissez-faire economics for the pottage of federal regulation, bureaucracy, and economic paternalism. They took him seriously —to the point that they broke rank, and seceded from the New Deal coalition. The organizing of the American Liberty League marked the rupture.

In large measure this response of businessmen to the New Deal was also psychological. It was embarrassing to businessmen in 1933 and 1934 to have to line up at the door with their hat in their hand. The egalitarianism implicit in Roosevelt's approach was humiliating. It was not just what Roosevelt was doing—not just the economic measures of the New Deal which eventually caused businessmen to go for his jugular. It was a sense of embarrassment, a feeling that their political influence and social prestige were ebbing away. When the economic crisis eased, businessmen had begun recovering their self-confidence. Typically, self-confident businessmen had a congenital distrust, or contempt, for government. In the 1930s they felt Roosevelt had ignored them, had failed to consult them in the planning of the New Deal. And by the standards of the 1920s they were correct.

In *Rendezvous with Destiny* Eric Goldman was on target on the psychological dimension of business reaction to the New Deal when he quoted a well-heeled liberal: "For quite a while I have lived in a commuter community that is rabidly anti-Roosevelt and I am convinced that the heart of their hatred is not economic. The real source of the venom is that Rooseveltism challenged their feeling that they were superior people, occupying by right a privileged position in the world. I am convinced that a lot of them would even have backed many of his economic measures if they had been permitted to believe the laws represented the fulfillment of their responsibility as 'superior people'!"

But business reaction was not solely one of fear inspired by rhetoric or of frustration accompanying a fall from grace. It was at least partly a response—a sincere response—to alleged economic heresies and the certain knowledge that at least some New Dealers were hostile toward large corporate business that led to businessmen fighting the New Deal like Knights Templar against the Saracens. Much of the heresy and hostility they traced to the Brain Trust, to the upstart lawyers and professors who "came flying into Washington from the four corners of the country, like crows to a dead horse, strange amorphous creatures, each of them seized and possessed of a complete and entirely different solution for every economic problem in the world."*

Whether New Deal economic policies were indeed heretical would continue to be a matter of opinion throughout the 1930s. Honorable

---

*Congressional Record, 75 Cong., 3 Sess. (1938), 6781. From a speech by Republican Representative Charles Eaton (N.J.), who went on to say that "These mysterious New Deal creatures have been roosting near the administration ever since and infecting it with their views, most of them impractical, un-American, and alien."

men could disagree, sometimes vehemently, on the subject. Certainly much of what seemed heretical to many then is commonplace now. At any rate, as the economic policies of the New Deal unfolded, many businessmen—as well as others—found much to deplore.

For example, suspension of the antitrust laws under the National Industrial Recovery Act gave businessmen a warm sense of well-being; but they were irritated by section 7(a), the collective bargaining provision, which was an open invitation to labor organization. Moreover, there was widespread feeling among small business operators that they had been handed the short end of the stick in the NRA codes. They had had little to do with drafting the codes in the first place. And they soon discovered that the codes discriminated against them, particularly in such areas as pricing and sales. Little wonder that they resented the opportunities for collusion which their larger competitors had under the codes, all in the name of economic recovery.

Businessmen likewise resented New Deal efforts to regulate banks and other forms of business activity. In fact, one historian of considerable reputation has asserted that "no single act did more to mobilize the business community against Roosevelt than his message of February 9, 1934, asking Congress for legislation to regulate the Stock Exchange."

Another conspicuous area that quickly came under attack was spending. Roosevelt had spoken of the need for economy, for balanced budgets; fiscal soundness, he said, was "the most direct and effective contribution the Government can make to business." And he meant it. After passage of the banking act, the first order of business in the 100 Days emergency session, Roosevelt turned to the matter of economy. The Economy Act of 1933 drastically cut federal spending by a quarter in an effort to balance the budget, largely by curtailing benefits to veterans and by cutting salaries of federal employees, including those of congressmen. Roosevelt finally achieved his elusive goal of a balanced budget in 1936-37. But, granting these exceptions, it is probably not unfair to say that during the New Deal there was neither economy nor balanced budgets.

Roosevelt certainly did not wish it to be that way. Despite the exaggerated tales of his prodigality, his resemblance to a drunken sailor on shore leave, his never having met a payroll, Roosevelt was never a convincing spender—certainly never a hot-eyed Keynesian, dedicated to the proposition of the English theorist, John Maynard Keynes, that massive government expenditures were the way to revive purchasing power. This was a bitter disappointment to some New Dealers, because Roosevelt was willing to spend enough to keep everybody's head above water but was steadfastly unwilling to spend enough to bring about the recovery promised by Keynesian theory.

A corollary to Roosevelt's spending policies was that of tampering with the currency. Currency manipulation in the early New Deal was an outgrowth of Roosevelt's understanding of the mature economy, that the closing of the frontier, restrictions on immigration, and sharp declines in the birth rate had removed self-starter mechanisms from the economy. The years of confident expansion were over; the ability of the system to produce goods and services far exceeded the capacity to consume. This imbalance was, in Roosevelt's judgment, the principal cause of the depression.

While there may have been options, the obvious (temptingly obvious) route to recovery, to higher prices, higher wages, increased purchasing power, and manageable surpluses was through limited production and controlled inflation. Roosevelt would learn the hard way that recovery could not be bought so cheaply. The notion of prosperity through limited production may have been his most egregious error.

But in 1933, anything seemed possible. The NIRA and the AAA were, of course, the principal devices for limiting production. Controlled inflation was a trickier piece of business. With the abandonment of the traditional gold standard, the dollar subsided to about eighty five cents in gold on international exchanges by the spring of 1933. This stimulated wholesale prices, and the entire economy appeared to stir.

Would Roosevelt back off, stabilize the dollar, let well enough alone? Or would he continue by other devices? Congress favored inflation. The Thomas Amendment of the AAA provided a half-dozen ways for the President to inflate the currency. It had taken all the king's horses and all the king's men to keep those inflationary devices discretionary rather than compulsory.

At the same time, Roosevelt was committed to the London Economic Conference, where the stabilization of currencies would have high priority. Roosevelt opted for inflation. By withholding cooperation, he shot the Conference out of the water. Not that it mattered much—the Conference was stricken before it began. What Roosevelt did was a mercy killing, not murder. Meanwhile he was proceeding with inflation plans of his own, based on the so-called commodity dollar of Professors George Warren and Frank Pearson, the "Gold Dust Twins"— or the "baloney dollar," as Al Smith described it.

Monkeying with the currency did not work for Roosevelt any better than it had worked in other countries, notably France and England, during the economic crises of the 1920s and early 1930s. About all Roosevelt had to show for his brief romance with currency tinkering was the indignant exodus of administration personnel like Lewis Douglas, Thomas Jefferson Coolidge, and Dean Acheson and the alienation of orthodox money men in the Democratic party.

After the stabilization of the dollar, there would be no more financial hocus-pocus; a managed currency, with carefully controlled inflation, would become the New Deal style for the rest of the decade. It was not that sound money people had won out and had forced Roosevelt into retreat. The traditional money doctrine had also lost its virtue along the way—had become thoroughly discredited, too. But the damage had been done; Roosevelt had acquired an image that was hard to shake. His fiscal policies would remain suspect and sound money men would continue to watch him with misgivings.

Roosevelt's tax policies were likewise suspect. Tax policies during the New Deal years passed through two phases. The first was a modestly successful effort to democratize the federal tax structure. But despite loud lamentations in the wake of the "soak the rich" revenue act of 1935, use of the taxing power during peacetime to attack the problem of concentrated wealth and to effect some redistribution of wealth produced minimal results. The second phase, comprising the numerous wartime revenue acts, was intended to curb inflation and war profiteering while raising revenue for the "pay as you go" war policy.

Wartime taxes likewise had long-range effects which carried over into the postwar years. For one thing, wartime tax measures, starting with the Revenue Act of 1942, affected just about everyone who worked for a living. Low incomes were tapped by lowering exemptions and raising the tax rates; for the largest incomes, the rates were virtually confiscatory. As a result, the thirteen million who paid income taxes in 1941 were joined by thirty-seven million more taxpayers in 1942.

Swelling the ranks of income taxpayers to fifty million meant that the revenue service could not possibly collect the tax by traditional methods. This led, in 1943, to adoption of the Ruml plan, a plan to collect the income tax at its source. Employers simply deducted the tax from payrolls and transferred the funds to the federal government. In 1944 Congress approved a plan whereby some thirty million taxpayers with annual incomes under $5,000 could file a simplified return. Other aspects of wartime taxation with lasting effects were the conflicts springing from efforts to plug tax "loopholes" and the policy adopted in 1945 of rebating substantial amounts of corporate taxation to aid business in the problems of reconversion.

Wartime taxes, which took tremendous hunks of personal and corporate income, set off the usual complaints, most of them unprintable. But the taxes were not suspect. With the country's usual predisposition to make any sacrifice during a war effort, most people, despite their bellyaching, were proud to pay their taxes, even heavy taxes. Use of the taxing power to waste the nation's resources in waging war was patriotic; use of the same power to redistribute wealth was dangerously subversive.

As the New Deal continued to unfold, critical talk turned to how Roosevelt's other economic policies meant browbeating industry, meant regimentation and strangling regulation by a bloated bureaucracy. Most of these criticisms were relative; they had a ring of truth only when compared to the late years of the nineteenth century or to the 1920s. As others saw it, the economic goals of the New Deal seemed hardly extreme, seemed only a well-meaning attempt to democratize industrial and finance capitalism, so as to see to it that its fruits were more fairly distributed, that its knavery was curbed. It was, as Herbert Agar put it, an economic program to promote widespread prosperity without the "obscenities of Big Business." And sympathetic observers might have added that most of Roosevelt's policies to restore prosperity and eradicate the "obscenities of Big Business" were intended, at the same time, to save capitalism.

A fair indication of Roosevelt's economic views and the goals of the New Deal came right at the outset, with the Emergency Banking Act. Roosevelt might have nationalized the banks. He chose, however, to save the existing private banking system, the most vital and sensitive part of the capitalist economy, and leave it in the hands of its traditional custodians. "The policies which vanquished the bank crisis," Raymond Moley wrote later, "were thoroughly conservative policies. The sole departure from convention lay in the swiftness and boldness with which they were carried out."

Subsequent legislation reaffirmed this economic stance of the New

Deal: the RFC financed business; commercial banking was separated from investment banking; the Truth-in-Securities and Securities Exchange acts left operation of stock exchanges in private hands but reduced speculation and various forms of hanky-panky; the Banking Act of 1935, the first important overhaul of the Federal Reserve System since its adoption in 1913, left that system essentially intact; the Public Utilities Holding Company Act of 1935, despite a spectacular lobbying campaign by its opponents (centering on what the act would do to widows and orphans), brought order for the first time to that wildly chaotic business.

Measures to enable farmers and city slickers alike to refinance their mortgages, efforts to spur construction by underwriting the mortgage market, relief programs to ease unemployment, youth programs like the NYA and the CCC to keep young people out of the labor market, public works to stimulate the construction trades, labor legislation like the Wagner Act to curb "unbalanced and radical" labor groups, generous use of subsidies—all indicated an economic philosophy as traditionally American as baseball and penny candy.

Public works, subsidies, and mortgage relief for farmers were old hat long before the New Deal. The others were somewhat innovative techniques to achieve traditional goals. They all reflected Roosevelt's old-fashioned American faith in the broad middle class and the need for its redemption. The techniques had grown out of more than half a century of serious discussion or practical experience. The goals, a rejuvenated middle class, were certainly consistent with Roosevelt's desire "to energize private enterprise" (to use his own words), with his belief that the capitalist system was worth saving.

Certainly the major New Deal steps to effect recovery—the Agricultural Adjustment Act and the National Industrial Recovery Act—despite the air of improvisation, the drama, the ballyhoo and hoopla that went with them, were based on the economic proposition that the way to recovery was through raising prices by restricting production, a thoroughly traditional tactic of businessmen. And it seems worth repeating that the AAA and the NIRA had the approval of the major farm organizations and businessmen, speaking through the Chamber of Commerce.

The New Deal coalition of businessmen, workers, and farmers began to crumble in the spring and summer of 1934. A large part of the business and industrial leadership, pouting because it could not control and dominate as in the past, came out in opposition to the administration's program, while the masses of voters—workers, farmers, ethnic groups, unemployed—rallied more overwhelmingly to Roosevelt in the congressional election of 1934 than they had done two years before.

Roosevelt had neither foreseen nor desired the realignment that occurred in late 1934 and early 1935. The administration had to undertake measures to allay the forces of discontent—of labor, the unemployed, the destitute, the aged, the farmers at the bottom of the haystack—or run the serious risk of being overwhelmed by those forces. Roosevelt moved swiftly to construct a new coalition and a program to match, a program to ameliorate the misfortunes of the masses through deficit spending, the redistribution of wealth, and the most far-reaching program of social and economic legislation in American history.

With the country behind him, with an eager Congress trying to outrun him, with nearly $5 billion in his pocket, Roosevelt set to work: the Works Progress Administration, with allied agencies, provided work relief for an average of more than two million unemployed, including some really "forgotten men"—musicians, actors, writers, artists, and even historians; the National Youth Administration; a stepped-up program for the Civilian Conservation Corps; the Social Security Act; and the National Labor Relations Act, reaffirming the collective bargaining principle of the defunct NIRA. Meanwhile, Congress was pushing other legislation extending federal power in various areas of the economy: the Guffey-Snyder Coal Conservation Act, the Alcohol Control Act, the Federal Power Act, and the Motor Carrier Act.

The deluge of social justice legislation was to continue, although somewhat diminished, through 1936 and into early 1937. It included the Walsh-Healey Act, requiring a minimum wage and a forty-hour work week of employers holding federal contracts. The Miller-Tydings Act permitted manufacturers to set "fair trade" prices, below which retailers could not sell, while the Robinson-Patman Act prohibited certain discriminatory practices. The Banking Act, Public Utilities Holding Company Act, Merchant Marine Act, and Revenue Act (discussed earlier) rounded out the legislative program of the so-called Second New Deal.

The victory of Roosevelt in 1936, despite its proportions, was followed by a meager harvest of economic reform legislation in 1937 and 1938. The motivation behind this legislation was impeccable; it was presumably a response to Roosevelt's appeal, in his second inaugural address, that something be done for the "one-third of a nation ill-housed, ill-clad, ill-nourished." "The test of our progress," he declared, is not whether we add more to the abundance of those who have much; it is whether we provide enough for those who have too little." What followed was a proposed legislative program that included additional public housing, reorganization of the executive branch and the judiciary, minimum wage and maximum hour legislation, and a revised version of the AAA.

As we have seen, the fight over judicial change in 1937 stalled the program for months, split the Democratic party badly, gave conservative Democrats an excuse for defying Roosevelt on other matters. Combining with the Republican minority, they succeeded in killing the executive reorganization plan for the time being, eliminated the "court packing" aspects of the judiciary plan before passing it, stalled the wages and hours legislation for another year. And, as noted in chapter 1, other proposals went down in defeat: child labor legislation, an anti-lynching bill, a stronger food and drug act, a ship safety bill, crop insurance, a proposal to make the Civilian Conservation Corps permanent, an extension of the TVA concept to other parts of the country, and the transfer of authority over air transportation to the Interstate Commerce Commission.

A few things were salvaged which Roosevelt could point to with pride: the Supreme Court Retirement Act, which permitted justices to retire at age seventy with full pay; the Judicial Procedure Reform Act (without the "court packing" aspects), which brought badly needed reforms at the lower court levels; the Guffey-Vinson Bituminous Coal Act, which reenacted most of the provisions of the Guffey-Snyder Act, (which had been struck down earlier by the court); the Wagner-Steagall National Housing Act; the second Agricultural Adjustment Act, which stabilized agriculture during the interval from 1938 to 1941; and the Bankhead-Jones Farm Tenancy Act.

The Bankhead-Jones Act, one tangible result of the investigation by the President's Committee on Farm Tenancy, was particularly noteworthy. The investigation had verified what everyone already knew, that tenancy was a problem of major proportions in all sections of the country. But it was acute in the South, where more than half of the farmers were tenants. The problem was compounded by the thousands of tenants who could not hang on, who, each year, slipped another rung on the economic ladder into the ranks of migrant farm workers. The Bankhead-Jones Act incorporated a recommendation of the President's Committee to reorganize the Resettlement Administration as the Farm Security Administration with lending power to help tenants acquire land and to help struggling farmers keep their land.

In 1939, as war erupted in Europe, the New Deal braced itself to meet the challenge of fascism. If Roosevelt had time to take stock, to look back, he would have noted with some satisfaction that, since 1935, American business had been forced to assume greater social consciousness, to curb at least some of its irresponsible behavior in such diverse areas as banking, public utilities, alcohol, coal, aviation, motor carriers, the merchant marine, wages and hours, collective bargaining, and fair trade practices. Some additional headway had been made on behalf of the "forgotten man"—in public housing, in attacking the farm tenancy problem, in humanizing the industrial system by abolishing child labor and the sweatshop, in providing a modicum of peace of mind through social security. At the Resettlement Administration, Rex Tugwell and Will Alexander were dreaming their brief dreams of generating a "back to the land" movement. And there were still the old standbys—work relief, the NYA, and the CCC.

But as the domestic New Deal yielded to demands of defense and war, one thing was clear: the third of a nation of which Roosevelt had spoken so eloquently in his second inaugural speech was still mute and dispirited, still empty handed. The New Deal legislative efforts in 1937 and 1938 (reviewed in the preceding section) emphasized that, had Congress passed Roosevelt's program in its entirety—which it did not— the consequences would not have disturbed the economic structure of the country. The best that could be said of the New Deal was that it had ameliorated some of the obvious excesses of the economic system. But the economic revolution which some predicted and many feared had not materialized.

Two developments in 1938 seemed to symbolize how far the New Deal had come economically since Roosevelt took office. In April, in what the late Richard Hofstadter described as "one of the most remark-

able economic documents that have ever come from the White House,"
Roosevelt called upon Congress to investigate the problem of monopoly. In urging such an investigation Roosevelt had already isolated the
dilemma. "The power of a few," he wrote, "to manage the economic
life of the Nation must be diffused among the many or be transferred
to the public and its democratically responsible government."

Two months later, the President assigned to the National Emergency
Council the task of preparing a report on the problems and needs of the
South, that area which Roosevelt had already identified as "the Na-
tion's No. 1 economic problem—the Nation's problem, not merely the
South's."

In July, Lowell Mellett, executive director of the National Emergency
Council, assembled a committee of prominent and knowledgeable
southerners, twenty-one men and one woman. It was a fine committee.
And with the redoubtable Lucy Randolph Mason, CIO representative
from Atlanta, on the committee, the sexes had the equivalent of equal
representation.

The *Report on Economic Conditions of the South*, fifteen sections in
all, covered a wide range of problems from resources, soil, and water to
health, education, and income, and everything in between. The committee was not dealing with any mystery as every agency of the government bulged with information on southern problems. Furthermore, the
solutions to the problems were not classified information. Thus it took
the committee only nineteen days to prepare the report. Nevertheless, a
three cent stamp and a letter to Howard Odum at the University of
North Carolina would probably have produced a better report by return
mail, for Odum and his colleagues had been grappling with southern
problems since the 1920s.

In December 1938 the O'Mahoney Committee—with the jaw-breaking
title of Temporary National Economic Committee—began its investigation of the extent and character of economic concentration. The hear-
ings continued intermittently until March 1941, the testimony filling
over thirty volumes and the economic studies by the TNEC staff ac-
counting for another forty-three volumes.

Nothing much came of either the study of southern economic problems or the study of monopoly. The easy explanation for this is simply
to say that nothing much *could* have come of them, that before anything could be done they were set aside—along with everything else.

World War II, even before the first American shot was fired, was becoming a pat answer that could excuse anything.

This was certainly the case with the work of the TNEC, which, after a long gestation period, gave birth to a mouse. Its final report commended free enterprise and condemned concentrated economic power; its principal recommendation was "the vigorous and vigilant enforcement of the anti-trust laws." What it amounted to was that, in six years, the New Deal had succeeded politically in dealing with the problem of monopoly; the barrage of rhetoric, and at least some of the legislation, satisfied the public that Roosevelt had accomplished much.

The fact was that economic concentration under the New Deal had never slowed down, and would accelerate during the war years. There is even reason to believe that the TNEC, together with the trust-busting activities of Thurman Arnold (which began in 1938), were devices for avoiding decisions, were intended—as Frank Freidel has suggested—"to forestall too drastic legislation in the Congress." And certainly Arnold's program, as Ellis Hawley has pointed out in *The New Deal and the Problem of Monopoly*, "made no real effort to rearrange the underlying industrial structure itself, no real attempt to dislodge vested interests, disrupt controls that were actual checks against deflation, or break up going concerns."

By the eve of World War II the New Deal had chastened business, had shamed it, and, in the process, had antagonized it; but the New Deal had made little change in the structure of American business or in the locus of economic power. It was one of the anomalies of the New Deal years that many businessmen could not understand that Roosevelt was their best protection for their long-range interests. They should have been friends. Businessmen, above all others, should have recognized the sincerity in Roosevelt's claim in 1937: "To preserve we had to reform. Wise and prudent men—intelligent conservatives—have long known that in a changing world worthy institutions can be conserved only by adjusting them to the changing time. In the words of the great essayist [Macaulay], 'The voice of great events is proclaiming to us, "Reform if you would preserve." ' I am that kind of conservative."

Concerning the problems cited in the report on conditions in the South, it could be said that the New Deal had, in six years, done much to alleviate the problems of the South but had made no appreciable headway toward solving them. Relative to other regions, it had received a greater share of benefit payments, higher prices, and increased income from New Deal farm programs. This was especially true in regard to tobacco and cotton. Tenancy declined and the conditions of southern farmers in general improved because of the New Deal. But agriculture in the pre-war South continued to lag well behind the rest of the country, as did industrialism, banking, and commerce.

Unionism made gratifying gains, but it involved only a minority of workers. There were still frustrating wage differentials, and racial discrimination persisted in the labor movement. Federal programs, although they improved the lot of southern blacks, were likewise tainted by racial discrimination. Certainly the New Deal made significant contributions to relief, welfare, public health, and education. And by encouraging state and local governments to cooperate with the New Deal, to engage in more intelligent planning, to undertake new public commitments—there was even a "Little New Deal" in Georgia—Roosevelt changed federal-state relations.

But, granting all this, on the eve of World War II the physical face of the South looked much the same as before. Except for TVA, Roosevelt seemed to be leaving the South about the way he had found it. The administration could pour in aid of every kind until the Second Coming and it would make little difference. Until there was major change in the social, political, and economic power structure of the South, the problems were unsolvable.

If the South *looked* the same, it nevertheless was not the same. Toward solving the real problems of the South, the material benefits of the New Deal—important as they may have been—were less important than the psychological benefits. The mood, the spirit of the New Deal gave heart to the disinherited of the South—the worker, the tenant and sharecropper, the black—marked the "first real stirring of the southern 'proletariat,' " in the words of one eminent historian.

The spirit of the New Deal threatened the power structure, frightened the traditional manipulators of that power structure, and thereby generated a formidable opposition within Roosevelt's own party. It may be that Roosevelt intended the economic report on the South as a prologue to significant change in the region, but, as we have already seen, Roosevelt retreated, unable to change the political system below the Potomac in any fundamental way. Nevertheless, the southern power structure, although it survived the New Deal intact, was shaken as it had never been before, shaken to the point that the scattered handful of southern liberals now had cause for optimism for the future.

World War II would prolong the assault on the strongholds of the southern system. Agriculture boomed, organized labor continued to grow, huge training camps, located in the South because of the congenial climate, invigorated local economies. The general standard of living in the South climbed to levels undreamed of before the war. War production also moved southward: shipbuilding, aircraft and ordnance, petrochemicals, and nonferrous metals.

The material benefits from the war—and they were enormous—were matched by the psychological effect of being needed, of being part of the great enterprise, of learning what the region was capable of doing, of feeling itself an integrated part of the union for the first time since the Civil War. When World War II ended, the South emerged, said one writer, "with more social change and more unfinished business than any other part of the country." Whether the process of change begun by the New Deal and intensified by the war emergency would continue remained to be seen.

The economic patterns that developed during the war were fairly clear. War mobilization stimulated government planning on a large scale, and the latter was justified in patriotic terms that silenced all but the bravest critics. On the home front, planning resulted in comprehensive controls on the economy unmatched by anything done during World War I or the desperate days of the 1930s. Americans soon learned that victory could not be bought cheap; along with wartime prosperity would come inconvenience and frustration in the form of rationing, rent control, restrictions on transportation and communication, regulation of agricultural prices and industrial wages, and priorities that sacrificed consumer goods to war production.

Planning for war meant that in the mixed public and private economy of the New Deal the emphasis was on the public sector. At least three-fourths of the capital for expansion of war production facilities came from government, largely through loans from the Reconstruction Finance Corporation. At other times the government built plants and leased them to private companies, the government keeping title to the properties.

Government likewise became the number one customer in the country, purchasing roughly half of all goods produced during the war years. And all of this buying and spending and funding was accompanied by power to control what was produced, by pressure to convert to war production, by authority to force industrial concentration or regional dispersal, and by standby power to "freeze" labor in any industry, to control hiring, to prevent strikes.

No major segment of the population escaped the impact of war planning. Labor and its unions gained strength and consolidated important gains during the war, as union membership swelled from ten and a half million to nearly fifteen million. When reminded that real wages (before taxes) were nearly double what they had been in 1939, labor could tolerate wartime restrictions on strikes and political activity, could look benignly on Rosie the Riveter and the hordes of her sisters, as well as teenagers and oldsters out of retirement, flocking into war plants.

Farm population declined sharply. Between 1940 and 1945 some five million (roughly one in seven)—mostly tenant and submarginal farmers —left the land to punch a time clock in a war plant or to greet each new dawn to a bugle solo. But with increased mechanization, better land utilization, fair weather, rising prices, and mountains of fertilizer, farm productivity increased more than 25 percent.

What probably interested farmers most were the rewards. By 1945— with fewer outstretched hands to share it—farm income was four times what it had been in 1940, reaching close to $10 billion the last year of the war. With enthusiastic support from the powerful farm bloc, Congress assured farmers a minimum price of 110 percent of parity for basic crops, a policy which certainly increased farm income but conflicted with Roosevelt's anti-inflation efforts. Farm mortgage debt declined $2 billion during the war, and farmers, besides enjoying a higher standard of living, accumulated $11 billion in savings.

But rewards were not obtained without a battle. The wartime fight between the President and the congressional farm bloc over farm prices was not won entirely by either side. Farmers successfully resisted efforts to alter the parity system, even while conceding it had been a crisis measure for dealing with the depression problems of surpluses and overproduction, not the wartime problems of underproduction.

They fought, again successfully, administration efforts to increase production by marginal and submarginal farmers. And when price incentives were not high enough to suit them—hog prices in 1944, for example—they cut production. Farmers were furious when, in April

1943, Roosevelt ordered price rollbacks and established a system of consumer price subsidies to fight inflation. Congress twice passed legislation undoing the consumer price subsidy plan; and twice Roosevelt used the veto. What farmers wanted during the war was the best of all worlds. They wanted a price floor, based on parity on one end, but no price ceilings on the other end. What the farmers and Roosevelt had to settle for was something in between.

War planning also resulted in a redistribution of wealth that could not have been accomplished in peacetime, depression or no depression. The magnitude of government spending during World War II boggled the mind. From 1941 to 1945, federal expenditures totaled some $321 billion—roughly twice the amount of all federal expenditures since 1789. To reduce inflationary pressure while raising revenue, the government urged the purchase of war bonds. The people responded, purchasing nearly $100 billion in bonds between 1941 and 1945! The rest of the capital for such staggering expenditures was raised by borrowing from Federal Reserve and commercial banks. And from taxation.

As already noted, the tax policy during the war required a major overhaul of the tax structure. Federal income taxes reached a maximum 94 percent of total net income, to say nothing of state and local taxes. As a consequence of tax changes in 1942 (what Roosevelt called "the greatest tax bill in history"), the 5 percent at the top of the economic pyramid saw a decline in its share of income from 25.7 percent in 1940 to 15.9 percent in 1944.

Even so, some people did very well during the war—were richer when it ended than when it began. But with an excess profits tax of 95 percent and corporation income taxes reaching a maximum of 50 percent, there was less "war profiteering" than might have been expected. While some businesses prospered for obvious reasons, net corporate income actually declined between 1941 and 1945, and dividends increased only slightly during the same period. It was still too little, many thought, but the war brought the most important redistribution of wealth in the nation's history.

The emergency of war planning also produced some lesser victories. The federal government vastly expanded public housing and the production of electrical power. And it entered industrial research in a decisive way, pioneering in such fields as synthetic rubber, electronics, and atomic energy.

But at least two developments were telltale signs that the war years would not be years of significant economic reform. Roosevelt relied on "dollar a year" industrialists to direct the war effort. Men like Donald Nelson, the Sears and Roebuck executive; William S. Knudsen, president of General Motors Corporation; Bernard Baruch; and what Harry Hopkins called his "tame millionaires," like Edward Stettinius of United States Steel, streamed into Washington as the New Deal types had done years before.

Roosevelt was loath to see the antitrust laws lapse for the duration of the war or to have industrialists exercise the kind of sweeping powers that had been delegated to them during World War I. But that is what happened. The most damning illustration was that of the sensitive Supplies Priorities and Allocations Board, headed by Donald Nelson. Nelson's board was the nerve center of the entire war-making apparatus until the spring of 1943; its decisions determined the supplies reaching the military, the civilians on the home front, and the allies, the Russians and the British.

Under Nelson, giant corporations all but monopolized war production—which is not to say, or even imply, that it was Nelson's fault. That the behemoths hogged war production contracts was neither surprising nor unexpected. The War and Navy Departments, grappling with the problems of rearming the country in a hurry, encouraged it, even promoted it. Their concern was getting production results, not worrying about equitable distribution of contracts. The rush to get production started meant turning to big companies that had plants, facilities, reserves of scarce materials, experienced management, and skilled labor.

By the time Harry Truman's special Senate committee investigating the situation finally blew the whistle, the one hundred largest corporations were getting (in dollar value) about 75 percent of the war contracts. "Gradually," wrote Eric Goldman in *Rendezvous with Destiny*, whether Roosevelt wished it or not, "the economic controls took on much of the 1917 pattern, with much the same consequences."

A second clue was the election of 1942. As we saw in chapter 1, the off-year election came at a low point in the war. During the eleven months since Pearl Harbor the United States had been on the defensive, had been humiliated by the loss of its empire in the western Pacific. At home, the anxieties of war were compounded by the inconveniences of shortages and rationing, increased taxes, higher prices, bottlenecks and foul-ups in transportation and production—altogether, the disruption of everybody's playhouse. The war, in all its ramifications, was causing the country to turn in upon itself. The result was a kind of storm-cellar conservatism and bruised caution, which was translated into a strong anti-administration trend in the voting.

In Congress, New Dealers were shot down all over. When the smoke cleared, Democrats had lost nine seats in the Senate and forty-five in the House. The defeat hardest to believe was that of Senator George Norris, who, despite his advanced age (he was eighty-one), had been Nebraska's man-in-Washington for thirty years. Strange things were happening, when George Norris could be beaten by a car dealer. The Congress that was elected in 1942 was easily the most conservative since 1928, and reduced Democratic majorities meant that southern Democrats, with their Republican allies, were more firmly in control than ever before during Roosevelt's years in office.

Roosevelt fought a rear-guard action to save the economic reform image of the New Deal. In his annual message in January 1944 he urged renegotiation of war contracts to curb what he considered exorbitant profits. And he criticized the Congress for rejecting Secretary Morgenthau's plan to raise wartime taxes according to ability to pay. He wanted, he said, "a realistic tax law—which would tax all unreasonable profits, both individual and corporate, and reduce the ultimate cost of the war to our sons and daughters."

Roosevelt also proposed what he called a "second Bill of Rights." Political rights, he insisted, were not enough; they must be balanced by economic rights. "Necessitous men are not free men," said the President. Included in his list of economic rights were social insurance, sickness and accident protection, medical care, education, and, above all, the right to "a useful and remuncrative job." Government, according to the President, had an obligation to provide full employment.

But Roosevelt's economic bill of rights would have to wait. War and reform did not mix, and Roosevelt accepted the inevitable. "Dr. Win-the-War" must replace old "Dr. New Deal," he told a press conference, a sign of tacit surrender that only added to the distress of his liberal supporters.

The decline of reformism during the war seemed a fair price to pay for a road map to the economic Holy Grail. Providing one did not linger too long at the biers of more than 290,000 young Americans, it might be argued that the war was a good thing.

For the United States, World War II meant the end of pessimism and despair, and in their places optimism and buoyancy. Quite literally, millions emerged from the war with new hope, with raised expectations, with a new sense of destiny. Despite their obvious occupational hazards, most of the fifteen million men who served in the armed forces lived better than they had ever lived before. Civilians—even with the fears and foreboding that went with the war, especially in its early stages—lived better than before. Wartime rationing and shortages were relative, as the economy of the country was never mobilized on a full wartime basis. Most civilians had more of everything than they had during the depression. There was—to use the expression of the time— plenty of both "guns and butter."

If for many people the war meant higher hopes, fuller bellies, and more amenities, it also meant putting people on the move. Americans were uprooted by the war. Servicemen, jerked from familiar surroundings, thrown together with every type and pedigree, and transported to strange and distant places, would never be the same afterward. Their parochialism was rubbed threadbare. And the slow process of ethnic assimilation—the "melting pot" ideal—which might otherwise have taken generations, was accomplished by Selective Service—the draft— almost inadvertently in the short span between Pearl Harbor and Hiroshima.

A steady stream of civilians poured out of the hamlets and countryside to take jobs in the cities. Housewives joined in forgoing the alleged rewards of home for the excitement of the assembly line. The black-power movement of later years was born during World War II, when Negroes discovered that they, too, were needed to help save the world from the threat of fascism. Once begun, there would be no turning back. The people would never retreat to farm and village; there would be no exodus from city and suburb. There would be no postwar "back to the land" movement. There would be no turning back for women and blacks, no voluntary return to inferiority, passivity, and a humdrum daily existence.

The war likewise meant a transfusion for America's industrial plant, bringing it back to robust health. The legacy, and the desired state of health, was full production, full employment, high wages, gratifying profits, and a vast expansion of facilities—with offices, plants, assembly lines, warehouses, and distribution networks poised to meet every need of postwar society.

Industrial capitalism survived depression and war, and twelve years of

Roosevelt and the New Deal. It had done *more* than survive. Along with federal government, corporate industrial capitalism emerged from the ordeal of depression and war as a dominant institution of American society. No one could seriously believe there would ever be a turning back here, either—a slow-down of corporate expansion, a significant revival of small business.

To be sure, it was not the capitalism of 1929, that highly structured, almost monolithic economy entrusted, by divine right, to an episcopacy of businessmen, financiers, and industrialists. What had emerged by 1945 was a mixed economy, a middle way, lying somewhere between laissez-faire capitalism and socialism, in which powerful "countervailing forces" (as John Kenneth Galbraith would call them)—business, agriculture, industry, labor, banking and finance, state and local government, the aged, ethnic minorities—would compete for advantage, for a fairer shake, for a larger slice of the national loaf, all the while yelling "Foul!" to that enlarged political arbiter, the federal government, which was armed with new powers to achieve economic reform by coercion.

It was a style of capitalism in which federal government likewise assumed responsibility for avoiding economic collapse, for the continuing good health, the robustness of the national economy, and for the safety, the security, the well-being of the individual member of society. The New Deal left a legacy of anti-depression devices which the public not only approved but demanded. By 1945 the observation made in 1935 by a British visitor, Sir Josiah Stamp, was an unquestioned article in the American creed: "Just as in 1929 the whole country was 'Wall Street-conscious' now it is 'Washington-conscious.' "

In assuming responsibility for the economy of the country the government was acting on a basic Rooseveltian premise. "Our Republican leaders tell us economic laws—sacred, inviolable, unchangeable—cause panics," Roosevelt had said during the campaign of 1932. "We must lay hold of the fact that economic laws are not made by nature. They are made by human beings." The experiences of eight years in office had not changed his mind on this point. "There were some in those days [before 1933] who chanted that nature had to run its course of misery," said Roosevelt in 1940, "that the depression was only the working of natural economic laws in a system of free enterprise. The American Government . . . decided to reject that philosophy."

Finally, what emerged from the New Deal and the war was a style of capitalism that would contribute much to the rootlessness, the impersonality, the alienation, and the dehumanizing frustrations that would characterize American society in later decades. But at the time, 1945, Americans—most of them, anyway—who may not have understood the subtleties of what had happened over the previous twelve years, liked what they saw. Like Roosevelt, they would not have restored that "ancient order" if they could.

During the New Deal years, those twelve years of Roosevelt's leadership, the economic consequences had been enormous. Roosevelt had preserved and rejuvenated capitalism, undertaken the first long strides toward a welfare state, and made economic security for the individual and governmental responsibility for the health of the national economy goals that were acceptable to nearly every shade of opinion. The effect of World War II was the acceleration of those economic trends beyond the imagination of everyone. The historian who writes an economic history of the war years would do well to start his first chapter with "In the beginning was World War II. . . . And the United States was without form, and void." The before-and-after contrast was that great.

CHAPTER FOUR

The Next Day and the Day After: The Social and Political Consequences of the New Deal

What the government's experiments in music, painting, and the theatre actually did ... was to work a sort of cultural revolution in America.
—Fortune *(May 1937)*

It is the problem of Government to harmonize the interests of these groups which are often divergent and opposing, to harmonize them in order to guarantee security and good for as many of their individual members as may be possible. The science of politics, indeed, may properly be said to be in large part the science of adjustment of conflicting group interest.
—Franklin D. Roosevelt at Rollins College (1936)

The issue is myself.
—Franklin D. Roosevelt (1936)

A massive cerebral hemorrhage at Warm Springs, Georgia, had ended a life, it may even have ended an era—the "Age of Roosevelt," Arthur Schlesinger, Jr., would call it—but it did not end the New Deal.

Roosevelt and the New Deal had changed the face of the United States, maybe its body chemistry, certainly its psyche. Some of the New Deal, of course, was mere cosmetics, a little plastic surgery, some shots of vitamins and hormones, a few placebos. More important, however, was Roosevelt's "bedside manner"—what it meant to national morale, the national convalescence. His real, most lasting contribution to the national rejuvenation was spiritual: a rekindled hope in the hearts of individuals; for the country, a renewed sense of destiny, a reaffirmation of the efficacy of democracy and capitalism in a tormented world.

In retrospect, it is now apparent that the New Deal cure outlasted the national malaise. Some of its economic, social, and political consequences were immediate; others were more subtle, a delayed action, cumulative in their impact. All were worth clinical review, a second look. In the preceding chapter we surveyed the economic consequences of the New Deal. It is now appropriate to turn to the social and political results.

The New Deal had a profound effect on the social and cultural life of the country, spreading into every corner of the American experience. In the 1930s the whole fabric of society and its culture responded to the interplay of the New Deal and the Great Depression.

After the Crash of 1929 the American people began to find their own ways of accommodating to the ensuing depression, of living with adversity and fear as constant companions. Many did the obvious; they turned to each other for reassurance. There developed a renewed sense of family togetherness, the art of conversation revived, people found strength in simple pleasures like strolling, picnicking, and neighborhood parties. They also sought less prosaic diversions.

The 1930s were not lacking in diversions. One craze which swept the country involved putting a golf ball through lengths of downspout and holes in pieces of wood. In 1930 and 1931, everyone who could afford a dime was playing miniature golf. Those who could not afford miniature golf could while away an evening at home playing backgammon.

There were still sports heroes left over from the 1920s to fire the imagination of sportswriters: Bobby Jones in golf, Babe Ruth in baseball. There would soon be others to take their places: Joe Louis, the black heavyweight, the improbable "Dizzy" Dean and the St. Louis Cardinals' "Gashouse Gang" in baseball, and others. And there were heroes of a lower order: flagpole sitters, marathon dancers, and fortune tellers—to soothe depression anxieties. Conservative estimates were that fortune tellers, preying on a public worried about an uncertain future, took in some $25 million in New York City alone in 1931.

As cultural influences on depression America, all of these were minor compared to radio and motion pictures. Both were democratic art forms, by-products of science and technology, and able to offer instant culture to unprecedented audiences. The 1930s were the golden age for both. Although the development of network radio meant an entire nation could enjoy music, drama, sports and comedy, could hear history being made on the spot, there was something a little disconcerting about millions laughing simultaneously at the same joke or getting political views predigested from the same commentator.

Symbolic of the hold of radio on the public taste was Freeman Gosden's and Charles Correll's show, "Amos 'n' Andy"; five nights weekly the country hung on the misadventures of two black owners of the Fresh Air Taxicab Company. What people heard was not always edifying; both Amos and Andy were humiliating caricatures of American blacks. But if the pervasive influence of network radio had everyone mimicking Andy's frustrated "I'se regusted," it also had them imitating Franklin Roosevelt's favorite radio salutation, "My friends."

Motion pictures capitalized on two things: an insatiable demand for movies exploiting the popular escape themes of love, sex, crime, and adventure, and the exciting, mysterious, glamorous lifestyles of the performers. The 1930s were the years of the "movie star," not the least of which was Mickey Mouse. But perhaps no performer better personified the mood of the American movie patron for escape than the precocious child actress, Shirley Temple.

Movie makers also produced some remarkably fine documentary films, such as *The Plow That Broke the Plains*, and the newsreels, a regular feature at every neighborhood theater, helped develop a heightened public sense of history. Nor did Hollywood shy away from depression themes. Movies depicting the seamier side of depression America included *Dead End*, a story of youth gangs in the urban ghetto, *Grapes of Wrath*, a classic film treatment of John Steinbeck's novel about victims of the Dust Bowl, and *Black Legion*, which portrayed the activities of a native fascist Klan-type organization in Detroit. The prospect of getting free dishes or winning a few dollars on Bank Night, along with a double feature—occasionally in Technicolor after 1935—made movies the favorite form of entertainment in the depression decade.

With the end of Prohibition (for which a thirsty nation gave the New Deal all the credit), social customs changed significantly. Once beer started flowing legally, neighborhood taverns suddenly appeared everywhere and became local centers for earnest talk and raucous laughter. In the social scale, the beer tavern was the private domain of the working male, a convivial place where a man could drink "with the boys."

Hard liquor produced the cocktail lounge, more sophisticated in decor than the tavern, where the clientele was expected to include women. Hard liquor also made profitable very large, very plush watering holes, the "night club," frequented by celebrities and featuring live entertainment. Indirectly, the return of liquor produced a whole new school of entertainers: dancers, singers, comedians, and musicians—the night club performer. The night club, along with radio, was the setting for an important musical development, a refinement of jazz called "swing." Swing ushered in the "big band" era, in which the "King of Swing," Benny Goodman, had no peer.

Beer and liquor became an indispensable part of the American social scene. Beer was available at every backyard party, every fishing trip, every ball game. Cocktails before dinner took on the mystique of a religious rite. And the cocktail party, among the more affluent, became an expensive substitute for more meaningful forms of social intercourse.

The depression and the response of the American people to it were revealed in other ways besides radio, movies, and booze. For example, the birth rate dropped sharply, to the lowest levels in our history up to that time; birth control and contraceptive methods, which obviously were widely practiced and used, acquired public acceptance and a new respectability. The depression also did damage to the male ego, to his self-esteem as the family provider, for it was often the woman who had to hold the family together. This strained normal family patterns and caused divorce rates to soar. Divorce ended nearly 18 of every 100 marriages by 1936, almost double the rate of a decade earlier.

Education was badly hurt. Declining tax revenues were translated into shorter school terms, fewer classrooms, and low-paid teachers. Sometimes teachers were not paid at all, or were paid in scrip, which was discounted at banks, sometimes as much as 10 percent. College enrollment, except at the graduate level, dropped alarmingly and many schools were forced to close. By 1933, according to the United States Office of Education, some 1,500 schools, mostly professional and vocational, had ceased operations.

This was also a time of staggering losses in church membership, so great that some observers believed the church as a social institution was on the way to extinction. Some of the reasons for the phenomenon were obvious—embarrassment at not having decent clothes and shoes to wear on Sunday, humiliation (especially among denominations like the Baptists, who stressed tithing and being "a cheerful giver") at not being able to contribute. But the ultimate reason may have been more serious, a disenchantment with a God who could let such a calamity afflict His believers. Americans were not all that accustomed to rationalizing the trials of Job.

This may have been particularly true of those of a more liberal persuasion, those who had embraced a "social gospel" theology that stressed progress and the capacity of man for self-improvement. Many liberal theologians found themselves arguing that the trouble was not spiritual but a failure of the economic system. Men like Harry F. Ward of Union Theological Seminary would come to a severe indictment of capitalism during the depression. On the other hand, the depression generated a resurgence of conservative theology, a neo-orthodoxy that explained the disaster in terms of punishment for having glorified man at the expense of God—as a way of reminding men of their frailty, their dependence, their sinfulness.

The depression, with its common sacrifices, had two other discernible effects on the religious life of America. Despite continuing friction between the champions of the social gospel and neo-orthodoxy, churches were drawn closer together. The 1930s were a time of considerable ecumenical activity, either for actual union (as in the case of the three major branches of Methodism) or for closer cooperation through a stronger Federal Council of Churches.

There was also an unusual growth by millennial sects, groups specializing in the imminence of a "Great Judgment" and having exclusive rights to cosmic answers directly from the Deity. The "I Am" group flourished until its leader, Guy Ballard, who claimed immortality, died of cirrhosis of the liver. The Peace Mission of Father Divine (whose salutation was "Peace, it's wonderful!") had headquarters in Harlem and integrated "Kingdoms" around the country that featured cheap food and lodging. Father Divine, an itinerant Baptist preacher who also claimed immortality, seriously jeopardized the future of his group by swearing the members to celibacy. But the group that made the greatest headway was Jehovah's Witnesses, headed by Judge Rutherford. The Jehovah's Witnesses thrived on persecution resulting from their severe criticism of other religious groups and their truculent opposition to the state, manifested in such things as refusing to salute the flag. Their simplistic faith that Judgment Day was at hand led them to prepare an expensive home in San Diego for Jesus to use after His Second Coming.

"When people are broke," said John Steinbeck, reminiscing about the experiences of being a writer during the depression, "the first things they give up are books." But if Americans stopped buying books, they did not stop reading. The circulation of newspapers and popular magazines stayed at about the same level as before, but there was a tremendous increase in the use of public libraries, where idle people could read—and stay warm.

The depression profoundly influenced American writers. At the outset there was an almost grim satisfaction among serious American writers, many of whom had deeply resented the vulgarities of Big Business in the 1920s. "One couldn't help being exhilarated at the sudden unexpected collapse of that stupid gigantic fraud [big business]," was the way Edmund Wilson expressed it. A few, including some who were quite prominent, turned to Marxist solutions and their conversion was evident in their writings. But the greater number rallied to their country. With depression at home and fascism abroad, American writers became less critical of the United States, and most gave sympathetic support to Roosevelt's efforts to deal with both.

Writers of the "Lost Generation," men such as Sinclair Lewis, F. Scott Fitzgerald, and Ernest Hemingway, coped none too successfully with the chaotic world of the 1930s. Lewis's experience was typical. In 1935 his *It Can't Happen Here* related the rise and triumph of fascism in the United States. It did not ring true, however, when the man who had built a literary career on ridiculing the middle class now had that middle class saving democracy from the fascists.

But other writers were emerging, offspring of the depression, who developed powerful economic and social themes. Notable among them were John Dos Passos, who had begun writing in the 1920s but did not achieve real fame until the publication in the 1930s of his trilogy *U.S.A.*; James T. Farrell, whose Studs Lonigan trilogy introduced the country to the argot of Chicago's South Side; and John Steinbeck, whose *Grapes of Wrath* (in 1939) may have been the most powerful novel written during the decade.

One literary phenomenon, no doubt a part of the identity crisis caused by the depression, was the rash of "uplift" and "self-help" books which usually combined street-corner psychology with a form of self-hypnosis to produce instant self-respect. Pathetic nobodies could gain confidence, could become somebody, if they read Dale Carnegie's *How to Win Friends and Influence People*, Walter Pitkin's *Life Begins at Forty*, or Emmet Fox's *Power through Constructive Thinking*.

The emergence of a new "protest" literature did not mean the total disappearance of genteel writing with more traditional themes. For example, the historical novel matured as an art form and was enormously popular in the 1930s. Among the best were Hervey Allen's *Anthony Adverse* (1934) and Margaret Mitchell's *Gone with the Wind* (1936), both runaway best sellers.

But the "angry" writers dominated the literary scene, just as "angry" playwrights dominated the live theater. There were dramatists like Maxwell Anderson, Marc Connelly, and Thornton Wilder, whose plays, *Winterset* (1935), *The Green Pastures* (1930), and *Our Town* (1938), stayed with broader themes; but the ones who got the most attention were those who used the stage to propagandize, to promote social protest. Among the most talented were Clifford Odets, Lillian Hellman, and Robert Sherwood. Sherwood, not so extreme in his alienation as some of the others, personified the trend of the decade among writers. In *The Petrified Forest* (1934) he argued, with eloquent despair, that reason was no match for a world dominated by brute force. But by 1938, in *Abe Lincoln in Illinois*, Sherwood was reaffirming his faith in reason and its handmaiden, democracy.

Before the advent of the depression and the New Deal the influence of the federal government on the cultural life of the country was minimal and for the most part unintentional. But the influence of the New Deal in the world of arts and letters was direct. Roosevelt made cultural goals a part of official policy; improving the quality of life was included in his definition of recovery and security. The Works Progress Administration was the obvious example. The WPA—acting on the assumption that people in the arts were entitled to eat—developed four major programs in art, theater, music, and writing that eventually employed approximately forty thousand people, most of whom were considered professionals in their fields.

The art program, coinciding with the massive public works program, triggered an exciting revival of mural painting, particularly in government buildings, and easel paintings, which were hung in government buildings, libraries, schools, veterans' hospitals, and United States embassies all over the world. Most of the murals and paintings had contemporary American themes and frequently were done in a critical vein reflecting the mood of the decade.

Before the art program was curtailed by Congress in 1939, more than 4,000 artists had been annually employed. Over 1,300 murals adorned public buildings, while more than 48,000 oils and water colors were on permanent loan. The program had likewise sponsored endless art exhibits, lectures, workshops, and free art lessons. One particularly noteworthy accomplishment of the art program was the compiling of an Index of American Design, which consisted of several thousand plates on which artists copied the design of American folk arts dating back to colonial times.

Many of the experimental projects and new plays of the Federal Theatre program had radical social or political themes, which eventually caused trouble with the House Un-American Activities Committee. In 1939, Congress cut off the funds; but until then the project had annually employed more than 10,000 performers and technicians and had sponsored more than 50,000 performances, involving more than 1,000 plays, vaudeville shows, dance and ballet troupes, puppet shows and circuses. Where else but in the Federal Theatre could the public have seen a budding Orson Welles, a production of *Macbeth* with an all-black cast, or a performance of T. S. Eliot's *Murder in the Cathedral* for fifty-five cents?

The music project may have been the most successful of the government-sponsored cultural programs, for at least two reasons. Music tended to be politically neutral and it could take advantage of radio, the obvious vehicle for mass culture. The music project, headed by Nikolai Sokoloff of the Cleveland Symphony, employed some 15,000 vocalists and musicians who staged, quite literally, thousands of concerts, operas, and radio shows. The project likewise sponsored a teaching program which reached children and adults who might otherwise have received no musical training.

At its peak, the writers' project employed about 6,000 people. A few, like John Steinbeck, had real talent, but most were of no more than average ability. Nonetheless, the project had two notable achievements: the American Guide Series and the Historical Records Survey. The guides, covering the history and geography of the states, major regions, and cities, were of unusually high quality. In some instances they are still considered the best local history available. The records survey was an attempt to inventory the records of the federal government, as well as state and local records, and in some cases private records of schools, churches, and the like. Although the survey was not completed in every instance—the depression did not last quite long enough—it has become an indispensable tool of the historian and researcher.

Across from the White House, in Lafayette Park, a stunned throng of people shuffled nervously and spoke to each other in whispers that December 7 Sunday. Then suddenly, unaccountably, they broke into a spontaneous chorus of "The Star Spangled Banner," followed by "My Country 'Tis of Thee" and "God Bless America."

The West Coast received word of the Japanese attack while many people were still at church. A number of congregations cut short their services, and after a prayer and a verse of "Onward Christian Soldiers" the churchgoers scattered quickly to their homes to listen to the news on radio. Thus did the war begin, affecting the lives of the American people even while the smoke of battle hung over Pearl Harbor. In the struggle of the next four years, which, according to Richard Polenberg, required "total danger, total sacrifice, total effort," the cultural shock would be as great as the depression had been.

What the war effort meant at home—"Use it up, wear it out, make it do or do without," or giving, as popular New York Mayor Fiorello LaGuardia exhorted, "an hour a day for the U.S.A.," and all the rest—

was a unity of action and purpose that had been considered impossible to achieve in a democracy. But the effort exacted its price.

War generated its own romantic notions about the uncertainty of life and imminent death; as a result, there were hasty marriages. The birth rate also zoomed, perhaps accounted for by some deep-seated reach for immortality by those presumably about to face death on the battle-field. On the less romantic side, nearly one out of every three marriages, by 1945, led from the altar to the divorce court. The incidence of venereal disease reached epidemic proportions, prostitution thrived (although law enforcement agencies waged continuous war against it around military bases), and the sexual promiscuity of young girls ("victory girls") was scandalous. Nearly 75 percent of all females who were arrested for sex offenses were under twenty-one years of age, and girls under nineteen accounted for over 40 percent of all reported cases of venereal disease.

One of the great instigators of these and other social and cultural changes during the war was the increased mobility of the population. Mobility, which reversed the "back to the land" trend during the de-pression, caused widespread social disorganization. The migration of more than 15 million swelled urban populations, created severe housing shortages, overtaxed recreation, transportation, and sanitation facilities, strained family relations, increased juvenile delinquency and crime (particularly crime against other persons, such as rape and assault), stirred racial tensions (there were race riots in Harlem and Detroit and lesser incidents in numerous other places), and aroused hostilities and conflicts between permanent residents and the hordes of newcomers.

Education was one of the war casualties in a special way. Crowding, particularly in defense centers, meant having to use makeshift facilities, abandoned buildings, and buildings in which needed repairs were impos-sible because of the shortages of materials and equipment. The burden of enrollment meant that many schools had to operate double shifts to meet the demand. But even this was not always possible because of the exodus of teachers from the profession. By 1945 approximately 350,000 teachers—roughly one in three of the nation's teaching force—had left for military service or for higher-paying jobs in business, indus-try, or government. The only alternatives were poorly prepared tempo-rary teachers, shorter school terms, and severely restricted curricula.

Generally, the programs that were popular on radio before the war remained popular during the war. However, the war spawned a new brand of humor, which relied heavily upon insulting the enemy, upon the supposed lack of amenities for American servicemen, and upon their superiority as fighters. No one mastered the new comedy themes more successfully than Bob Hope. Many programs incorporated war themes in which authorities no longer chased run-of-the-mill robbers but enemy agents and ration book counterfeiters. Coverage of the war greatly increased the size of news departments, as well as the air time allotted to war news, and developed an exciting new breed of expert on-the-spot radio journalists, such as Edward R. Murrow.

Music, especially on radio, reflected the war influence. Military march music was understandably in vogue. And there were songs with titles like "Praise the Lord and Pass the Ammunition," "Coming In on a Wing and a Prayer," "At the Stage Door Canteen," and "Boogie Woogie Bugle Boy of Company B." Most of it was incredibly bad, but the dubious honor of being the worst perhaps should have gone to "When the Yanks Raised the Stars and Stripes on Iwo Jima Isle."

Hollywood likewise supported the war effort with enthusiasm. Instead of the serious social themes of the 1930s, the recurring themes in movies during the war were the total depravity of the Germans and Japanese, the moral superiority of the American cause, the superior fighting qualities of the American armed forces, the sterling virtues of America's allies, the British and the Russians, and how wonderful everything was going to be "when the lights go on again all over the world." There was also a revival of movies with religious themes, possibly the best being *The Song of Bernadette.*

It was not just in the movies that there was a renewed interest in religion, for the war reversed the trend of the 1930s and church membership began to rise once again. Every major religious body (except the Jews) grew at a faster rate than the general population. The most remarkable gains were among the fanatically orthodox, aggressively evangelical fringe denominations that appealed most strongly to lower income groups and especially the uprooted and transplanted who felt isolated and threatened in their new urban surroundings. Storefront churches in the big cities had a unique appeal to such people. The unusual gains in church membership during the war, exceeding the gains by Jews and Roman Catholics, reinforced the essentially Protestant character of the country.

The war years also witnessed the mobilization of America's intellectuals and men of arts and letters. There had been some agonized soul searching in the late years when war was drawing ever nearer; for many, the thought of war was wicked and repulsive. Some railed against it. "Roosevelt will horn into the war at the first chance," H. L. Mencken wrote to Ezra Pound. "He is, to be sure, still bellowing about keeping the United States out of it, but no rational man takes such talk seriously." But when the time came, most supported the common cause. The hysteria of war, however, was not conducive to artistic creativity. The war years produced only a minuscule amount of music, art, drama, or literature that mattered. Only one playwright, Tennessee Williams, showed any real distinction.

But one book written during the war—a small 206-page volume—sold one million copies in the first seven weeks after publication, only the third book since 1900 to sell that many (H. G. Wells' *Outline of History* and Dale Carnegie's *How to Win Friends and Influence People* were the other two). Wendell Willkie's *One World* eventually topped two million, was translated into nearly every language, and even became a best seller in postwar Germany.

In the fall of 1942 Willkie had undertaken a trip around the world at the request of President Roosevelt, covering more than 31,000 miles in a stripped-down Liberator bomber, the *Gulliver. One World* was a hastily written report of the trip by Willkie, an amateur statesman who had never held public office and was beaten by Roosevelt in 1940 in his only attempt in politics, yet his honesty and earnest sincerity ("I speak for myself alone and I say what I damn please," he told the press) captured the imagination of the whole world.

Willkie's simple message was that the United States' view of the rest of the world had for too long been childishly parochial. There are "no distant points in the world any longer," said Willkie; "our thinking in the future must be world-wide." He forecast the postwar drive for freedom in underdeveloped parts of the world: "Men and women all over the world are on the march, physically, intellectually and spiritually. . . . They are resolved, as we must be, that there is no more place for imperialism. . . . The big house on the hill surrounded by mud huts has lost its awesome charm."

In what one writer has called "the most widely read and discussed non-fiction book of the century," Willkie was preparing the American people psychologically for a role in the United Nations and a role in the world that would make isolationism for all time an anachronism.

One should not be misled by the radical and revolutionary signs and gestures in the depression decade. With his New Deal program, which emphasized individual security, Roosevelt understood the American people better than the "angry voices" did. People *did* want security, security that was rooted in a reaffirmation of traditional values that had become tarnished in the 1920s. Sociological and psychological studies of the 1930s appear to support the conclusion that the essence of the traditional value system remained remarkably stable. People wanted jobs, a dependable income, marriage, family, home, friends. To satisfy this deep yearning, perhaps it is fair to say that something akin to Roosevelt's New Deal was inevitable under the circumstances.

Although the depression was evoking a revival of traditional values, there was one major casualty: the depression hung a wreath on the Horatio Alger concept. "Security," *Fortune* magazine's survey discovered, "is the *summum bonum* of the present college generation. The present day average undergraduate is no chancy gambler." If the country had set its jaw to whip the depression, it was not so its youth could resume extravagant talk about making a million dollars, marrying the boss's daughter, and becoming president of the company.

If the depression did nothing else, it dramatized the shallowness of a culture in which excessive materialism was the dominant force. Americans in increasing numbers seemed to be learning the lesson that making a living was a means, not an end in itself. The good life depended as much upon nurturing the intangibles of the spirit as upon filling one's belly. While the New Deal was sparking a new kind of hope in the land, there was an almost measurable deflation of faith in "progress" and the jaunty kind of optimism and adventuresome spirit which, in the past, had fired fierce political independence, phenomenal economic expansion, and social mobility. In the 1930s the paternalism implicit in the New Deal had contributed to the weakening of the tradition of acquisitive self-reliance and "rugged individualism." In the future, collective social action would be the style.

In a very positive way, the New Deal had contributed to the cultural development of America—first, by making esthetic goals an acceptable part of the enlarged responsibility of government and, second, by supporting the traditional custodians of American culture. It may be argued that this was only coincidental, deriving from the New Deal idea that such custodians needed help the same as workers, farmers, and businessmen. Whatever may have been the motive, the fact is that the government patronized and subsidized the arts against the withering effect of depression.

This new role of concerned patron in the cultural life of the country was reciprocated by those who benefited from it. This, however, is not to say that arts and letters became a servant of the state as in countries like Nazi Germany or the Soviet Union. On the contrary, there continued to be dissident voices, often with strong Marxist overtones, raised in protest against American society, politics, and economics. But even though the New Deal refrained from exerting any appreciable censorship or seeking to propagandize, there was a discernible "nationalizing" of American cultural life, enough to make some observers apprehensive.

Perhaps this was inevitable. Certainly there could be no ignoring the depression crisis of the 1930s and, as the decade ended, the sense of foreboding aroused by the international situation. The all-inclusive way in which Roosevelt dealt with the depression meant that the artist, the writer, the intellectual encountered the New Deal at every turn. In adversity, the cultural life of America began to reflect a new pride in the country and its institutions, as well as in its government, which was apparently trying to redeem both.

The war years continued the process, the cultural life of the country becoming increasingly patriotic, increasingly "official" in its orientation. The needs of the state to defeat its enemies took priority in science, in education. The federal government poured millions of dollars into universities for research and development, an alliance that would be hard to terminate in later years. The needs of the state to promote patriotism, loyalty, and "good Americanism" likewise had high priority in such diverse cultural areas as radio, the movies, and the theater. Even religion, the vehicle for entreating a divine providence to bring victory in a righteous cause, did not escape. War work such as running canteens, providing entertainment, contributing blood plasma, and the like became a substitute for more traditional religious activities, particularly for churches located near military installations.

Although some were concerned about these developments, there still seemed to be cause for optimism, for hope of a better future. In a world plagued by depression and war, by fascism and communism, by dictatorship and tyranny, Roosevelt seemed to be succeeding in providing leadership which perpetuated, perhaps even strengthened, the democratic ideal in matters cultural as well as economic and political.

Thomas Jefferson, with the finality that comes of being wiser than most men, could say that that government governs best which governs least. Calvin Coolidge, for quite different reasons, could observe wryly that the federal government could quit functioning altogether and it would be "a considerable length of time" before anybody noticed. H. L. Mencken had his own version of Coolidge's position. "Coolidge," he wrote, "slept more than any other President in this century." And not quite as an afterthought, he added: "He also did less when he was awake."

Jefferson and Coolidge were not of the same political persuasion, nor were they saying the same thing. But even if they had been, the New Deal put an end to all such talk about the minor, supporting role of government in the American scheme of things. With the coming of the New Deal, and after, whenever people spoke of "the government" there was no doubt in anyone's mind what they meant. They did not mean Austin, or Albany, or Pierre. They meant Washington, D.C. And they meant that Washington was not only the political capital but, under Roosevelt, the economic capital as well.

Under Roosevelt, federal government became the principal creative force in American society. While some governments in other countries sat helpless, and mute, as if transfixed by the deepening world crisis, and while other governments were toppling from within from subversive forces—not for attempting too much but for attempting too little—Roosevelt was seizing the initiative, striking out boldly. And if his goals seemed long familiar, his techniques at least created the illusion of action. We shall "wage a war" against the depression as if we were "in fact invaded by a foreign foe," Roosevelt had said in his inaugural address. The metaphor of war was reassuring; it struck a responsive chord among a people desperate for leadership.

People descended on Washington from every direction, all sorts of people—people with all kinds of ideas, people promoting all sorts of causes, people whose fires of hope had burned low since the days of

Wilson: professors; the college-bred class; thousands of devoted and able people; and not a few who should not have been let out after dark. Roosevelt listened; Roosevelt picked their brains. Roosevelt sorted and arranged, discarded and chose, reconciled unreconcilables. What mattered, after Hoover, was that somebody paid attention, that somebody gave a damn.

The reaction of people who lived through the Crash of 1929, the ominous gloom of the Great Depression, the hallelujah spirit of the change in administrations, the tumultuous carrying-on of the first 100 Days, depended largely on the state of their nerves. Some were tempted to call these events revolutionary, the end of Western civilization as they knew it (theirs was the kind of mentality that had the secret police mounting the stairs three at a time). Others applauded, shouting joyfully that it was about time.

This was partly because much of the unfinished business of reform, things that should have been done years ago, things that usually took political eons to accomplish, were now being compressed, condensed, streamlined in the name of crisis and emergency. All may have seemed revolutionary but it was not. Eventually the pace slackened; in later years the New Deal would march to a slower beat. But throughout there remained some of that "hell-for-leather, try-anything" mood of the early days.

 Considering the new, creative role of government under Roosevelt, the miracle of the New Deal may well be that compared to Europe, the United States emerged from the Great Depression without revolution, its social, political, and economic institutions modified but still intact.

In assuming charge of that creative force—the federal government—Roosevelt fashioned something new of the office of President. Clinton Rossiter, in *The American Presidency* (1956), has concluded: "Only Washington, who made the office, and Jackson, who remade it, did more than [Roosevelt] to raise it to its present condition of strength, dignity, and independence."

It was not just that Roosevelt was a strong leader; it was his rare gift of being able to reach people, move people (move them sometimes to heroic heights), inspire trust; it was his ability to "personalize" his leadership. It is probably true that no President, before or since, was able to evoke such an outpouring of popular support and confidence.

The "fireside chat," a stroke of genius from the leadership stand-point, was a symbol of the love affair between Roosevelt and the American people. Frances Perkins recalled that, as he spoke over the radio, "his head would nod and his hands would move in simple, natural, comfortable gestures. His face would smile and light up as though he were actually sitting on the front porch or in the parlor with them."

Eleanor Roosevelt related that, after the death of her husband, people would stop her on the street to say "they missed the way the President used to talk to them. They'd say 'He used to talk to me about my government.' " There was, said Mrs. Roosevelt, "a real dialogue between Franklin and the people."

One can only speculate what might have been his hold on the people had there been the intimacy of television in the 1930s. The resonant voice, the infectious smile, the toss of the head, and the profile would likely have carried him to the top of all the television polls.

In any case, Roosevelt was converting the presidency into folk hero dimensions even in his own time. Other Presidents had been heroes—heroes of a sort, anyway: Jackson, Lincoln, Theodore Roosevelt, and maybe others. But no other President had been the kind of hero that Franklin Roosevelt became. That he became a hero was remarkable; there was little anywhere in his background that suggested it. And there was genuine skepticism concerning his talents, a skepticism best sum-marized, perhaps, by Walter Lippmann's comment in 1932 that Roose-velt was "no crusader . . . no tribune of the people . . . no enemy of entrenched privilege . . . a pleasant man who, without any important qualification for the office, would very much like to be President."

Lippmann may have had a point. During the campaign of 1932 Roosevelt generated enthusiasm, but not the kind of idolatry that would come later. He was no Isaiah, nor a William Jennings Bryan. He was no John the Baptist, crying in the wilderness; he was too sophisti-cated, too urbane. There was not even a log cabin in his background, much less locusts and wild honey. With such credentials—or lack of them—he did not qualify as a folk hero in the Jackson or Lincoln style. Yet Roosevelt used the presidency as the vehicle for becoming Ameri-ca's greatest popular hero of modern times, for sketching a new dimen-sion of the office that all Presidents since have ignored at their peril.

The starting point of this enormous popularity can be documented. It began in Miami on February 15, 1933. It began when the deranged Joseph Zangara, a Hackensack, New Jersey, bricklayer fired at nearly point-blank range into the presidential car. Zangara missed Roosevelt but mortally wounded Chicago's Mayor Anton Cermak. The President-elect remained remarkably poised throughout the ordeal, and the country, applauding the display of courage, pondered just how much it was counting on Roosevelt after all. Surviving assassination attempts is the raw material from which heroes are made—at least as good as marathon dancing, flagpole sitting, or even solo nonstop flights to Paris.

But there was more. Roosevelt was a cripple. There are those who build a pretty good case that it was Roosevelt's being struck down in his prime by polio that not only developed important but latent qualities of character—courage, capacity for pain, tenacity, a sense of the tragic, a fatalism producing calmness under pressure, a self-assuredness about always winning out no matter the odds (others would consistently refer to the Roosevelt "luck")—but, more important, inspired a realization that there were things over which one had no control. And they could happen to anybody. They could happen to Franklin Roosevelt. High fever, paralyzed legs, and a painful recovery had perhaps turned an arrogant, supercilious young man into a compassionate human being with deep feeling for his fellow man.

Certainly the influence of his wife had something to do with the change in Roosevelt. Eleanor's life had not been a happy one. Her lonely childhood and growing awareness that she was unattractive, that she was awkward and homely and lacking in the social graces, made her early years miserable. The one bright spot was her marriage to the handsome young Franklin. Eleanor marveled at her good fortune. But the marriage was not a good one. The early years of having babies (six in all), of living under the critical eye of a domineering mother-in-law, of always having under foot her husband's possessive friend, Louis Howe, and, finally, the shattering knowledge of Franklin's relationship with Lucy Mercer Rutherfurd left a deep sense of self-sacrifice and betrayal.

When Roosevelt went to Washington in 1914 as Assistant Secretary of the Navy, Eleanor had employed Lucy Mercer as a part-time secretary. For the inexperienced Eleanor, the beautiful and charming Lucy Mercer was the ideal choice. She understood the rituals and nuances of formal Washington society, knew everybody who was anybody, and, with her family connections, was herself a part of Washington society. In time, Roosevelt became strongly attracted to her. There seems little doubt that Roosevelt fell in love with Lucy, and that his love was reciprocated. The romance continued until the autumn of 1918, when Roosevelt returned, seriously ill, from a trip to Europe. Taking care of his mail during his illness, Eleanor came upon letters from Lucy confirming what she had long only suspected. There was a confrontation of Eleanor, Franklin, and Lucy in which the latter agreed to stop seeing each other. But the Roosevelt marriage had very nearly ended in divorce.

Lucy Mercer later married Winthrop Rutherfurd, in 1920. Even so, Roosevelt and Lucy Mercer Rutherfurd continued a relationship over the years—one that was eventually more a friendship than a romance. And, as already noted, she was visiting at Warm Springs when he died.

In 1921, when Roosevelt was stricken, Eleanor was really needed; for the first time in her life someone was really counting on her. The stamina and courage had always been there. Eleanor Roosevelt matured quickly, became the eyes and ears and right hand for her husband, walked and talked in his place. But more, she became his conscience, and after 1933 the conscience of the New Deal as well.

In time, maybe Roosevelt would have mellowed anyway. But it is true, nonetheless, that polio slowed him down in a hurry, provided time for reflection at a critical juncture in his career, gave him a different perspective on life. There was something moving, something ironic about all this. From deepest despair and desperation the American people were turning for leadership to a man who could not walk. Overcoming such adversity was the stuff of which heroes are made.

The Roosevelt personality left few people neutral. Not a few of those who were moved by the Roosevelt personality took pen in hand, and the result was an avalanche of mail that arrived at the White House by the truckload. During the last two years of his administration, Hoover received an average of 600 letters a day, the number dropping occasionally as low as 100. Roosevelt received 450,000 letters during the first week after his inauguration in 1933. According to Louis Howe, the President averaged 6,500 letters daily during his first year in office. The volume declined somewhat in later years; but the fact remains that Roosevelt received more mail, far more mail, than any previous President.

As we have noted, some of the writers were unbelievably vicious in what they said. But most of the people wrote to President Roosevelt as they would write to their father, to a dear friend, to a favorite uncle, to their priest. He had captured their imagination; had included them; had made them part of the team in a worthy enterprise; had made them feel—even the most humble—that they shared the great destiny of the country; had called upon them for sacrifice. In the first fireside chat he had said: "It is your problem no less than mine. Together we cannot fail."

"He was in a very special sense the people's President," Supreme Court Justice William O. Douglas has written, "because he made them feel that with him in the White House they shared the Presidency. The sense of sharing the Presidency gave even the most humble citizen a lively sense of belonging." It is rare when challenge, sacrificial challenge, does not bring out the best in people; every great leader knows this. If the results are successful, people cast their hero in bronze and erect statues in the parks.

Roosevelt likewise became a hero in his own time because he was dramatic; could make dramatic that which was not dramatic; had, as one observer put it, the "imperial gesture." In Roosevelt's Washington there was no dull status quo, no quietude and piety. When Roosevelt's Washington came alive, began to hum, it was not the steady, consistent, predictable motions of a factory assembly line; it was the orderly chaos of the battlefield. Roosevelt had the capacity for making all of the day-in, day-out mundane business of government appear dramatic, crucially significant. He had an inspired sense of timing, the theatrical instincts of a Barrymore. The fact—or at least the illusion—was such action, such drama, such derring-do as had not been seen since Douglas Fairbanks.

An important aspect of Roosevelt's skill at dramatizing government developed from his relationship with the working press. Roosevelt dominated the headlines of the newspapers as no President before or since has done. At his first press conference he abandoned the traditional written questions and informed the reporters that they could ask him anything.

Throughout the years, and even after the country went to war, Roosevelt continued his informal press conferences, usually twice a week. A hundred or more reporters huddled around the President's desk in the White House as Roosevelt leaned back in his chair fielding questions, his cigarette holder at a jaunty angle, and became a familiar and reassuring picture in the newspapers and newsreels. Because most of their publishers were hostile to him, Roosevelt wisely cultivated the working press, knew them by their first names, joked with them, traded stories, took them into his confidence with "off the record" information. But in the process Roosevelt was making news, was educating the public, was dramatizing the affairs of government.

The Constitution is silent on heroes and heroics; Article II does not mention them as qualifications for office. But Roosevelt had made them qualifications all the same. In the future, he who would aspire to the presidency would have to display, in his own fashion and in his own style, that he, too, was more than mere mortal.

The President would have to be, in addition to all other things, a man who could fire the imagination, produce at least the illusion of vigorous action, dramatize government, make of government an institution directly experienced by the people, be almost a Renaissance man—as Roosevelt surely was -in his knowledge of economics, geography, history, and much more, or he was courting failure. He must be a heroic figure, one who could win hearts as well as elections—something Lyndon Johnson and Richard Nixon would never quite comprehend.

Much of Roosevelt's personalized style of leadership was carried on through his position in the Democratic party. Despite appearances, Roosevelt was never really much of a party man. He believed more could be accomplished as President by remaining above the pull and tug, beyond the half-a-loaf compromising approach of party politics.

Lack of commitment to party accounts in part for his lack of compunction about excluding prominent party leaders and wheelhorses from the New Deal team, for his willingness to include people who could hardly be classified as old-line Democrats. Little wonder that Al Smith, deeply wounded at not being invited into Roosevelt's holy of holies, eventually exploded: "Who is Ickes? Who is Tugwell? And who is Hopkins and where did he blow from? If LaGuardia is a Democrat then I am a Chinaman with a haircut."

Lack of devotion to party also helps explain Roosevelt's desire not just to be elected but to be virtually anointed. In each of his campaigns mere victory was not enough. He coveted a mandate like the "Grand

Ratification" of 1936. Consequently, he avoided references to party, avoided party labels, and sought instead to be leader of all the people, above the partisanship of party feeling.

This style of leadership left little room for competitors; and Roosevelt was preparing no one as successor. He left his party—just as he found it—in chaos, disorganized, in wild disarray. Roosevelt had succeeded in wooing the majority into the Democratic camp (most voters, by 1945, were at least nominally Democrats), but Truman inherited a party machinery in a state of collapse, which meant that his difficulties in getting elected in 1948 were nòt solely of his own making.

Roosevelt used the party, of course, as a means to an end. And whether he liked it or not, whether he meant it to be that way or not, Roosevelt *was* the Democratic party. The breakdown of party lines, the diminishing dependence upon traditional party politics, the rebirth of issue politics with vital principles at stake, the amount of work done on Roosevelt's behalf by people outside the party, and the relative decline in eminence of party leaders all led to a festering uneasiness among many Democrats. "Let one man die," wrote one disillusioned Democrat, "and the New Deal structure may well collapse overnight." Roosevelt died; but the New Deal did not collapse. The disillusioned Democrat, reflecting a feeling not uncommon at the time, was proved wrong.

Roosevelt always saw his relationship to the people as one in which they were choosing a leader, not signing a chattel mortgage on the issues. But both Roosevelt and the unidentified Democrat were expressing the lack of real commitment between the New Deal and the Democratic party.

Another dimension of Roosevelt's personal leadership style was reflected in the nature of the advisers he relied on. Everyone soon heard about the Brain Trust—which was not nearly so formalized as mythology would have it, certainly not so shifty and sinister as the critics warned. What it amounted to was Roosevelt's willingly seeking advice from those who normally did not show up on the Washington landscape: tweedy types who smoked pipes, read books, liked good music, were shy with people but at ease with ideas, had brains, carried their Ph.Ds and professorial ranks lightly. All of which should have automatically disqualified them from government.

And it did, to hear some people tell it. Harold Ickes, Secretary of the Interior, later had some sarcastic things to say about the attitude of many toward the Brain Trust:

You will recall that one of the funniest things that the Roosevelt administration ever did was to reach the insane conclusion that if there were brains available and for hire they could not be used to better advantage than in the service of their country. That elicited shrieks of derisive laughter. The country was not prepared for any such silly proposal. The first synonym of brains is "college professor," but who in the world would ever think of asking a college professor to formulate a sane opinion about the more serious affairs of government? It is notorious that college professors usually sit in their bathtubs with their hats on, or go to bed without taking off their shoes. Certainly, we shouldn't trust them to run the public's business.

Donald Richberg, counsel to the National Recovery Administration and later its chairman, was likewise irritated by the attitude of some toward the Brain Trust approach: "When any man ventures to scoff at the use of brains in government he should be asked to explain by what part of the anatomy he believes human affairs should be conducted."

But Roosevelt did not consider college teaching a felony, or even a laughing matter. He was willing to listen to and use such people; the only criterion was expertise. The significance of this breach of orthodoxy was that Roosevelt's personalized style of leadership meant relying for advice on men outside the traditional circumference of political influence.

Roosevelt's personalized style of leadership, the "President of all the people" approach, also meant that he became legislator-in-chief. People with long memories associated "my policies" with an earlier Roosevelt who thought the pronoun *I* had been invented specially for him. The later Roosevelt soon introduced them to "must" legislation. Congressmen were frightened, bewildered, and sometimes angered by the swarm of hot-eyed young New Dealers who ascended Capitol Hill, each claiming to have just left Roosevelt's bosom with a legislative proposal he wanted passed posthaste.

During the emergency of the 100 Days, Congress acquiesced. Congress was as jumpy as everybody else; it was prepared to approve anything Roosevelt wanted. As the crisis eased and the death-bed mood of Congress dissipated, there was more resistance to Roosevelt in his role of lawmaker. But the style had been set.

Congress now expected the President to have "a program." Special messages to Congress, pressure on the party caucus, drafts of bills prepared by Brain Trusters, letters and telephone calls to committee chairmen, leaders being summoned to the White House, arm twisting by presidential lobbyists, patronage dangled under their noses, all this and more became a standard part of the President's repertoire for getting what he wanted from the Congress. Subsequent Presidents, indeed even Roosevelt himself, had to modify their techniques; but, like it or not, the chief executive had become chief legislator, and even so popular a President as Dwight Eisenhower could not change it.

A neglected aspect of Roosevelt's personal style of leadership was the length of time involved. Years passed. The Great Depression receded. All hell broke loose in Europe and China. Through it all the bonds of trust and affection between Roosevelt and the people grew, grew to the point of believing that only Roosevelt could handle the job. Critics could talk, with some accuracy, about his being President for life—he *was* President for life. And an entire generation seemed grateful for something it could depend on besides "Amos 'n' Andy" and the *Saturday Evening Post*.

Roosevelt's remarkable feat of longevity relegated the two-term tradition to the footnotes of textbooks. It also stimulated passage of the Twenty-second Amendment, which limits a President to two terms (unless he was Vice President when something happened to his predecessor, in which case he could serve as long as ten years less one day). The amendment was probably a mistake; the punishment did not fit the crime. It means that the President who wins a second term is, in fact, condemned rather than rewarded. When he places his hand on the Bible at his second inauguration, he is already a lame duck. The retreat begins with the unhitching of political wagons from the fading star and is followed by the eye gouging and elbowing to become the successor.

As if from the grave, Roosevelt removed the sobering possibility of a third term—sobering for those with thoughts of getting too cavalier with a second-term President.

Despite his lukewarm attitude toward the party and the absence of serious commitment between the New Deal and the old democracy, Roosevelt left an indelible mark on the American party system.

With Roosevelt, the Democratic party became the majority party. Before he arrived on the scene, Democrats had entered the White House without knocking only twice since 1860. Grover Cleveland won in 1884 by the slimmest of margins, and again in 1892 as a reaction to a depression which hit bottom the next year—the Panic of 1893. Woodrow Wilson won in 1912 as a minority President, thanks to the bloodletting between Taft and Theodore Roosevelt, and again in 1916 by the grace of Hiram Johnson and Kaiser Wilhelm. An alleged snub of California's Governor Johnson by the Republican candidate, Charles Evans Hughes (Hughes failed to call on Johnson when both men were staying at the Virginia Hotel in Long Beach), is the usual simplistic explanation for that state's going to Wilson, the margin of victory in the election. And, fortunately for Wilson, Wilhelm did not order the resumption of unrestricted submarine warfare until after the election, which gave the Democratic slogan "He kept us out of war" a ring of truth.

There was more to it, of course. Wilson, by coming out unequivocally for Progressive reforms and by linking those reforms to the issue of peace, forged a coalition that converted the Democratic minority party temporarily into the majority. To the Democratic faithful were added independents, many Progressives who had supported Theodore Roosevelt in 1912, women (in those states that had woman's suffrage), and radicals who usually voted for the Socialist ticket. The wholesale defection to Wilson of Socialist supporters in California may have been as crucial as the Johnson snub in swinging that state to the Democratic column.

At any rate, since 1860 the Democratic party had spent more time wandering the political wilderness than the Children of Israel. For the Democratic party, Roosevelt was a latter-day Joshua; the Promised Land was at hand. Since Roosevelt, even Republican Presidents know they will likely face a Democratic Congress.

Roosevelt also demolished the party's hillbilly image. The Democratic party had been held responsible for everything from Sumter to Appomattox. For years the taint of treason and blame for the Civil War hung heavy over the party; for years the "bloody shirt" kept Democrats on the defensive. The Democratic party was a genuinely national party with support from all parts of the country. It always had been a national party. But while memory of the war faded, the party became saddled with a "Solid South" and cotton-tobacco-peanuts image. Despite dependable and sizable strength in the Midwest and East and support from Irish-dominated political machines in some of the major cities, the Democratic party projected a rural image in a changing society of rapid industrialization, urbanization, and all that went with it.

The Republican party on the other hand, had discovered the Industrial Revolution early. It had formed an open alliance with business, worked with it, for it, and became clearly identified as the "party of business." As the process of economic centralization went on, the Republican party became the "party of Big Business," a fact of political life that was a source of pride, a boast.

Not until the Crash of 1929 and the Great Depression did pointing out the obvious—that the Republican party was the party of Big Business—become a reproach. So long as its ally, business, could deliver prosperity and consistent economic boom, the Republican party could deliver matching political victories. It virtually acquired squatter's rights to the White House, usually dominated Congress, had its business-oriented views translated into holy writ by the courts. Big Business and the Republican party were an unbeatable tandem.

The process by which the Democratic party began to lose its strong agrarian coloration probably began with Al Smith, the four-time governor of New York who represented something novel in the Democratic party. Smith represented the East, urban sprawl, the new immigrant, minority ethnic groups, Catholics, Jews, the sidewalks of New York— and something strong to wash it down. He despised the "noble experiment" of Prohibition and said so. He did not win in 1928, of course; but as already noted, he polled more votes than any other Democratic presidential candidate, winner or loser, up to that time. He carried important eastern cities—New York, Jersey City, Boston, Providence, New Haven—and relaxed the Republican stranglehold on others across the country.

He also picked a national party chairman, John J. Raskob, who defied tradition. Raskob, wealthier than most men, an executive of DuPont and General Motors, and a Republican, had fully expected to vote for Hoover. At least until his friendship with Smith, based on their mutual distaste for Prohibition and their common fealty to the Church of Rome and the Knights of Columbus, changed his mind. Raskob did not know beans about running a political party. He did not get on well with the party professionals. But he made two very practical contributions. Among his businessmen friends, he soothed their fears of the

Democratic party. And he kept the national party headquarters in business between elections. Traditionally, the national headquarters functioned only during presidential election years.

There was no way of defeating Hoover in 1928, short of divine intervention. Since that did not happen, the next best thing was Raskob's fateful decision to keep the national headquarters operating, paying the expenses out of his own pocket. It was a stroke of good fortune. When the Crash came, Raskob and the veteran newspaperman Charles Michelson, Democratic publicity director, engineered a successful "smear Hoover" campaign, pinning the rap on the Republican party for the Great Depression.

Victory was all but certain for the Democrats in 1932. In the four years since 1928, Smith and Raskob had led the party a long way from its bib-overall, Bible Belt image; the Crash, the Great Depression, and Franklin Roosevelt did the rest.

"The rest" included shaking off the stranglehold of the South on the Democratic party. Looking no further than the Democratic convention and the campaign of 1932, one might get the impression that nothing much had changed with the Democrats. The convention produced a ticket, Roosevelt-Garner, on which the South had exercised its usual negative influence. And during the campaign Roosevelt devoted an inordinate amount of time to buttering up the agrarian wing of the party.

Southern support, after all, had been decisive in his nomination. In 1932, southerners—men like Cordell Hull, Alben Barkley, Josephus Daniels, John Rankin, Pat Harrison, Huey Long, and others—worked untiringly for Roosevelt. By convention time they had succeeded in putting all the southern delegations in his column except Maryland, Virginia, and Texas—a total of 210 convention votes of a possible 296. And it was well they had. With the two-thirds rule still alive and well, Roosevelt had to have the South to win nomination.

If southerners had any second thoughts about Roosevelt, they kept still. They had reason to feel secure; John Nance Garner would be looking after their interests. As one Texas delegate had put it at Chicago, the Roosevelt-Garner pairing was a "kangaroo ticket, stronger in the hindquarter than in front." The lisping Tennessean, Cordell Hull, would be in the cabinet; and the Congress, where only tenure and seniority counted, would be dominated by southern Democrats who had consistently survived the long drought since Woodrow Wilson.

The South and West nominated Roosevelt in 1932, but the South certainly did not elect him. Had Hoover carried every southern state, Roosevelt would still have won. The mid-term elections of 1934 further diminished Roosevelt's dependency on the South. Of 69 Democratic senators, the South had but 24; of the 322 Democratic representatives, the South had only 108.

The signs were clear. The classical Democratic party was yielding to one that was more northern than southern, more urban than rural. It was a new combination of forces that appealed to labor, to traditionally Republican Negroes, to the ethnic groups of the New Immigration, to women, and to intellectuals. Roosevelt was constructing a new political edifice—one in which the South was the frieze, not the cornerstone.

In 1936 a significant erosion of southern influence developed at the Democratic National Convention in Philadelphia. In the case of the South, as singleminded as an alcoholic about its political goals, the two-thirds rule had meant the same as a minority veto. The hasty, ill-conceived effort of the Roosevelt forces to eliminate the rule in 1932 had failed. But in 1936 Jim Farley's disciplined convention voted the century-old rule into oblivion with a minimum of fireworks; even southern opposition was perfunctory, listless, spiritless. With the two-thirds rule went the South's last important hold on the party.

Abolishing the two-thirds rule also meant that Champ Clark had, at long last, been avenged. In 1912 Clark (of Missouri), then Speaker of the House of Representatives, had been the leading contender for the Democratic nomination. At the national convention in Baltimore he forged to an early lead, and eventually mustered a majority, but never the necessary two-thirds. Clark's support slowly eroded and, after forty-six ballots, Woodrow Wilson received the nomination. In an ironic touch, it was Missouri Senator Bennett Champ Clark, son of the victim of the rule in 1912, who had the satisfaction of moving adoption of the simple majority rule at Philadelphia in 1936.

That the South continued to support Roosevelt at the ballot box did not change the fact that he now had on his hands a dissident group of old professionals, at odds with the strange assortment of new leaders emerging within Democratic ranks: leaders with pigmented skin, thick accents, the smell of mine and factory about them, or the cultured pallor of the college classroom; new leaders with ideas as alien to southern traditionalists as if the former were from another planet.

"Democrats, Democrats," muttered Virginia's salty Senator Carter Glass of the New Dealers in 1935; "Why, Thomas Jefferson would not speak to these people."

Glass was right; his caustic remark went to the heart of the matter. Roosevelt's approach to the nation's troubles stirred the hopes of classes of people who had been untouched by the main currents of politics since the golden days of Progressivism, and the South was being singled out for special attention as the "economic problem No. 1 of the nation." This appraisal of the South was not remarkable; anyone, assuming he was not half-witted, could see that it was true.

In the last chapter it was noted that the economic changes brought about by the New Deal constituted a threat to the traditional power structure, a threat which took several forms. Federally financed and administered relief and public works involved patronage on an unprecedented scale, sufficient to make any good Democrat smile in his sleep. But it was federal; the administration expected, in exchange, a certain amount of gratitude, visible gratitude, which, incidentally, it did not always get. Nor were the beneficiaries of federal largess apt to forget where to locate the source of the manna. It was not coming from the county judge or the sheriff's office.

This meant that the New Deal was undermining that southern tenet of the faith, states' rights. Men like Governor O. Max Gardner of North Carolina warned that the New Deal was destroying local government and substituting an "all-powerful federal authority similar to the current dictatorship in several European countries." Albert Ritchie, former governor of Maryland, saw in the New Deal a trend that would soon make the federal government "master of our souls." The transfer of power from the states to the federal government, according to Ritchie, was "the complete reversal of the Jeffersonian theory of government." "It was not Ulysses S. Grant who effected the near-destruction of 'States' Rights,' " mourned one prominent southerner, "but rather the man who invented 'Federal Aid.' " "What has become of the old Jeffersonian Democracy?" asked Congressman Will Taylor of Tennessee. "Alas! it has gone the way of the dodo, the mastodon, and the ichthyosaurus. States' rights is now only a memory, and subsidy and centralized government are sweet morsels which our Democratic brethren roll on their tongues with increasing glee and gratification."

Whatever the ideological objections of southerners to the New Deal, and however justifiable these may have seemed, there were some who feared it and attacked it for less admirable reasons. The New Deal was having a profound effect on forgotten men all over the nation. In the South, this meant the black. Whites, too; but particularly the black. In other words, the New Deal was playing hob with white supremacy. The change in the economic status of blacks through direct relief, work relief, and federal jobs was immediate.

This is not to say that Roosevelt was consciously trying to undermine the racial status quo in the South or that he was even particularly concerned with the plight of blacks. "Roosevelt's actual commitments to the American Negro were slim," according to Leslie Fishel, Jr., a scholar of black-white relations. Roosevelt was "more a symbol than an activist." The New Deal, for all its class-oriented legislation, was surprisingly lacking in measures specifically designed to help blacks. Their status was improved only as a by-product of New Deal programs, only to the extent that New Deal programs did not exclude them.

The Roosevelt administration tolerated discrimination: in wages, in promotions, in hiring for supervisory jobs, in permitting what amounted to quota systems. For example, the percentage of blacks on relief and in relief work was consistently lower than the percentage of blacks in the total number of unemployed. Or, to put it another way, considering the number who needed assistance, a higher percentage of whites received help from the federal government than blacks.

Furthermore, when Roosevelt took office there were five anti-lynching bills in congressional committees. But he never gave more than lukewarm support to anti-lynching legislation. Three years later, the editors of *Crisis* noted: "Since Mr. Roosevelt took office . . . seventy persons have been killed by mobs . . . at the rate of one every fifteen days. The President has spoken over the radio about lynching, but he has not spoken the right words to congressional leaders." This failure, *Crisis* remarked, "is all the more glaring when it is remembered that in the House there are more than enough votes to pass such a bill without a single Southern vote." Walter White, president of the NAACP, urged Roosevelt on several occasions to speak out against lynching, to give support to federal anti-lynching legislation. But Eleanor Roosevelt admitted that "though Franklin was in favor of [that] measure, [it] never became 'must' legislation."

In June 1934 a bill with great potential for federal prosecution of lynching cases became law. The Lindbergh law, it was called. It made kidnapping a federal offense when "the kidnapped person was knowingly transported in interstate or foreign commerce and held for ransom, reward or otherwise." Should the kidnapped person be missing for more than seven days, it would be assumed that he had been carried across state lines.

In October 1934, after a Georgia black had been abducted and not been discovered for more than seven days, NAACP representatives approached the Department of Justice. They were told there was "nothing to indicate that the person alleged to be kidnapped was transported in interstate commerce and was held for ransom, reward or otherwise," and that the case would be left in the hands of Georgia authorities.

Three weeks later, a black was kidnapped from an Alabama jail, was carried away in a car bearing Florida license plates, and was later found in Florida brutally and obscenely mutilated and lynched. Before the NAACP could act, the Department of Justice issued a statement claiming that lynching was not included in the meaning of "otherwise."

Such evasions continued throughout the New Deal. To Roosevelt's silence on lynching, as well as on other glaring injustices—the neglect of their right to own land and property, to live where they chose, to get jobs for which their skills fitted them and the pay which their jobs deserved—blacks reacted with a remarkable lack of bitterness or reproach. Walter White's most strongly worded criticism of Roosevelt merely pointed to the irony of three men having been lynched in one week "in the United States of America during the regime of the world's greatest liberal—Franklin Delano Roosevelt." The newspaper the *Afro-American* was not so kind. It claimed that "the only difference between the President and the South is Mr. Roosevelt has violated the Constitution for four years and Dixie for forty."

But such attacks were uncommon, compared to the many glowing resolutions by black groups and organizations endorsing the New Deal and its programs. Or to statements such as that of Robert Weaver: "The New Deal is for the Negro." Even W. E. B. DuBois, more militant than most, agreed that the black had benefited more from the New Deal than from any other administration except Lincoln's.

Paul Robeson, a black singer with few equals, recounted that in 1936 John D. M. Hamilton, national chairman of the Republican party, approached him in London, where Robeson had taken residence, the first step of his self-imposed exile. Hamilton urged Robeson to return to the United States and campaign among blacks for Alf Landon, in return for which Robeson "could write his own ticket in Hollywood contracts." Robeson turned down the offer. Recalling the offer, Robeson wrote later, he "would smile at the thought that anyone could imagine his stumping the country, urging Negroes to turn against the New Deal."

Despite its shortcomings where blacks were concerned—and there were serious shortcomings—blacks nonetheless found sufficient reason for supporting the New Deal. It gave them hope. It offered something else, too. Perhaps its most valuable contribution was that of demonstrating that the federal government and federal power could be an alternative to statism and localism; for all their limitations, the nature of New Deal programs established precedents that challenged local white control over blacks. W. E. B. DuBois did not let this fact escape him:

A new and direct connection between the federal government and the individual arose such as the South had never experienced before, but much more than that, there came a direct connection between politics and industry, between government and work, between voting and wages, such as the South was born believing was absolutely impossible and absolutely wrong.*

The political effect of the New Deal on the black was slower, perhaps more subtle, although the success of Roosevelt in wooing him from his traditional allegiance to the Republican party was obvious. In 1936, for the first time in history, the majority of black voters supported the Democratic candidate. This meant northern blacks—southern blacks simply did not vote. But the lesson of 1936 was not lost on southerners, white or black. The handwriting was on the wall, and the *Grovey* v. *Townsend* decision of 1935, upholding the white primary, could not erase it. The New Deal was hastening the day when the southern black would be a voter, when he would be a citizen in fact as well as in theory. It was also hastening the day when the southern politician

---

*W.E.B. DuBois, "Federal Action Programs and Community Action in the South," *Social Forces*, XIX (March 1941), 377.

could no longer count on using the black to frighten the masses half to death.

World War II accelerated the process the New Deal had started. But there were still plenty of indignities, of course. The armed forces remained segregated. And so did Red Cross blood banks. There were race riots in New York. And in Detroit, where Roosevelt finally intervened with federal troops to halt the havoc, but not before some twenty-five blacks had lost their lives. There were racial tensions everywhere during the war years as more than a million blacks swarmed from the back country into southern industrialized cities, then moved on—to Los Angeles, St. Louis, Chicago, Detroit, Pittsburgh, New York—in search of jobs, in search of new opportunity. So incendiary were race relations in the South, wrote the eminent southern sociologist Howard Odum, that "the South and the Negro, in the early 1940s, faced their greatest crisis since the days of the reconstruction."

All the same, there was progress. Lynching had about stopped; there was but one in 1945. Blacks, in areas outside the South, became politically more active. And as they did, both major parties began to show increasing concern with civil rights and Jim Crow. Finally, in 1944, in *Smith* v. *Allwright*, the Supreme Court—the "New Deal Court," some were calling it—reversed *Grovey* v. *Townsend*. The party primary was an essential part of the state electoral process, ruled the court, and blacks could not be excluded.

But the greatest progress of blacks during the war was on the economic front. Roosevelt did little to help blacks benefit from the defense spending boom until he was threatened by a protest march on Washington. In the spring of 1941, A. Philip Randolph, head of the Brotherhood of Sleeping Car Porters, rallied the support of some 50,000 blacks for a demonstration to protest their exclusion from defense jobs. Randolph called off the demonstration when Roosevelt countered with an executive order on June 25, 1941, an order which admitted blacks to federal job-training programs and forbade racial discrimination by companies doing federal defense contract work. The order likewise provided for a Fair Employment Practices Committee to investigate violations.

The threatened march on Washington and Roosevelt's Executive Order 8802 got results. By 1945, nearly two million blacks were working in defense industries all over the country, including the South. And the Fair Employment Practices Committee, through its fifteen regional offices, resolved more than 8,000 complaints before the end of the war.

It was unfortunate that with many southerners centralized government, moderation in race relations, economic planning, and a face lifting of the Democratic party were so ominous in their implications that they precluded serious discussion of the New Deal on its merits. But they did. And so Roosevelt and the South moved toward a showdown, the "purge" of 1938.

As we saw in an earlier chapter, the purge was a dismal failure. The South and the Democratic party were still legally wed; but the long romance between them would never again be quite the same. By altering the traditional conservative orientation of the Democratic party, "the New Deal had alienated the affections of Southern leadership; the New Deal had created the eternal triangle."

The changes and alterations that took place in the Democratic party at the hands of Roosevelt may have been more apparent than real. Until quite late in the game, until the purge of 1938, Roosevelt thought it necessary to cooperate with the southern wing of the party in Congress. There was a practicality in this, an expediency that may have been necessary. The seniority system guaranteed that when Democrats had a majority in either or both houses, southern Democrats would dominate the standing committees, exercising very nearly a life-and-death control over the flow of legislation.

For the sake of his legislative program, as well as foreign-policy considerations, Roosevelt felt he could not risk the total alienation of southern Democrats. This helps explain his ambivalent position toward anti-lynching legislation. It also helps explain his willingness to work with state and local political machines, with the Hagues, Kelly-Nashes, Pendergasts, Crumps, and other politically odoriferous types who could not have cared less about good government, who compromised the reform idealism of the New Deal.

The usual explanation for this association is put in terms of New Deal goals, of Roosevelt's ambition to "nationalize" politics and issues. It is the first lesson that every beginner in politics learns: If you do not get elected you forfeit the chance to implement your goals, no matter how noble those goals may be. Once elected, you still may not achieve broader goals unless you remain sensitive to parochial issues. Roosevelt's dilemma was that he did not need southerners to get elected; he carried every southern state each time he ran, but he would have been elected each time had every southern state gone Republican. But he needed southerners in the Congress. Political machines presented no grave problem in the Congress—but he needed them to get elected.

Roosevelt's lack of real concern for the Democratic party, his willingness to cooperate with Democratic machines, with the southern conservatives, all for the sake of nationalizing issues, probably made sense at the time. But it meant leaving power in the hands of men who could not have exercised power in any other, non-machine way. It made sense because, at that time, race relations were not causing the kinds of problems they would cause thirty-five years later. Southern blacks had no political power. Northern blacks were grateful to Roosevelt for a handout, for petty relief jobs, for some degree of security, security for the first time in their memories. That they were entitled to more had not occurred to them; in the 1930s, civil rights were not an issue.

Southern whites in Congress did not give a damn about civil rights; neither did they give a damn about the problems of northern urban centers. Like civil rights, the problems of the cities were also scanted in the 1930s; urban unemployment and the industrial slump were all that mattered. Southern Democrats sometimes had to swallow hard, had to acquiesce in objectionable parts of the New Deal, which jarred southern sensibilities, to get what they wanted: relief, subsidies, supports for cotton, tobacco, peanuts, sugar cane, citrus fruits, and TVA with its jobs and cheap power—pet projects dear to the old Confederacy.

But they could not have cared less about urban problems—slums, ghettoes, crime, environmental pollution, transportation—problems that would haunt the nation in later years. Despite the fact that any number of southerners seemed in the forefront of the New Deal—Joe Robinson, Pat Harrison, and others—the relationship was always a tenuous one, uncomfortable, not a little embarrassing for Roosevelt, and for them too.

The point is not that Roosevelt expected to solve civil rights and urban problems—or even that others expected him to solve them. The point is that Roosevelt had to confront men whose real concerns were regional before they were national, singleminded men whose fears for the preservation of the "southern way of life" could arouse a formidable opposition. As we have seen, the time would come when Roosevelt would run afoul of them on other issues, when a coalition of Republicans and southern Democrats in the Congress would stymie his program, would stop the New Deal in its tracks.

Roosevelt's failure to do anything about reorienting the political party system when he might have, when the country may have been ready for a two-party system that had a different meaning, would make things much more difficult later. In the 1930s, the spectacle of a determined minority in the Congress being handed the power to frustrate the will of the majority seemed quite normal. Even in the anguish of depression the anomoly of the minority dominating the majority in Congress was dismissed as one of the prices the country paid for federalism and its alleged blessings.

So long as Roosevelt stayed with broad issues, those that were "national" in their implications, the coalition approach to Democratic party politics seemed to work. When it came to the more difficult task of challenging the party status quo at the state and local level, the coalition approach broke down.

A party that was not rebuilt at the grass roots, not committed to liberalism at the grass roots, was not going to change much at the local levels. Blacks would ride in the back of the bus, when they were not being lynched. Sharecroppers would still be swindled by local landowners. Political decisions would still be made by minions of political bosses lounging around brass spittoons in the court house, by lobbyists supplying the liquor and girls in the state capitals. And Roosevelt's "economic royalists" would still buy or browbeat their way out of behaving themselves and paying their taxes.

All of this is by way of saying that Roosevelt failed to remake the Democratic party into an effective instrument of liberalism. In fact, it does not appear that the thought even crossed his mind, at least not until the purge of 1938, by which time it was probably too late anyway. Despite overwhelming and uninterrupted victories, the Democratic party was actually a coalition riding on Roosevelt's personal popularity, a coalition which included both liberal and conservative elements. The party that won elections at the polls was not the same party that ran the Congress.

There was more to Roosevelt's "nationalizing" of politics than met the eye. By some method he isolated and identified the one great strength of a national party leader—the opportunity to define the terms, the dimensions, of the power struggle in society. What Roosevelt tried to do, and to a large measure succeeded in doing, was eliminate certain conflicts from national politics completely and drastically reshape the nature of others. He undertook to broaden the horizon of politics, to involve the whole nation around one major proposition: that prosperity would be the business of national government.

To achieve that, he meticulously avoided specifics, avoided ideological stereotypes, avoided labels, as one would avoid evil companions. With Roosevelt, things were "social," not "socialistic." He defined "liberalism" so broadly that it would include nearly anybody. "New Deal" may have been spontaneous, an off-the-top-of-the-head kind of political accident; but for effectiveness, for suiting Roosevelt's purposes, the Oracle of Delphi could not have created a better one. It implied action but it was as neutral as Switzerland. It had none of the value orientation of, say, the New Nationalism or the New Freedom or even a Return to Normalcy.

A major object of his technique was to replace hoary conflicts of the past—sound money, tariff, civil service, immigration, liquor, clean government, sectionalism, religion, imperialism, trusts—with a new vision, a new understanding of the power struggle in society.

The object was to avoid people versus people confrontations, the many against the few, the "haves" fending off the "have nots," and substitute the whole nation against an inscrutable nature. Against a nature that could pound the crops of entire states into the ground with hail as big as golfballs, that could send rivers boiling out of their banks for miles, that could burn up the plains and turn them into dust bowls, that could hurl lightning bolts that would scorch entire forests, that could send howling winds that threatened to tear the Gulf Coast and Florida loose from the continent.

Substitute the nation not only against an inscrutable nature but against an indifferent economic system, an economic system that seemed as equally beyond control as nature. The New Deal, then, would be a crusade against evil, not against people; against injustice, not for unfair advantage. It was to unite all Americans against a common foe—natural disaster and economic collapse. "The new assumption," said Roosevelt in 1936, "must be that the community, the State, and the Nation must so cooperate in controlling the conditions which cause calamities that these will be eliminated, or at least substantially reduced."

At the outset the technique seemed to work. Roosevelt *did* inspire confidence, *did* rally the American people, *did* define immediate goals, *did* begin the attack on natural disaster and economic collapse—with the whole country cheering him on. But the time was not far off when he would have to live with the institutionalization of the new political technique he was managing. Decisions had to be made; people had to be hurt, disappointed, disillusioned. After all, the country could not continue indefinitely, as some critics sneered, on government-by-elocution. Or, as some of his enemies put it, Roosevelt could not grin the country back to prosperity.

There were defections; class politics reasserted itself. Although Roosevelt was to prove that he was better than any previous President at reconciling unreconcilables—the New Nationalism and the New Freedom, farm and city, labor and management, regulation and trust busting, producers and processors, competition and monopoly, and all the rest—he nonetheless found himself increasingly in the business of juggling interests he could no longer override. Consensus at the verbal level was one thing; consensus at the administrative level was something else. What began to emerge from the New Deal was consensus government, implemented with more radical political techniques and with saltier language, in which "economic royalists" and "malefactors of great wealth" became the spook words in the New Deal vocabulary.

Roosevelt gave the country a glimpse of what could be accomplished when politics was able to rise above, to transcend, special interests. The nationalizing of politics had developed a momentum which carried Roosevelt through the lean years, a momentum which would bind a whole generation of voters to the Democratic party. But he faltered before the challenge of his own politics when he lost the natural issue of crisis. And he failed to point the way for his successors to a sure-fire technique of managing the politics of national interest except with the advantage of crisis.

One major by-product of Roosevelt's attempt to nationalize politics was the development of "big labor," matching "big business" and "big government."

It is surprising that the greatest gains of labor in the United States since the start of the Industrial Revolution were made during a time of intense economic distress. Staggering unemployment during the first years of the depression drained the anemic strength of the labor movement; union membership declined precipitously; dues fell off; unions curtailed their activities; racketeers moved in, took over. Unions, incapable of calling strikes except in sheer desperation, were powerless to improve wages or working conditions, or even hold the line, for that matter.

Yet, despite all this, labor made headway, significant headway. The explanation seems to be that, in attempting to get business off dead center through the National Industrial Recovery Act, a provision was included that gave labor a glimmer of what might be. Section 7(a) gave legal sanction to collective bargaining.

Section 7(a) also showed the door to the company union, the mother-in-law who had lived in the house of labor, had dominated and browbeaten labor for years. Little matter that section 7(a) was too often honored in the breach. Little matter that when the Supreme Court, in late May 1935, declared that the NRA was living in constitutional sin, collective bargaining was banished with it. It was immediately revived, in stronger form, by the Wagner Act, which became law early in July 1935.

With passage of the Wagner Act, labor began an unprecedented period of growth. In 1933, fewer than three million workers belonged to unions; on the eve of World War II, the combined membership of the AFL and CIO was well beyond nine million.

But Roosevelt had been no vigorous friend to labor, and in 1932 labor unions had made virtually no contributions to his victory. Hence Roosevelt owed the labor movement nothing for his victory. As President, he had on occasion hung back on pro-labor legislative matters, had on occasion sided with management (as when he ruled in favor of the automobile manufacturers, that the NIRA did not require that workers join a trade union to secure their rights under the law; they could join a company union if they voted to). And Roosevelt had contributed little to the passage of the Wagner Act until late in the fourth quarter of the game, when he was convinced it was the political thing to do.

Nevertheless, after 1932 labor consistently supported Roosevelt, worked for him, voted for him in overwhelming numbers. Workers sensed that Roosevelt was at least not hostile toward them, that the mood of the New Deal was not openly anti-labor as administrations of the past had been. For labor, the New Deal meant that in the future the decision-making power in great hunks of American industry, where the voice of labor had never been more than a whisper, would have to be shared with unions. The New Deal gave labor the right to pound on the table. The trade union movement was destined to enjoy a higher status in American life than ever before. In return, labor became the reliable ally of the Democratic party.

As "big labor" emerged in the 1930s—due in part to the boost given it by the Roosevelt administration, in part to a monumental bootstraps effort—it received a major assist from the courts. Quite apart from the image the Supreme Court may have projected during those years—a "thin black line" saving the country, or "nine old men" obstructing progress—a major change was under way in constitutional law. The courts retreated from the traditional position that the Constitution was preoccupied with protecting private property, with defending a man's fences and safe deposit box against his fellow man and a menacing federal government. The judicial retreat cleared the way for federal government to become actively involved in defending and protecting the civil liberties of labor in the 1930s.

The La Follette Civil Liberties Committee investigation provided proof that both state and local governments, as well as private interests, had often ignored the civil liberties of workers—bloody heads, labor spies, union-busting "scabs," and private arsenals of machine guns and vomit gas were the evidence. It was a time when many who had feared the federal government realized that it could be a friend of civil liberties rather than a foe, that federal government could and should be used to defend civil liberties.

With the federal government assuming the role of protector of the civil liberties of labor in the 1930s, others in later years turned to the federal government for similar protection—blacks, college students, war protestors, welfare mothers, religious nuts, and social outcasts of one sort or another who found themselves in the clutches of the local constabulary. From protector of labor to guardian of misfits and people of no consequence was not too great a step for the courts.

It was not just in the area of civil liberties that the federal judiciary began to yield under pressure of the New Deal years. In the early stages of the New Deal, Roosevelt and the judiciary had been headed for collision, which finally came in 1937 with Roosevelt's court plan. Although the plan failed of its immediate purpose, the Supreme Court nevertheless surrendered. In a remarkable series of opinions, beginning in 1937, it approved major New Deal reform measures, including some that had been passed to replace those that the court had previously invalidated.

In quick succession the court turned thumbs up on a state minimum wage law, the Farm Mortgage Act of 1935, the amended Railway Labor Act of 1934, the 1935 National Labor Relations Act, and the Social Security Act. And, in so doing, the court wrote a new body of constitutional law which laid to rest the conflict between dual federalism and liberal nationalism.

The capitulation by the Supreme Court in 1937 marked the beginning of a new era in federalism. Dual federalism had apparently gone the way of the Saturday night bath and silent movies. The notion that the federal government and the states were two mutually exclusive systems of power, that both were supreme within their respective orbits, that neither could intrude, even incidentally, upon the areas reserved to the other, was passing into the historical file. The Supreme Court, in *United States* v. *Darby* (1941), specifically repudiated the doctrine of dual federalism in favor of national supremacy. In other words, since federal law is superior to state law, the Congress cannot be hamstrung in the exercise of its powers merely because it may intrude upon an area traditionally reserved to states.

One obvious consequence has been the permanent expansion of federal power. Whole areas formerly reserved to state governments—or to no government—became fair game for federal action. Agricultural production, agricultural marketing, the sale of securities, labor-management relations, and flood control are among the important new areas of federal interest. While none of these has been entirely closed to states (they are still in the picture), it is true that federal policy has become far more important than state policy. This enlargement in federal authority has apparently been accepted by both major political parties, by all shades of political opinion.

The New Deal likewise worked a permanent change in Washington's responsibility for the national economy. Other administrations, especially during the Progressive era, had occasionally asserted the need, here and there, for federal control over some part of the national economy. But, as we noted earlier, Roosevelt was the first to assume that it was the federal government's duty to take responsibility for the whole business. By contrast with earlier years, the degree to which the court accepted this singular proposition was truly remarkable.

None of this is to say that the expansion of federal power and the demise of dual federalism has destroyed the federal system or jeopardized the position of the states in the system. As federal action has increased since 1933, state activities have not declined in some devilish geometric progression. On the contrary, state functions increased substantially with the inception of the New Deal.

Part of that increase in state functions could be attributed at least indirectly to a change in the attitude of the Supreme Court. The waning interest of the Supreme Court in substantive due process of law, especially after 1937, opened up new areas for experimentation in state social legislation. Substantive due process—which has to do with the content of law, its reasonableness and fairness—had, for years, been used by conservative-oriented courts to judge state social welfare legislation "unreasonable" and, hence, unconstitutional. During the 1930s, the Supreme Court wavered, and finally yielded to the criticism that when it substituted its own opinion of "unreasonableness" for that of the legislature it was usurping a legislative prerogative. After 1937, it virtually abandoned substantive due process as a restraint on legislative regulation of the economy and social behavior.

Furthermore, much New Deal legislation depended upon the states for implementation. The New Deal required a new state-federal partnership, a "cooperative federalism," for the attainment of common goals. In cooperative federalism the states had a vital role to play as agents of national policy.

Cooperative federalism meant federal government and states complementing each other in mutually beneficial enterprises. It meant a decline in the importance of states as compared to the past. But it was only a relative decline. It also meant a fairly certain way of getting states to act, especially in social areas where they had never acted before, and in areas where they were not likely to act except by dint of federal government's gigging them in the tail. Much of the New Deal program was implemented on this basis—the federal government provided the ideas, the initiative, the guidelines, the general supervision, and—above all—the money; the states provided the personnel, the physical facilities, and kept house.

What it amounted to was this. Faced with the Great Depression of the 1930s, the states had neither financial resources to handle relief nor power over a wide enough geographical area to stimulate recovery. Federal government, with greater tax resources, with almost unlimited borrowing power, was literally forced to act.

The relative decline of the states under the New Deal was inevitable in the sense that because the problems were national, the approach had to be national—and under Roosevelt they were purposefully made national. States, with limited resources, limited capabilities, and even less will, were unable to retain the loyalty of large numbers of their citizens. Some time later, J. Melville Broughton, former governor of North Carolina, about said it all when he wrote:

> Those of us who believe in the fundamental principles of states' rights and local self-government may as well concede frankly that much of the almost terrifying expansion of federal encroachment upon the original domain of the states has come about because state governments failed to meet the challenge of the new day. Inadequate educational opportunities, archaic labor laws and regulations, unrelieved hardships and inequities suffered by the working people, low-pitched politics and unjust class and race discriminations have, all too frequently, caused the people to . . . call for relief from the Federal Government.

Cooperative federalism was not entirely an unmixed blessing, of course. There were tremendous political implications, and associated dangers, lurking all over the place. There were, after all, state administrations unfriendly to the national administration, hostile to what Roosevelt was trying to accomplish. There were senators who turned green and blew smoke through their ears at the thought of handing over that kind of patronage to state politicos. And, of course, if Washington did not stay on its toes there was the risk of federal influence and money falling into the hands of local power groups and vested interests. None of these possibilities was a source of comfort. But be that as it may, in all of the new relationships resulting from cooperative federalism developed under the New Deal the national judiciary acquiesced.

The importance of crisis to Roosevelt in the nationalizing process has already been reviewed. While most people admired, even applauded Roosevelt's swift response to the crisis of the depression, many resented and feared the tendency to develop and perpetuate an entirely new method of conducting the business of government based on crisis. It was their sincere conviction that the President's constant practice of couching his program (it seemed) in terms of emergency, of national peril, of grave danger, of critical urgency, or other scare phrases ("government by crisis" they called it) was altogether unhealthy, and probably dangerous.

In March 1939 Congressman Bruce Barton pointed out that Roosevelt had used the terms "emergency," "crisis," "disaster," and "national peril" thirty-nine times in his speeches and state papers, which, commented Barton, meant that some dreadful fate had been confronting the country every seven weeks for six years. "Any national administration is entitled to one or two emergencies in a term of six years," said Barton. "But an emergency every seven weeks means plain bad management."

Eventually (and this was particularly true after the election of 1936), to "government by crisis" was added "government by mandate." Because of the magnitude of Roosevelt's victories his friends found it easy to brush aside all objections, to justify almost anything on the grounds that the New Deal had a "mandate" from the voters. Roosevelt used and perfected the techniques of mandate and crisis to promote the public interest, to nationalize politics.

The fact, nevertheless, was that Roosevelt *did* confront a great crisis. To have failed to act—not to have met the crisis and turned it into an advantage—could have been fatal to America. The crisis Roosevelt faced was not nominal, was not made up of "viewing with alarm," "America at the crossroads," "in our hour of peril," "a dim and uncertain future," and the other scare words of the political lexicon, the usual excesses and exaggerations which had always characterized American politics, particularly during hotly contested campaigns. The country faced real crisis in the 1930s.

Not only that. From the Crash of 1929 to the Cambodian invasion, from the Bonus March to the Moratorium March, from the assassination of Mayor Cermak to the assassination of John Kennedy, Martin Luther King and Robert Kennedy, from Watts to Harlem, from Hiroshima and the Bomb to the Berlin Wall, and finally to outer space, the country has faced more than forty years of terrifying, unrelenting, emotionally exhausting crisis.

Other Presidents would look back to Roosevelt for guidance and inspiration in the constant struggle. And in meeting those crises the granting of powers, the delegating of authority, the endorsing and underwriting of executive action by the Congress, first begun during the New Deal, would become a way of life.

The crises of depression and war might have overwhelmed lesser men, but Roosevelt had met the challenge of both. We have already examined how Roosevelt guided important economic changes which yielded a modified capitalist system that was stronger than ever before. In the process he had revised the political system as well. Through his gift of the dramatic touch, his ability to isolate and nationalize issues, his steady dialogue with the press and the people, his skillful use of crisis and mandate, his personalized style of leadership, Roosevelt had created something new of the presidency, an office with greater dignity and infinitely greater power. That new power enabled him to cut deep into the legislative and judicial processes.

Roosevelt, by his strong appeal to ethnic groups of the New Immigration, to blacks, labor, and intellectuals, had democratized politics and broadened the base of the electorate. The reward was a Democratic party that was not only the majority party but also the party with an image of action, liberalism, and reform. Even the negative influence of the South could not tarnish that new image.

Roosevelt had altered not only the relationship between the major political parties and among the branches of the federal government, but the federal-state relationship as well. It seemed certain that cooperative federalism would continue to make serious inroads into traditional states' rights.

Finally, after the twelve years of Roosevelt and the New Deal, it seems beyond serious argument that the federal government had emerged as the driving, creative force in the economic, political, and social life of the nation. Given the new roles of federal government at home and abroad, it is little wonder that future Presidents would look back to Roosevelt with admiration and no small amount of envy.

Epilogue

The Meaning of the New Deal: A Personal Note

*He had no answers that were good
for a hundred years. But in a six-month crisis
he always had a six-month answer.*
—Samuel Grafton, New York Post *(1945)*

*Stall for time. Trade dollars for time. Time.
Time for the country to collect its wits.
Time for the people to pull themselves together,
shake their fears, recover their sense of humor,
take heart. Time so that America would not
default to madmen and lunatics and their wicked dreams.
Time so that honest men could find solid answers
to pressing problems that the country had been
ignoring and fending off for years. Time to
vindicate Roosevelt's dream of the middle way.*
—George Wolfskill and John A. Hudson,
All but the People *(1969)*

Would it be too fanciful to suppose that in the year 2033, the centennial of the New Deal, the American Historical Association will appoint a distinguished commission of historians with the task of evaluating the New Deal and its impact on the destiny of the United States? Should that happen, the likelihood is that there will be as many different verdicts as commission members. The New Deal was like that.

Complex and controversial as it may have been, there are some observations which, in retrospect, can be made about Roosevelt and the New Deal with at least some degree of certitude. It appears fairly certain that there were some things the New Deal was *not*. It was not, for example, communism, socialism, fascism, or any other identifiable "ism." Granted that a lot of people thought it was one or the other of these at the time. And some of them said so—loud and often. But a lot of people thought the NRA blue eagle was the Mark of the Beast and Mussolini was the anti-Christ, too.

It was important to pay attention to who was saying what. It does not matter much today that the chairman of the board of a bank or the president of a large corporation called the New Deal communistic. The board chairman and the corporation president were unlikely to have recognized a Communist had they met one on the first tee at the country club. It seems more important that William Z. Foster and Earl Browder knew that Roosevelt was no Communist, and said so. Norman Thomas, one of Roosevelt's bitterest critics, knew Roosevelt was no Socialist—that was the pity of it, as Thomas saw it. Every native fascist lunatic, dreaming his dream of being America's *führer*, knew very well that Roosevelt was no fascist—if for no other reason than that Roosevelt was a Jew, was he not?

If Roosevelt was on the receiving end of attacks from both ends of the political spectrum, if he caught it from both sides of the political street, it may be fair to assume that he stood somewhere in the shifting, ill-defined, political center. This is where Roosevelt *thought* he stood— somewhere slightly left of center, according to his own definition. If this be the case, the New Deal was no revolution, and those who insist it was are stretching the definition too far. The New Deal brought change, but change is not revolution.

If it is possible to say what the New Deal was not, it also seems possible to say what it was—if not in its entirety, at least in some of its particulars. For example, it now seems clear that the New Deal was a spirited attempt to rescue the capitalist system, was committed to the basic institutions of that system, and, from the first, intended to redeem industrial capitalism and democracy.

There is no convincing evidence that Roosevelt ever considered doing anything else. Conversely, this is what he thought he had done. "It was this Administration," Roosevelt told a Chicago audience during the campaign of 1936, "which saved the system of private profit and free enterprise after it had been dragged to the brink of ruin." Roosevelt certainly had no mandate to do anything else. The millions who cheered him on and four times voted him into office may have been voting for change; but change to them obviously meant improving, refurbishing, reforming capitalism and democracy, not destroying them.

For all the twists and turns, the zigs and zags, that were an everyday part of the New Deal, the technique for rescuing capitalism and democracy remained remarkably constant. The technique was that of steering an uncertain course between laissez-faire economics and socialism, of finding a middle way between the either/or choices thrust forward by dogmatists and ideologues.

The middle way would obviously have to start with an enlarged conception of government responsibility. Roosevelt had that. And he also was willing to develop new tools of government to meet the enlarged responsibility: planning, economic regulation, aids and services, government ownership. But he also faced crisis, prolonged crisis, crisis grown chronic under Hoover. There had to be action; there *was* action—so much that Alfred Rollins would subtitle one of his books on the New Deal *The Age of Action*. Under Roosevelt, positive action became a fundamental part of governmental policy.

But the action required unseemly haste. "Fast action" was a euphemistic way of describing New Deal experimentation. "The country demands bold, persistent experimentation," Roosevelt had said. And that is what it got. While crisis persisted, a major part of New Deal action was prolonged, sometimes ingenious, improvisation. The scenario would be repeated often during the 1930s: some new crisis, a plausible solution served up by a calm and reassuring Roosevelt, fast action, and measurable improvement. But New Deal solutions were admittedly tentative. Roosevelt was not promising the kind of solutions that were supposed to endure for a thousand years.

Besides, Roosevelt was realist enough to know there may be some problems for which there are no solutions, despite the romantic American notion that all problems have solutions. If the solution is not immediately self-evident, send people to school a little longer and then take a show of hands; in our democracy there are no insoluble problems. At least some of the New Dealers, practical as most of them were in their daily behavior, were imbued with a certain amount of that utopianism.

But that kind of idealism seldom got in the way. It did not get in Roosevelt's way. Roosevelt did not view the New Deal as the start of the millennium, the City of God come down to earth. The New Deal was but another moment in history, with men struggling against forces they did not always comprehend, trying to be—in the language of one of Roosevelt's favorite poems—the captains of their fate.

So there was a healthy skepticism about the New Deal, a suspicion about final answers, about dogmas, about utopian solutions. "I am for experimenting . . . trying out schemes which are supported by reasonable people and see if they work," Harry Hopkins once said. "If they do not work, the world will not come to an end." This kind of realism kept Roosevelt from ever becoming a "true believing" New Dealer.

Roosevelt was distracted in his quest for the middle way by the pressure of crises demanding the untried, crises which left little time for thinking things through, for judicious trial and error. The New Deal came to power during an economic disaster. Which meant that, unlike previous reform periods, the emphasis, the thrust, had to be on combating depression.

Day-to-day preoccupation with immediate problems of depression precluded not only careful thought and probing but also the expenditure of energies on the usual objects of reform wrath: trusts, city machines, bankers, and other miscreants on the reformer's list. "Indeed," wrote one historian, "the New Deal episode marks the first in the history of reform movements when a leader of the reform party took the reins of a government confronted above all by the problems of a sick economy." What it amounted to was that the New Deal's middle-way approach, as a reform movement, would inevitably differ from earlier reform movements because its central task was restoring prosperity, not sharing it; saving the system, not democratizing it.

Although he counted on their votes, Roosevelt was indifferent toward the big-city political machines—indifferent in the sense that he did not seem to worry much about how they compromised the idealism of reform. Roosevelt was only too willing to cooperate with machines and bosses if *they* were willing to cooperate. He was ambivalent toward the trusts—willing to waive antitrust laws during the early stages of the New Deal, resorting to ritualistic rhetoric devoid of any real action to damn the trusts later on, and altogether forgiving for the sake of winning World War II.

This attitude toward trusts and political machines was a good example of a kind of amorality that characterized the New Deal, and that worried more than one oldtime reformer. There was little "uplift" in the New Deal, either in its language or its action. Roosevelt, with regularity, worked the "do-good" language of Theodore Roosevelt and the old Progressives into his public statements. How serious he was about it—he called it "God stuff" in private—is another matter.

At any rate, from first to last the New Deal seemed much more interested in making people feel better than in making them behave better. We are trying "to reform the structure of things," Aubrey Williams explained to a group of NYA administrators, "rather than try to reform the people."

Roosevelt was likewise handicapped in the search for a middle way by the scarcity of trained personnel to assume direction of an enlarged governmental responsibility and by the absence of administrative precedent to guide his own activities as chief executive.

Part of this problem was of his own making. Roosevelt's approach to administration was normally disorganized and chaotic; what he did not know about efficient administration would have filled volumes. Unable to bring himself to fire anybody, he tolerated more incompetence than he should have. And his penchant for overlapping authority and assignments, for postponing hard decisions, for excessive bureaucracy, was notorious. "At times Roosevelt acted as if a new agency were almost a new solution. His addiction to new organizations," writes Arthur Schlesinger, Jr., "became a kind of nervous tic which disturbed even avid New Dealers."

Yet, somehow, the day-to-day job of administration got done. And more. The new people whom Roosevelt attracted to Washington—able for the most part and fiercely loyal—eventually solved the personnel problem and at the same time invested the old departments with a zest and an air of excitement they had never had before. Roosevelt's un-orthodox techniques of administration inspired new ideas, creativity, and a daring spirit of improvisation, innovation, and chance taking.

His organizational charts may have been a shambles, but, what was more important, he knew how to keep open the lines of communication. Roosevelt, writes William Leuchtenburg, "encouraged men to feel that their own beliefs might win the day." "You would be surprised ... the remarkable ideas that have been turned loose," Leuchtenburg quotes Utah's Senator Elbert Thomas as saying, "just because men have felt that they can get a hearing."

One consequence of the lack of precedents was the enormous expansion of administrative lawmaking by the executive branch so as to fill the void, to compensate for the new, positive role of government. A by-product of the New Deal was an enlarged body of administrative law, often vague and uncertain, and sometimes resented because, not having been enacted by Congress, it was by its nature arbitrary legislation. What may have been more important was its general acceptance, the acquiescence in this erosion of congressional independence.

Roosevelt was certainly handicapped in the search for a middle way by the lack of a coherent New Deal ideology, or even a philosopher who could explain it. Some people deplored the lack of any discernible goal except that of providing security through a massive dose of government action.

This understanding of the New Deal purpose, perhaps more than any other thing, set the New Deal apart in the public mind from traditional reformism. The earlier style of American reformism took the form of political protest on behalf of those with their noses pressed against the window of the economic system—farmers, small businessmen, professionals, occasionally artisans and skilled workers—all wanting a larger share of the good life. Their goals were that of putting a halter on Big Business, rooting out privilege for the "fat cats," curbing monopoly, clearing the way for newcomers, hard strivers, those with their dreams on the stars. What they were after was a chance, an opportunity, a glorious opportunity to compete on equal terms, to play with an honest deck according to honest rules of the game.

They glorified the competitive order, the open marketplace, free enterprise. The proper role of government was essentially negative, preventive, a cop on the beat, an umpire who moralized and enforced the rules of the game with aloof impartiality. Granted that in the past some advanced thinkers among reformers had urged a more vigorous, more positive role for government. But their proposals for government's taking a hand in the economic affairs of men were usually the reforms that had the most strenuous opposition, the least acceptance.

Even the Progressives, with whom New Dealers were so often compared, did not stray far from this historical pattern of reform. For all their emphasis on "uplift" and "do-goodism," what William Leuchtenburg has aptly called "Methodist-parsonage morality," the real concern of Progressives was the chance to stay in the race. Being ground to bits between big business and militant labor was their overriding fear. Historically, reform was tied to the opportunity to compete, and government was supposed to see that men had that opportunity unimpaired.

The New Deal's middle way seemed to mean a different emphasis in the reform tradition. With the New Deal, reform meant *economic* reform, with the federal government both the maker and the enforcer of the rules, as well as a player on the field, helping first one side and then the other, and the manager of all the teams. "If the state was believed neutral in the days of T.R. because its leaders claimed to sanction favors for no one," to quote Richard Hofstadter's neat aphorism, "the state under F.D.R. could be called neutral only in the sense that it offered favors to everyone."

The object of all the hectic activity by government was to guarantee the continuous health of the economy and the security of the individual against economic adversity. "These three great objectives—the security of the home, the security of livelihood, and the security of social insurance," Roosevelt told the country in 1934, constituted "a minimum of the promise that we can offer to the American people." At the risk of oversimplification, it is fair to say that the New Deal's economic reform emphasis gave security priority over opportunity.

The middle-way approach, with its emphasis on economic reform and security, also meant creating long-term commitments which no administration or Congress would dare repudiate. For example, to do other than extend and enhance the social security system would be unthinkable. Other programs, initiated by the New Deal for such things as agricultural parity, for guaranteeing the rights of labor (particularly collective bargaining), for maintaining minimum wage and maximum hour standards—the list is indeed a long one—created obligations which seemed likely to bind succeeding administrations. Each of these required the exercise by government of a regulatory function in creating a vested interest which later administrations would find virtually impossible to undo.

Under Roosevelt's leadership the middle way took on a life and character of its own. And if it was no revolution, no great watershed, no great discontinuity with the reform tradition in America, what was it? The crucial question remains: Where did we come out?

Some conclusions appear incontrovertible. For one thing, Roosevelt's New Deal did not demonstrate that it could bring the country full employment and lasting prosperity in peacetime. If one is an apologist, he can argue that Roosevelt did not have enough opportunity, enough time. Before Roosevelt had a chance to shift from the despair of depression economics to the joy of prosperity economics, he ran afoul of a revived Republican party, insubordination and treachery within his own party (particularly by the southern wing), massive opposition from business, a recalcitrant Congress, a fossilized Supreme Court, and a rising international peril.

All of these demurrers may have some validity. But it seems inescapable that full employment and prosperity were not restored short of war, that in some sense the New Deal was rescued by involvement in World War II. Thus it is regrettable that Emperor Hirohito may have had more to do with economic recovery in the United States than Franklin Roosevelt.

It also appears that industrial capitalism survived the New Deal somewhat shaken, and perhaps chastened, but unharmed. It, too, found a middle way—in accommodating to the New Deal changes. Capitalism, of course, was not the same as it had been in 1929. There had been consistent intervention by government—what Norman Thomas described as a system of "state capitalism." But government intervention, on the whole, had been on behalf of and for the benefit of the private profit system. The New Deal had also promoted "big labor," "big agriculture," and, of course, "big government" to compete with "big business" as countervailing forces. From this emerged what one historian has called "collectivistic capitalism."

That may be. But more important was the matter of economic power. As a consequence of the New Deal, business was going to be required to share at least some of its economic power. But there was no appreciable shift of power. Anyone who doubts that should be required to look at the report of the TNEC, the Senate investigation into monopoly and concentrated economic power. The crowning irony was that during World War II big business would consolidate its power, grip the economy more firmly, resort to practices that had for years reduced economic reformers to tears.

A tentative welfare state likewise emerged from the New Deal. One observer has said: "During the ten years between 1929 and 1939 more progress was made in public welfare and relief than in the three hundred years after this country was first settled." Equally significant was the fact that Roosevelt believed welfare was a matter of right, not charity. It may be that it had been too long in coming, that even states of Europe not noted for their humanitarianism or democracy had had these symbols of individual security for years. And it may also be that the degree of welfarism was much too small, that it did little more (as some historians now claim) than "create an aura of good will." And it may also be that welfarism was only an expediency, a necessary concession to the masses so that the corporate stranglehold on the economy could endure.

In any case, what emerged from the New Deal was at least the beginnings of a welfare state superimposed upon a capitalist foundation. This was accomplished by a middle-way approach to economics in which the country was shaken from its dedication to a laissez-faire philosophy, both real and imaginary, but without going to the other extreme, without embracing socialism. In pursuing a middle way, writes a prominent historian, Roosevelt "was able at once to preserve capitalism and at the same time disarm both its revolutionary and reactionary critics." The economy which emerged under New Deal policies, he concluded, was "an interesting mixture, an amalgam of private enterprise and government controls, an American version of state capitalism and social democracy."* And at the heart of the matter was Roosevelt's conviction that the profit system was compatible with governmental help and security for the individual, for his "forgotten man."

Roosevelt was not going to get the chance to find out whether a

*Arthur A. Ekirch, Jr., *Ideologies and Utopias* (Chicago: Quadrangle Books, 1969), p. 104.

welfare capitalism state based on a mixed economy would work, whether it would eventually produce prosperity and full employment. The circumstances and the rush of events precluded that. In retrospect, then, a good definition of the New Deal might be that it provided breathing space, a reprieve, that it obviated the possibility of more violent and extreme solutions to the nation's ills, that it was a transition from serious economic crisis to a time when the country would have the chance to attack problems without the pressure of crisis.

If this is a valid appraisal, then it is altogether possible that the best definition of the New Deal is still the one contained in an obituary written by Samuel Grafton of the New York *Post* the night Roosevelt died. "He had no answers that were good for a hundred years. But in a six-month crisis he always had a six-month answer." Grafton was saying that the New Deal, whatever else it may have been, was a delaying tactic, a "Grand Postponement," a tentative, partial solution to problems that could not have been solved under the circumstances in so short a time, perhaps not even by revolutionary methods.

So the growing, festering political and economic problems besetting the land were still without permanent answers. Nor were they to come soon; World War II would see to that. The problems remained. And the day was coming when, modified and in some instances intensified by the experiences of World War II, they would confront America once more—more chronic than ever, multiplied, pressed down and running over—problems that would convulse the land in the 1960s and 1970s.

In a 'sense—and one nearly gags in saying it—World War II was the salvation of the New Deal. War and the eventual involvement of the United States in it certainly meant the end of unemployment and the return of prosperity. The war meant the creation of millions of new jobs. Industrial production reached astounding levels with government taking great hunks of the production for the war effort. Corporate profits (after taxes) still remained impressive.

War also resulted in a somewhat fairer distribution of income, changes in the dreary pattern of rural life, a consolidation of gains in trade union strength. With the wartime intrusion of government into the economic life of the country—well beyond that of the New Deal of the depression years, and far beyond anything before that—romantic talk about business policing itself, about "industrial self-government," vanished from serious conversation. The country was approaching the degree of economic planning that New Dealers like Rexford Tugwell had been urging for years.

The war meant acquiescence in government programs and projects which, in peacetime, would probably have been opposed as more needless New Deal meddling. This was particularly true in such matters as public housing and labor relations. At the same time, the war made it possible for Roosevelt to liquidate some old, well-worn New Deal programs made obsolete by wartime prosperity. The country would hardly seem the same without the CCC, the NYA, and WPA and PWA projects all over the place.

The war, in an important sense, revitalized the waning reform spirit of the New Deal in ways that seemed to assure that reformism would not suffer the same fate as after World War I. Obviously, the winning of the war took priority over domestic reform. That much could be expected. The need for maximum production meant soft pedaling antitrust action, so dear to the heart of most reformers. And the reliance upon "dollar a year" industrialists for active management of the war effort, men who had never shown much interest in reform, was not reassuring.

All the same, the vast expansion of government regulation of the national economy continued the eroding process, the weakening of ideological resistance to federal control. The vast shifts of population, the growing demand for equality by blacks, and the rapid changes and leap into economic prominence of the South and particularly the West Coast caused by the war meant, surely, that there could be no postwar "return to normalcy."

And if the idealism of the war (not so lofty this time as saving the world for democracy, but only attempting to make the world safe for the "common man") meant anything at all, it meant that the country could not tolerate a postwar land of joblessness, poverty, and insecurity. There was more than a little reason for hope when Roosevelt pleaded for an economic bill of rights that included the federal government's assuming responsibility for full employment. President Truman would take the proposal seriously; but that is another story.

So World War II saved the New Deal, if by "saving" it we mean that it took the hurt of mankind at war to bring full employment and prosperity. Again, the war saved the New Deal if we mean that the war, in some ironic and perverse fashion, kept alive the New Deal reform spirit that would carry over into the postwar years.

But the war certainly did not save the New Deal in the sense that would cause Senator Robert Taft of Ohio to warn that "the New Dealers are determined to make the country over under the cover of war if they can." Quite the contrary. The toll was heavy. The war would unleash passions, would cause pain in the heart and a storm in the soul. The war, the reaction to war, and the dream (held in other and alien hands) would slow down, would jeopardize the vindication of the Roosevelt vision. But perhaps not to the degree that caused the editor of *The New Republic*, Malcolm Cowley, to write despondently during the war: "The New Dealers are a vanishing tribe; and the money-changers who were driven from the temple are now quietly established in government offices."

The truth appears to fall somewhere between Taft and Cowley. The New Deal, more a state of mind than an ideology, more a direction than a goal, never produced a utopian America. But it did reverse the pessimism of the depression era and restore faith in capitalism and democracy. It projected the country a long way down the road from its "rugged individualism" heritage toward a more humane, collective social action. It preserved freedom at home in a world made delirious by the fever of fascism and dictatorship. Without espousing revolutionary goals or resorting to radical methods, the New Deal achieved a level of individual security and well-being undreamed of as late as the 1920s. Its spirit is the driving force behind that deep yearning still abroad in the land for social change, for getting on with the task of perfecting a yet unfinished, imperfect society.

Paul Conkin, certainly no admirer of Roosevelt and the New Deal, was perhaps saying it better than he knew when he recently wrote: "A subsidized, regulated, welfare capitalism still stands, thirty years later, as the core of American domestic policy. . . . Thus, the changes of the thirties were not only numerous but prophetic, setting the themes for subsequent political discourse."*

Not every administration could claim as much. Now, thirty years later, it remains to be seen whether Roosevelt's dream of the middle

*Paul K. Conkin, *The New Deal* (New York: Thomas Y. Crowell Company, 1967), p. 103.

way is still intact, as Conkin claims, or whether it is to remain forever unfulfilled, done to death by self-serving centralized power, stifling bureaucracy, and—worst of all—indifference.

The Way
It Seems Now:
A Bibliographical Essay

*I long ago knew that it was my good fortune
to work for a man of straightforward simplicity, courage,
passion and honesty—one of the great souls of history.*
—Grace Tully, FDR, My Boss *(1949)*

*Little by little a nature, not greatly unlike
many well-considered public men of his type,
disintegrated, until power corrupted him. In the
end it corrupted him utterly.*
—John T. Flynn, The Roosevelt Myth *(1948)*

The Crash, the Great Depression, even World War II,
have begun to blur. Events once part of an unknown and
uncertain future are past. They are history. For many
people that means they are as remote in time as the
Hanging Gardens of Babylon.

It does not seem possible that nearly half the population of the United States—of the whole world, for that matter—was not alive on April 12, 1945, the day Franklin Roosevelt died. What they—and millions more who were only children—know of Roosevelt and the New Deal they know vicariously. Even for people who lived through those years, the Roosevelt years, for whom the New Deal was a part of their daily lives, memories have become hazy, unreliable.

Tempers have cooled; emotion has dissipated; personal involvement hardly matters any more; perspective has changed. But perspective is often a bigger liar than an eyewitness. Morrie Brickman, editorial cartoonist for the Washington Star Syndicate, knew that. In 1969 he drew a cartoon in which two woebegone legislators—southern-looking types— are gazing wistfully off into space, with the Capitol dome looming in the background. One is saying to the other: "Sometimes I wish we could return to the solid, sound conservative principles of Franklin D. Roosevelt." Perry Barlow, cartoonist for *The New Yorker*, likewise understood perspective. In one of his cartoons in 1960 an elderly gentleman, obviously at home in board rooms, looks as if he has just smelled something long overdue for burial. His grand-daughter is saying: "History test tomorrow, Granddaddy. Will you see if I can recite the achievements of the Franklin D. Roosevelt administrations?"

It is the historian who has now taken over, who has assumed responsibility for keeping the record. However, it sometimes seems doubtful that the historian has done any better job of understanding the New Deal than Brickman's legislators or Barlow's "granddaddy."

This is certainly the case with historians who write survey textbooks. From time to time I have had my graduate seminar analyze several of the more popular surveys to find out how authors have handled certain controversial questions. How, for example, have they treated the United Nations, the Yalta agreements, the unconditional surrender policy of World War II? How do they interpret Progressivism, World War I, and the Great Depression? What do they say about civil rights and the role of the black in United States history? And so on. Included, of course, is the question of New Deal interpretation.

This simple exercise has been an eye opener. The students have found that textbook writers, on the whole, tend to play everything down the middle. They may go all out with maps, pictures, bibliographies, study guides, suggested readings, and sample quiz questions. Their product may be bigger, thicker, more elaborately bound, more handsome in its dust jacket than the next fellow's. But they will likely have two things in common: uninspired prose and inoffensive interpretations.

Which means that survey textbooks in United States history tend to be dull and uninteresting. I will not elaborate on a dark suspicion, developed over nearly thirty years behind the desk, that authors and publishers do not want to make anybody mad. They both know what sells textbooks. Since selling textbooks is big business, the strategy is not to antagonize customers.

Four basic themes appear in nearly every textbook treatment of the New Deal. Usually much is made of the so-called three *R*s of the New Deal—relief, recovery, reform—an orderly (but not always reliable) way of classifying New Deal legislation. And most textbooks subscribe in varying degree to the First-Second New Deal interpretation: the proposition that shortly after the elections of 1934 Roosevelt veered from fairly standard techniques of recovery to a program of left-of-center reforms with emphasis on security for the individual. Most also stress continuity, explaining the New Deal as some reincarnation of pre-World War I Progressivism, often by inference: Franklin Roosevelt was a relative of Theodore Roosevelt and an admirer of Woodrow Wilson. And, finally, there is usually emphasis on the salutary course of the New Deal compared to what happened in other countries. Whatever the New Deal may have been, whatever it may have done to the country, it looked good compared to Nazi Germany, Fascist Italy, Communist Russia, Imperial Japan.

The seminar students were bemused by several things: textbook writers approached the New Deal with the blandness of an ulcer diet; they also seemed to ignore much significant New Deal literature, literature with conflicting views of the New Deal; and some textbook authors often had a different story to tell in their specialized writings about the New Deal!

But I digress.

New Deal literature is enormous, and continues to grow like the national debt. In general, it falls into three categories—broad, sweeping interpretations of the New Deal period; memoirs, reminiscences, personal recollections, and backstair gossip by everyone from cabinet officers to White House secretaries; and specialized works on specific aspects of the New Deal.

Those who have studied the New Deal with care, who have written about it with serious purpose, tend to treat Roosevelt kindly, limiting criticism to specific errors of judgment or specific mistakes. Until the recent arrival on the scene of what are being called writers of the New Left, those who were openly hostile to Roosevelt have been scarce.

Writers of general works have usually concerned themselves with at least three major themes. Was the New Deal evolutionary or revolutionary; was it consistent with American tradition or was it a significant break with the past? What were its antecedents; was it home grown, imported, or altogether spontaneous? Did it have a philosophy, a consistent set of goals, or was it improvisation; did it change directions; was there more than one New Deal?

For the origins of the New Deal and whether it was revolution or evolution, one might profitably turn to Carl Degler, *Out of Our Past* (New York, 1959). Degler argues that the New Deal departed in fundamental ways from past political practices and traditions. Under the spell of Roosevelt, America "abandoned, once and for all, the doctrine of laissez-faire."

"The conclusion seems inescapable," writes Degler, "that, traditional as the words may have been in which the New Deal expressed itself, in actuality it was a revolutionary response to a revolutionary situation." The New Deal (the "Third Revolution," Degler calls it, rating it in importance with the Revolutionary War and the Civil War) "marked the crossing of a divide from which, it would seem, there could be no turning back." The "divide" means the federal government passed from the role of regulator to that of guarantor; the New Deal resulted in what Degler calls the "Guarantor State."

Another who pioneered the New Deal-as-revolution theme is the late Richard Hofstadter. In his prize-winning book, *The Age of Reform* (New York, 1955), Hofstadter concluded: "Still, granting that absolute discontinuities do not occur in history, and viewing the history of the New Deal as a whole, what seems outstanding about it is the drastic new departure that it marks in the history of American reformism. The New Deal was different from anything that had yet happened in the United States." In terms of its antecedents, Hofstadter obviously minimized Populist and Progressive influences on the New Deal.

In taking the position that the New Deal was revolutionary, Degler and Hofstadter were echoing the sentiment of Samuel Lubell, a prominent political analyst, who may have been the first writer with national prestige to say it out loud. In *The Future of American Politics* (New York, 1951), Lubell had said: "The distinctive feature of the political revolution which Franklin D. Roosevelt began and Truman inherited lies not in the resemblance to the political wars of Andrew Jackson or Thomas Jefferson, but in its abrupt break with the continuity of the past."

William Leuchtenburg is another scholar with impressive credentials who comes down on the side of revolution. In *Franklin D. Roosevelt and the New Deal* (New York, 1963), a volume in the New American Nation Series (and generally conceded to be the best one-volume history of the New Deal so far), Leuchtenburg argues that the New Deal was "a radically new departure." "Yet such considerations should not obscure the more important point," writes Leuchtenburg, "that the New Deal, however conservative it was in some respects and however much it owed to the past, marked a radically new departure." In the next line Leuchtenburg quotes Degler's statement that the New Deal was "a revolutionary response to a revolutionary situation."

Other eminent historians disagree. Eric Goldman for one. In *Rendezvous with Destiny* (New York, 1952), Goldman develops the thesis that the dilemma of the reformer in history has not been resisting expansion of government but, rather, determining the extent and nature of government's participation in affairs. The goal of governmental participation changed from time to time; but, in general, it progressed from liberty, to opportunity, to security for the individual. In this progression has run a thread of continuity through the activities of what Goldman calls the "Reform Darwinists" (in the years after the Civil War), through Populism, Progressivism, the Associational Activities (of trade associations) in the 1920s, and the New Deal. Each wave of reformism, writes Goldman, is "reborn in a new wave." In this context, the New Deal was evolutionary, a logical progression in the reform tradition.

Frank Freidel, the major biographer of Franklin Roosevelt, concurs. Freidel's most succinct statement on his interpretation of the New Deal is contained in *The New Deal in Historical Perspective* (Washington, D.C., 1965). He sees much stronger New Deal ties with Progressivism than with the other reform eras. "How sharply," he asks, "did it [New Deal legislation] break with earlier American political traditions?" Not sharply at all, according to Freidel; it "was based squarely on American objectives and experience in the Progressive Era and during the first World War." Like Freidel, Leuchtenburg concedes that the New Deal borrowed heavily from earlier reform movements, especially Progressivism, and in this sense there may have been some kind of continuity. "Nonetheless," writes Leuchtenburg—in conflict with Freidel—"the spirit of the 1930s seems to me to be quite different from that of the Progressive era."

There are those, then, who explain the New Deal in terms of its antecedents, who trace its roots back at least to the post-Civil War reformers, the Populists, the Progressives, even the more virtuous aspects of the trade association movement in the 1920s. There is a case—sometimes a persuasive case—for arguing that the New Deal was some logical fulfillment of the reform tradition in America. And there are those who deny the continuity of the New Deal, who stress change, who see it as a break with the past, a sufficiently significant break to call it revolutionary.

The student who wishes to pursue these aspects of the New Deal would do well to start with two articles by Richard Kirkendall, "The Great Depression: Another Watershed in American History?" in John Braeman et al. (eds.), *Change and Continuity in Twentieth-Century America* (Columbus, 1964), and "The New Deal as Watershed: The Recent Literature," in the *Journal of American History* LIV (March 1968). Kirkendall, while presenting evidence supporting both points of view, finally takes the position that the New Deal was not revolutionary, not a watershed. It was but another episode on the road to what he calls "collectivistic capitalism," by which he means a system of large private economic units, organized for the public interest under government direction. To this end the New Deal promoted big government, big labor, and big agriculture—to compete with big business.

For the case of continuity by someone close to Roosevelt, see the articles by Rexford Tugwell in *Ethics* (October 1953 and July 1954): "The Progressive Orthodoxy of Franklin D. Roosevelt" and "The Sources of New Deal Reformism." The ideas in these two articles are developed in greater substance and detail in Tugwell's prize-winning book, *The Democratic Roosevelt* (Garden City, 1957).

On the relationship of Progressivism and the New Deal, the student will do himself a great disservice if he does not read Edgar Kemler, *The Deflation of American Ideals* (Washington, D.C., 1941), Otis L.

Graham, Jr., *An Encore for Reform* (New York, 1967), and Andrew M. Scott, "The Progressive Era in Perspective," *Journal of Politics* XXI (November 1959). Another useful article dealing with New Deal antecedents is Arthur M. Schlesinger, Jr., "Sources of the New Deal: Reflections on the Temper of a Time," *Columbia University Forum* II (Fall 1959).

Those who approve its antecedents are inclined to agree that the New Deal underwent internal changes: there was some ideological gear shifting; there was more than one New Deal.

For this aspect a good place to start would be with a pioneer work by Basil Rauch, *The History of the New Deal, 1933-1938* (New York, 1944). Rauch assumes that the New Deal was evolutionary and its roots were deep in Progressivism. But the book is significant because it is Rauch who originated the First-Second New Deal concept. As Rauch sees it, the first New Deal was a fairly conservative effort to cure the Great Depression. By implication, the relative failure of the first New Deal and intense pressure from the left forced Roosevelt, after 1934, into a second New Deal, a liberal program of social and economic reforms.

Both Goldman and Freidel agree with Rauch that there were two New Deals—the first, with its emphasis on relief and recovery, combined fairly conservative techniques and consensus politics with dramatic timing and Hollywood hoopla; the second, relying on class politics for its thrust, aimed at reform and social justice. Both Goldman and Freidel agree that the first New Deal gave way to the second under pressure from the left, from the Longs and Townsends and others who espoused more extreme solutions for the problems in the 1930s. And both would agree that probably the major contribution of the New Deal was that of making security for the individual an acceptable part of American political thinking.

Tugwell does not believe the internal changes in the New Deal came about as the result of pressure from either the left or the right. It was a conscious choice. Roosevelt, wrote Tugwell, regretted that his early approach through the AAA and NIRA had alienated old Progressives like Wheeler, Borah, and Cutting—"all progressives out of the West." He was determined to win them over, according to Tugwell, but to do so meant going back to "an accepted version of the progressive position," which "believed in bearing down on Big Business and encouraging little business." An "obsolete social philosophy," said Tugwell, had proved more attractive to Roosevelt than centralization and planning; "progressivism had returned to the White House"; and "the old Justice [Brandeis] who knew what he wanted" had triumphed.

James MacGregor Burns (*Roosevelt: The Lion and the Fox* [New York, 1956]), who falls in the category of a sympathetic critic of Roosevelt, accepts the Rauch thesis in its broader terms. But Burns argues that the shift from a first to a second New Deal was not nearly so clear cut as Rauch implies, and that it lacked inspiration and conviction. Roosevelt, as Burns sees him, was no liberal; he moved reluctantly, not because of pressure from the left but only after the desertion of conservatives both in and out of Congress. Burns believes Roosevelt was trying to steer the New Deal in the direction of "a middle way" between individualistic capitalism and socialism.

While sympathetic to Roosevelt, Burns is nonetheless devastating. Roosevelt, Burns concludes, missed the "middle way" for at least three reasons. In the first place, Roosevelt balked at total commitment to Keynesian economics; he was willing to spend to produce economic improvement, but not enough to end the depression. He accepted political support from diverse groups and interests but faltered at remaking the Democratic party into an effective, disciplined coalition for liberal reform. Finally, Burns accuses Roosevelt of being the captive of an intellectual quirk that sought gratification in reconciling opposites. He was, says Burns, "captive to his habit of mediating among pressures rather than reshaping them." While this might prove that he was, in Burns' words, "a skillful manipulator," it also meant that the New Deal was allowed to deteriorate into "broker politics."

In the first three volumes of the *Age of Roosevelt* (Boston, 1957-1960), which carry the account forward to 1937, Arthur Schlesinger, Jr., likewise accepts most of the Rauch thesis. Unlike Burns, Schlesinger admires Roosevelt unabashedly. He is enamored of the "great man" concept and the ability of great men to shape the course of events. Schlesinger sees Roosevelt in this role, as a heroic figure rescuing democracy and capitalism from between the railroad tracks at the last possible second.

Schlesinger agrees that the New Deal followed logically the path of reformism since the late nineteenth century. And he agrees that Roosevelt was a master at reconciling internal contradictions in that reform heritage—reconciling the New Nationalism with the New Freedom, regulation with trust busting, urban with rural goals, business with labor. This talent, which Burns scorns as the "broker politics" of a "skillful manipulator," is, in Schlesinger's interpretation, one of Roosevelt's major talents, one of his greatest strengths.

Schlesinger likewise agrees with Burns that the goal of the New Deal was "a middle way." "Was no middle way possible between freedom and tyranny?" Schlesinger asks rhetorically. "Rejecting the platonic distinction between 'capitalism' and 'socialism,' " writes Schlesinger, "he [Roosevelt] led the way toward a new society which took elements from each and rendered both obsolescent. It was this freedom from dogma which outraged the angry, logical men who saw everything with dazzling certitude."

In developing the First-Second New Deal theme, Schlesinger parts company with some other New Deal writers. He argues that the overriding characteristic of the first New Deal was national planning that required government to assume a special responsibility for resources, prices, and markets—areas traditionally off limits to government, areas which had been left to the catch-as-catch-can of the marketplace. Schlesinger characterizes the second New Deal as "neo-Brandeisian"—government continuing its dynamic role in the economy but shifting its emphasis from national planning to a restoration of competition.

This interpretation puts Schlesinger at odds with the standard version, which has it that the New Deal shift was from conservative to more liberal economic politics. Schlesinger argues, as does Tugwell, that it was the other way around. National planning was radical, the return to competition was conservative. The misunderstanding on this point, writes Schlesinger, is caused by Roosevelt's abuse of "economic royalists," leading to the mistaken belief that Roosevelt was moving leftward. What it really meant, says Schlesinger, was that the New Deal was pursuing conservative economic aims by a more radical political strategy.

A corollary to this also sets Schlesinger apart. Rauch and others, including Tugwell, account for the shift in 1935 by at least implying that the first New Deal was a relative failure because prosperity was not restored. Roosevelt, Tugwell would later write, spent "a lot of time . . . planting shrubbery on the slopes of a volcano." Something more had to be done. Schlesinger insists that the opposite was the case: the relative success of the first New Deal made a less strenuous economic policy possible.

Goldman combines the First-Second New Deal thesis and the continuity theme by representing the shift as New Nationalism and New Freedom phases of the New Deal. The NIRA, AAA, temporary suspension of the antitrust laws, emphasis on business-government cooperation, and "regulated monopoly" were reminiscent of Theodore Roosevelt and the New Nationalism. Regulatory legislation, a revival of trust busting under Thurman Arnold, heavy taxes on the wealthy, and the apparent chastisement of business suggested that Brandeis and the "regulated competition" orientation of Wilson's New Freedom were back in vogue.

Leuchtenburg takes issue with the First-Second New Deal interpretation, arguing that the New Deal was such a mixed bag, so pragmatic, so consistently inconsistent, that it is futile to try to blueprint it. "At no time," writes Leuchtenburg, contradicting Schlesinger, "had Roosevelt seriously considered the creation of a planned economy."

"Even the most precedent-breaking New Deal projects," he continues, "reflected capitalist thinking and deferred to business sensibilities." And any number of measures offered as evidence of the shift in the New Deal were on their way through the legislative mill before 1935.

If there is a consistent theme in the New Deal, Leuchtenburg argues, it is that Roosevelt's program "rested on the assumption that a just society could be secured by imposing a welfare state on a capitalist foundation." According to Leuchtenburg, then, the First-Second New Deal thesis is largely myth, 1935 is an artificial dividing line, and the alleged shift in policy was, to use his words, "confusing shadow with substance."

Leuchtenburg also chides his fellow historians for failing to see the importance of the World War I experience on Roosevelt and the New Deal—what Leuchtenburg calls the "analogue of war" theme which runs fairly consistently through the New Deal. (See William Leuchtenburg, "The New Deal and the Analogue of War," in John Braeman et al. [eds.], *Change and Continuity in Twentieth-Century America* [Columbus, 1964].)

The student who wishes to try his hand at unscrambling the historical

speculation which Rauch started with his First-Second New Deal inter-
pretation should consult William H. Wilson, "The Two New Deals: A
Valid Concept?" *The Historian* XXVIII (February 1966), and Otis L.
Graham, Jr., "Historians and the New Deals, 1944-1960," *Social
Studies* LIV (April 1963).

Roosevelt has recently had his feet put to the fire by a group of
revisionist historians sometimes described as Radical or New Left. The
New Left viewpoint has not yet made much headway in the survey
textbooks, except at one point. It is beginning to appear in the "Suggested Readings," either at the end of chapters on the New Deal or at
the back of the book, somewhere between the list of chief justices of
the Supreme Court and the picture credits.

Suggested Readings are part of the ritual of textbook writing, somewhat like playing the national anthem at sporting events—everybody
expects it; it does not add much, but neither does it do any particular
harm. I have often pondered their reason for being. Authors do not
really expect students to pay any attention to them; most authors,
being teachers, know by experience that even getting students to read
the textbook is a miracle only slightly less difficult than turning water
into wine.

It may be that Suggested Readings are included to give a textbook a
little class. Or it may be that the author thinks they make him "look
good," although he knows that we know that he has not even started to
read all those books. A cynical guess is that Suggested Readings repre-
sent the collective efforts of faithful graduate assistants with overactive
glands. (I am also aware that this bibliographical essay might just as
readily have been titled "Suggested Readings.") But again I digress.

The literature of the New Left is characterized by indignation,
anguish, and self-pity that dwell on what the New Deal did not do, that
disregard the circumstances in which it operated, and that discount its
accomplishments. But New Left historians should not be dismissed
lightly as mere faultfinders abusing the advantage of hindsight. Their
premise—that the New Deal was essentially conservative rather than
radical or revolutionary and was intended to save the system rather
than seriously amend it—is shared by a great many historians who are
by no means New Left. That which probably sets the New Left historians apart from their peers is their tendency to accept a class warfare

interpretation of the 1930s, and a willingness—perhaps too great a willingness—to accept what amounts to a "conspiracy" interpretation of the New Deal: Roosevelt, while trying to get out of the worst of the Great Depression, was deliberately turning the country into a huge Indian reservation with Big Business jealously guarding the medicine. This has become the New Left theme, which has it that the New Deal did not go far enough, and had no intention of going far enough, to make significant changes in the economic and social structure of the United States.

The New Left thesis is not entirely new. It was anticipated as early as 1935 by people like Benjamin Stolberg and Warren Jay Vinton, men whose identification with radical causes was well known. In *The Economic Consequences of the New Deal* (New York, 1935), Stolberg and Vinton wrote that the New Deal "in trying to move in every direction at once . . . betrays the fact that it has no policy." "The unconscious philosophy of the New Deal," they said, "is not far removed from the crude economic ignorance of Andrew Mellon."

The concluding paragraph of their book might very easily have come from the contemporary writing of the New Left: "There is nothing the New Deal has so far done that could not have been done better by an earthquake. A first-rate earthquake from coast to coast could have reestablished scarcity much more effectively, and put all the survivors to work for the greater glory of Big Business—with far more speed and far less noise than the New Deal."

In later books, books like Broadus Mitchell's *Depression Decade* (New York, 1947) and Dixon Wecter's *The Age of the Great Depression, 1929-1941* (New York, 1948), there is also melancholia over the shortcomings of the New Deal that suggests the mood of the New Left writers.

An appraisal of New Left literature should probably begin with Paul Conkin's *The New Deal* (New York, 1967). Conkin set the tone for what was coming with his verdict that "the story of the New Deal is a sad story, the ever recurring story of what might have been." New Left historians, expanding on the Conkin thesis, do not much care whether the New Deal was evolutionary or revolutionary, what its antecedents were, whether or not it was consistent with the reform tradition, whether there was more than one New Deal, what its philosophy may or may not have been—whatever. The only relevant test is how far the

New Deal advanced the country toward a brighter future; and Roosevelt flunked their test.

Howard Zinn, in "The Limits of the New Deal," an essay in his *Politics of History* (Boston, 1970), and in his introduction to *New Deal Thought* (New York, 1966) typifies New Left unconcern with historical continuities: "It is fruitless today to debate 'interpretations' of the New Deal." "We can no longer vote for or against Roosevelt. We can only affect the world around us."

One senses very quickly where New Left interpretation is headed when Zinn asserts that the New Deal "had no clearly defined goals," that its ideals did not project "very far beyond the traditional structure of the American economy," that all the New Deal accomplished was "to refurbish middle-class America" and that it did just enough for those at the bottom of the heap "to create an aura of good will."

The New Deal, writes Zinn, failed to curtail the power of corporate business, did not make much headway toward redistributing wealth or giving the lower classes a fair shake, did not provide the individual real security for an uncertain future. To put it bluntly, the New Deal had failed to touch the real problem, the fundamental problem of improving "the environment of millions of Americans clawing for subsistence in the richest country in the world."

Barton Bernstein, editor of *Towards a New Past* (New York, 1968), inserted an essay of his own, "The New Deal: The Conservative Achievements of Liberal Reform," and his melancholy conclusion. "The liberal reforms of the New Deal did not transform the American system; they conserved and protected American corporate capitalism, occasionally by absorbing parts of threatening programs. There was no significant redistribution of power in American society, only limited recognition of other organized groups." The New Deal, says Bernstein in his final indictment, "failed to solve the problem of depression, it failed to raise the impoverished, it failed to redistribute income, it failed to extend equality and generally countenanced racial discrimination and segregation."

A superb summation of the New Left position may be found in "The Myth of the New Deal" by Ronald Radosh in *A New History of Leviathan* (New York, 1972), edited by Radosh and Murray Rothbard. "The myth of a New Deal revolution, or a new departure, or a basic watershed, call it what you will, dies hard," writes Radosh. His dissection of the "myth" leads to the conclusion that New Deal policies "were only a change in the way of doing things. They were a means of working out new arrangements to bolster the existing order." With uncommon candor, Radosh flings a challenge to his colleagues of the New Left: "Understanding how the New Deal worked will enable us to resist policies based on further extensions of the Welfare State, and to commit ourselves instead to the collective effort to forge a socialist community in America."

If the New Left interpretation by Radosh and the others of Roosevelt and the New Deal is accepted at face value, the next logical step would appear inevitable, sooner or later: Franklin Roosevelt was, after all, a "social fascist."

For a more thorough (and quite critical) assessment of New Left literature it would be useful to read Jerold Auerbach, "New Deal, Old Deal, or Raw Deal: Some Thoughts on New Left Historiography," in the *Journal of Southern History* XXXV (February 1969).

Books hostile to Roosevelt, but written from the perspective of a conservative, might include Edgar E. Robinson, *The Roosevelt Leadership, 1933-1945* (Philadelphia, 1955), and John T. Flynn, *Country Squire in the White House* (New York, 1940) and *The Roosevelt Myth* (New York, 1948).

Rooseveltian literature of the memoir and reminiscence type is quite extensive and, as might be expected, fluctuates wildly in quality. I confess the only criteria for including the following are that I have read them and that they have proved useful in my own research.

A place to start might be with two books by Eleanor Roosevelt, *This Is My Story* (New York, 1937), for the pre-1933 years, and *This I Remember* (New York, 1949), for the presidential years. Useful books by people of cabinet rank probably should include James A. Farley, *Behind the Ballots* (New York, 1938), written while he and Roosevelt were still on good terms, and his *Jim Farley's Story* (New York, 1948), written after disenchantment had set in; Cordell Hull, *Memoirs* (New York, 2 vols., 1948); Harold L. Ickes, *The Secret Diary of Harold L. Ickes* (New York, 3 vols., 1953); Frances Perkins, *The Roosevelt I Knew* (New York, 1946); and John Morton Blum, *From the Morgenthau Diaries: Years of Crisis, 1928-1938* (Boston, 3 vols., 1959).

Worth-while books by others in the administration—associates, Brain

Trusters, those close to Roosevelt—are Robert Sherwood, *Roosevelt and Hopkins* (New York, 1948), Rexford Tugwell, *The Democratic Roosevelt* (Garden City, 1957) (referred to earlier in this essay) and *The Brains Trust* (New York, 1968), Raymond Moley, *After Seven Years* (New York, 1939) and *The First New Deal* (New York, 1966), Samuel I. Rosenman, *Working with Roosevelt* (London, 1952), Grace Tully, *FDR, My Boss* (New York, 1949), and Joseph P. Lash, *Eleanor and Franklin* (New York, 1971).

For specific aspects of the New Deal, there are a few books that stand out either because of the significance of their topic or because of the excellent treatment of the topic, or sometimes both. I especially recommend David Daniel Fusfeld, *The Economic Thought of Franklin D. Roosevelt and the Origins of the New Deal* (New York, 1956), David E. Conrad, *The Forgotten Farmers* (Urbana, 1965), Richard S. Kirkendall, *Social Scientists and Farm Politics in the Age of Roosevelt* (Columbia, 1966), Ellis W. Hawley, *The New Deal and the Problem of Monopoly* (Princeton, 1966), James T. Patterson, *Congressional Conservatism and the New Deal* (Lexington, 1967), Jerold Auerbach, *Labor and Liberty: The La Follette Committee and the New Deal* (Indianapolis, 1966), George Wolfskill and John A. Hudson, *All but the People: Franklin D. Roosevelt and His Critics, 1933-39* (New York, 1969), and Alfred B. Rollins, *Roosevelt and Howe* (New York, 1964).

Literature on the New Deal and the war is still somewhat spotty, but there are a few things worth looking at. A good starting point might be Eric Goldman's *Rendezvous with Destiny*, which contains a chapter ". . . Much of What Not to Do," and Broadus Mitchell's *Depression Decade*, which has a chapter titled "War to the Rescue," both of which I consider almost seminal on the subject of what war meant to the New Deal. See also Bruce Catton, *The War Lords of Washington* (New York, 1948), and Roland Young, *Congressional Politics in the Second World War* (New York, 1956). Richard Polenberg (ed.), *America at War: The Home Front, 1941-1945* (Englewood Cliffs, 1968), and Geoffrey Perrett, *Days of Sadness, Years of Triumph* (New York, 1973), contain some really provocative views on the subject, as does Alonzo L. Hamby, "Sixty Million Jobs and the People's Revolution: The Liberals, the New Deal, and World War II," *The Historian* XXX (August 1968). On Roosevelt's leadership during the war years, see James MacGregor Burns, *Roosevelt: The Soldier of Freedom* (New York, 1970), and Richard

Polenberg, *War and Society: The United States, 1941-1945* (Philadelphia, 1972).

This is about as far as I am willing to go with bibliography; much more would be pretentious. There is little here about foreign affairs, diplomacy, and the military side of World War II because they are not what this book has been about. I have also omitted references to correspondence, collected papers, documents, and archival materials on the assumption that they do not belong in a bibliography intended primarily for undergraduate students.

If the student wishes to explore the scope and variety of New Deal literature still further, I suggest he consult such sources as Richard L. Watson, "Franklin D. Roosevelt in Historical Writing, 1950-1957," *South Atlantic Quarterly* LVII (Winter 1958); the article cited earlier, Richard Kirkendall, "The New Deal as Watershed: The Recent Literature," *Journal of American History* LIV (March 1968); Frank Freidel, "The New Deal, 1929-1941," *Yearbook of the National Council for Social Studies* XXXI (1961); William J. Stewart, *The Era of Franklin D. Roosevelt: A Selected Bibliography of Periodical and Dissertation Literature, 1945-1966* (Hyde Park, 1967); Clarke Chambers, "FDR, Pragmatist-Idealist: An Essay in Historiography," *Pacific Northwest Quarterly* LII (April 1961); and Basil Rauch, "Roosevelt and the Historians," *Yale Review*, new series, XLIV (Summer 1958).

And it is not unprofessional or undignified to consult the impressive bibliographies in the books by Robinson, Burns, Leuchtenburg, and a few others. Maybe even the Suggested Readings in survey textbooks.

Index